Why Privacy
Isn't Everything

feminist constructions

Series Editors: Hilde Lindemann Nelson, Sara Ruddick, and Margaret Urban Walker

Feminist Constructions publishes accessible books that send feminist ethics in promising new directions. Feminist ethics has excelled at critique, identifying masculinist bias in social practice and in the moral theory that is used to justify that practice. The series continues the work of critique, but its emphasis falls on construction. Moving beyond critique, the series aims to build a positive body of theory that extends feminist moral understandings.

Feminists Doing Ethics
    edited by Peggy DesAutels and Joanne Waugh
Gender Struggles: Practical Approaches to Contemporary Feminism
    edited by Constance L. Mui and Julien S. Murphy
"Sympathy and Solidarity" and Other Essays
    by Sandra Lee Bartky
The Subject of Violence: Arendtean Exercises in Understanding
    by Bat-Ami Bar On
How Can I Be Trusted? A Virtue Theory of Trustworthiness
    by Nancy Nyquist Potter
Moral Contexts
    by Margaret Urban Walker
Recognition, Responsibility, and Rights: Feminist Ethics & Social Theory
    edited by Robin N. Fiore and Hilde Lindemann Nelson
The Philosopher Queen: Feminist Essays on War, Love, and Knowledge
    by Chris Cuomo
The Subject of Care: Feminist Perspectives on Dependency
    edited by Eva Feder Kittay and Ellen K. Feder
Pilgrimages/Peregrinajes: Theorizing Coalition Against Multiple Oppressions
    by María Lugones
Why Privacy Isn't Everything: Feminist Reflections on Personal Accountability
    by Anita L. Allen

Forthcoming books in the series by

Amy R. Baehr; Joan Mason-Grant; Diana Tietjens Meyers; Robin Schott

Why Privacy Isn't Everything

Feminist Reflections on Personal Accountability

Anita L. Allen

ROWMAN & LITTLEFIELD PUBLISHERS, INC.
Lanham • Boulder • New York • Oxford

ROWMAN & LITTLEFIELD PUBLISHERS, INC.

Published in the United States of America
by Rowman & Littlefield Publishers, Inc.
A Member of the Rowman & Littlefield Publishing Group
4501 Forbes Boulevard, Suite 200, Lanham, Maryland 20706
www.rowmanlittlefield.com

PO Box 317
Oxford
OX2 9RU, UK

British Library Cataloguing in Publication Information Available

Library of Congress Cataloging-in-Publication Data

Allen, Anita L., 1953–
  Why privacy isn't everything : feminist reflections on personal accountability
  / Anita L. Allen.
    p. cm.—(Feminist constructions)
  Includes bibliographical references and index.
    ISBN 0-7425-1408-0 (cloth : alk. paper)—ISBN 0-7425-1409-9 (pbk. : alk. paper)
    1. Social norms—Philosophy. 2. Ethics—United States. 3. Responsibility—United
  States. 4. Privacy—United States. I. Title. II. Series.
  HM676 .A45 2003
  303.3'72—dc21

                                                                        2002014948
Printed in the United States of America

♾™ The paper used in this publication meets the minimum requirements of American
National Standard for Information Sciences—Permanence of Paper for Printed Library
Materials, ANSI/NISO Z39.48-1992.

To Monica Lynne Allen Newell

Contents

Introduction

Accountability for conduct is a pervasive feature of human association.[1] For example, along with explicit concerns about its proper means and ends, accountability operates implicitly in the fields of public administration and corporate governance.[2] Accountability imperatives drive the law of tort and crime. Accountability should not and cannot be total in any domain short of dystopia. Still, in every sector of society a degree of accountability for conduct is critical. It "is an essential and undismissable desideratum for orderly social interaction" without which "it is impossible to conceive of a society resembling an organized interlocking of individual actions, or for that matter maintaining sociality and intersubjectivity."[3] In the United States, as in other places, accountability and concerns about accountability range beyond the affairs of government and business enterprises whose stakeholders decry daft decision making and disappointing bottom lines.

Accountability and accountability concerns also extend into what Americans call "private life." Yet, how can that be? "Accountability for private life" is surely an oxymoron. After all, calling a realm or activity "private" is one of the ways to signal that answering to another earthly being is not required. It seems that, by definition, we are supposed to be unaccountable for what we term "private" life and accountable for the less precious rest of life.[4]

So the story goes. And it is something of a story, one that some of us sometimes imagine to be true. When designating certain realms or activities "private," "personal," and the like, we imagine ourselves as citizens of a free society, each entitled to enjoy a number of states, feelings, thoughts, acts, and relationships for which we owe others no accounting. Although others have a say in what we do in our capacities as managers, employees, and driver's license holders, they have no similar say in what we do as private persons. We imagine that other people are allowed to share in our private lives or not, at our discretion and on our terms, subject to very few exceptions. We often think and talk this way, drawing a sharp divide between public and private. The political philosophies some of us hold dear pay tribute to *On Liberty,* the classic essay in which John Stuart Mill famously wrote: "The individual is not accountable to society for his actions, in so far as these concern the interests of no person but himself."[5] American jurisprudence on occasion prominently echos Mill's sentiment. Dissenting in *Poe v. Ullman,* Justice John Marshall Harlan exploited the familiar political ideal of the private home, marriage, and family to build a revolutionary constitutional case for reproductive freedom that set the stage for *Griswold v. Connecticut* and *Roe v. Wade.*[6] Justice Harlan vigorously attacked Connecticut statutes on the grounds that laws criminalizing contraception intrude "into the very heart of marital privacy" and require "husband and wife to render account before a criminal tribunal the uses of . . . intimacy."[7]

However, accountability for the uses of intimacy is a common imperative, expectation, and deeply felt obligation in our society. As individuals, couples, families, and communities we live lives enmeshed in webs of accountability for conduct that include accountability for intimacies relating to sex, health, child rearing, finances, and other matters termed private. We are accountable for nominally private conduct both to persons with whom we have personal ties and to persons with whom we do not have personal ties. We are accountable to the government, and we are accountable to nongovernment actors. We are accountable for plainly harmful conduct and other-regarding conduct in our nominally private lives (for example, date rape) and we are accountable for the best candidates we have for harmless and self-regarding conduct (for example, consensual oral sex between monogamous partners in their own bedroom). We do not simply face others' "advice, instruction, persuasion, and avoidance,"—devices Mill approved.[8] We face social and legal demands for sanctions and other reckoning he disapproved. Mill's assertion that individuals are "not accountable to society" for actions that concern only themselves is debatable as a matter of ethics or political morality and flatly inaccurate as a matter of fact. Not only are we held accountable for what is commonly termed private life, but our accountability for some personal, arguably self-regarding, conduct extends to the extreme of criminal liability.

NO OXYMORON

Accountability for and in private life is thus no mere oxymoron or confusion. Social norms of every category—religious, ethical, moral, legal, and customary—foster accountability. We are held accountable, and we hold others accountable. We feel accountable, and we feel owed accountability. As citizens and scholars we debate what is and is not private and what should and should not be private, always against the backdrop of a culture in which accountability subsists in virtually every corner of our lives. Although some tolerant individuals try to avoid the most overtly moralistic accountability discourses and practices, it is nonetheless fair to say:

> In our private lives we wade in a constant stream of accountability initiatives. People hold their children, parents, partners, friends, neighbors, colleagues, and fellow citizens accountable for any kind of presumptive misbehavior—for political incorrectness, insubordination, disorderliness, bad memory, drinking and smoking, sexual misconduct, sinful behavior, lack of courtesy, strategic errors, factual ignorance, whatever. Because there are lots of rules that guide our private lives, there are lots of opportunities for private agents of accountability to step in and monitor and enforce compliance.[9]

Accountability for private life means that the broad areas of individual and group life regularly labeled as private are not walled off. We do not label dimensions of life private because they are immune from scrutiny and judgment by official and unofficial or public and private "agents of accountability." Flourishing accountability practices and policies—including the legal, moral, and other social norms central to this book—examine and evaluate what goes on in the personal and intimate arenas.

My point is that accountability for virtually all personal and intimate behavior is the rule rather than the exception in the United States. Accountability for private life is as common as dirt. It requires that everyone answer to a plethora of government and nongovernment actors for personal matters. A great many rules, commitments, and relationships entail accountability for both conduct and perceived misconduct. Hence, teenagers living with their parents are often accountable to them both for facts relating to dating ("conduct") and for facts relating to illegal drug use ("misconduct"). And, of course, the laws regarding sex and controlled substances render youths accountable to government for conduct and misconduct, too. The propriety of some accountability practices and policies is taken for granted; the status of others elicits extremes of controversy. An obvious pair of examples of the latter is laws establishing criminal accountability for intimate, adult heterosexual conduct and laws restricting homosexuals from the military.

ACCOUNTABILITY AND THE LIBERAL SPIRIT

Legal liability for sex and sexual orientation is one of the most emotionally charged forms of accountability. Philosophers, like legal theorists, understandably focus on the implications of legal accountability because of the onerous, coercive nature of civil and criminal sanction.[10] Legal liability for personal choices can feel particularly unjust when the individual expected to account does not share the moral, ethical, or religious outlook of the person demanding the accounting. But nonlegal sanctions for conduct are potentially coercive and punitive, too. It wounds the soul to suffer the social sanctions of censure and isolation.

Liability to sanction is but one form of accountability. Accountable individuals are called upon to reckon with others for acts and omissions that violate norms, in several other important senses introduced in chapter 1 of this book. An observer would miss a stark feature of American life were he or she to allow pervasive liberal values, aspirations, and rhetoric—much of which I find congenial—to obscure the richly diverse ways in which we are constantly called upon to report, explain, justify, and otherwise answer to others for the choices we make about our own lives.

In the spirit of toleration for individual differences, political liberals are skeptical of collective interference with individuals' own assessments concerning their affairs. Liberals are for leaving people alone, living and letting live. But a society cannot afford to fully leave people alone. The practical reality that the nonjudgmental outlook fosters mischief is captured in "Accountability," an ironic poem crafted in an imagined African American slave dialect by Paul Laurence Dunbar. The poem begins:

> Folks ain't got no right to censuah othah folks about dey habits;
> Him dat giv' de squir'ls de bushtails made de bobtails fu' de rabbits.
> . . .
> We is all constructed diff'ent, d'ain't no two of us de same;
> We cain't he'p ouah likes an' dislikes, ef we'se bad we ain't to blame.[11]
> . . .

The words of the poem's narrator make the case against accountability, while the actions of the narrator as revealed in an unquoted final stanza illustrate the case for it. People not subject to "censuah" may lack incentives for avoiding antisocial behavior. The poem's narrator delivers a lovely philosophical argument for respecting what he characterizes as God-given human differences; but it turns out that the narrator's tribute to toleration is merely a ploy to deflect criticism for having broken the law. His words are a self-serving rationalization. He is about to dine on a stolen chicken, "one o' mastah's chickens," to be exact.[12]

Accountability makes sense to committed liberals when the master's chickens begin to disappear. Liberals recognize reasons to hold others accountable for personal matters if harm can thereby be averted. The fights are about what constitutes the relevant sorts of harm. Sex and health are considered very per-

sonal. Yet, accountability makes sense in the case of a public official whose flagrant sexual immoralities impair public duties, or a sexually active man who has concealed his AIDS from unsuspecting partners. And many liberals are prepared to recognize situations in which "personal" and "self-regarding" acts are also social and other-regarding, for example, recreational drug use and casino gambling.

AIMS

This book is a group of essays about accountability in and for private life in the United States. My main goal is a series of thick descriptions of the say that others have in our nominally private lives. It is nothing new to point out that government has a complex and thoroughgoing say. Nor is it novel to note that our employers, insurance companies, and families have a say. But I hope to contribute a fuller sense of how, why, and to whom we are accountable for our personal lives, stressing more that others have both the varieties of accountability and the variety of people to whom we are expected to answer. The picture that will emerge from my discussions is that of highly social actors enmeshed in flexible but sticky webs of accountability that restrain without curtailing most individual freedoms. So long as we stick without, in the main, getting stuck, we remain personally and politically free.

My aims are not entirely descriptive. I will venture normative perspectives on a number of situations in which I believe people ought to hold others accountable but do not, and in which I believe people should not hold others accountable but do. Rather than attempt to work self-consciously from within the confines of a specified, overarching normative theory, I express normative considerations in familiar moral, ethical, and political vocabularies, contributing to normative debates surrounding the accountability practices and policies I describe. My highly contextual discussions will seek to illuminate accountability for private life demanded of intimacy and gender equality; family and ethno-racial community; and public trust and leadership.

WHAT ABOUT PRIVACY?

In the final decades of the past century, concerns about privacy emerged as pervasive themes in public policy. One such concern was about the overall quantity of personal privacy in the United States. Some observers, the privacy skeptics, expressed the concern that Americans enjoy too much privacy. Skeptics contended that the United States legal system confers individual privacy rights at the expense of public safety, public health, and law enforcement.[13] Privacy skeptics worried that an unbounded quest for individual privacy fosters neglect of group interests, civic virtues, and the common good.[14] Other observers, the privacy advocates, voiced the concern that Americans enjoy too little privacy. Responding to developments in information technology, mass communication, and health sciences, privacy advocates charged that the United States legal system permits daily assaults on individual privacy perpetrated by data-hungry governments, corporations, and media.[15] Fearing that Americans will grow indifferent to privacy, some privacy advocates called for public policies specifically designed to shore up privacy preferences and expectations.[16]

In a bevy of previous publications, I often emphasized the positive value of privacy.[17] I have been a friend of privacy. The financial burdens of federally mandated information privacy protections have won privacy few new friends. The most conspicuous of these protections, the Financial Services Modernization Act, the Health Insurance Portability and Accountability Act, and the Children's Online Privacy Protection Act, forced the commercial sector to overhaul their business practices to protect consumers.[18] The specter of terrorism on American soil led many Americans to view privacy as a dispensable luxury, a tool of the enemy. The USA PATRIOT Act and other "homeland security" measures adopted by the federal government after September 11, 2001, enhance the power of government to intercept communications and hold suspects captive.[19]

Unpopular in the world of corporate and government practice, privacy is also remarkably friendless in the world of theory:

> Contemporary views are uniformly critical: privacy is judged an incoherent and confused value, a poisonous public philosophy, a perverse and infantile demand, a masculinist prerogative that only enhances the vulnerability and powerlessness of women, and once enshrined as a "right," a positive hindrance to any more expansive notion of social good or more lasting kind of social peace.[20]

Against this current of opinion, I have remained privacy's friend, urging critical rethinking while defending as legitimate some of the core of the traditional privacy claims we assert in liberal societies to be free of unwanted accountability with respect to intimacy, sexuality, health, and finances.

Indeed, accountability for private life can be arbitrary, unjust, oppressive, and humiliating, robbing people of basic dignity and liberty. There are even a few things, such as the continuous stream of thought and feeling, for which no one should have to be accountable in the normal course of events. The prison guard who can strip-search, body cavity–search, and cell-search virtually at will has no authority to know his charges' thoughts and emotions. Because of the importance of personal privacy, government and nongovernment actors should carefully attend to the accountability norms fostered by their attitudes, decisions, policies, and practices affecting matters commonly considered private. People should neither give up nor be deprived of such privacy casually.

Here, though, I try to locate the positive value of modes of accountability in and for private life. I am not switching sides: although privacy is important, accountability is important too. Both in their own way render us more fit for valued forms of social participation. Privacy is our repose and intimate accountability our engagement. One is entitled to say "None of your business!" in response to some requests for answers, but not others. It is important to understand that and to understand why some privacy claims, even some that relate to archetypical "private" and "personal" realms, are not clearly legitimate. Robust regard for privacy does not eliminate the desirability of many forms of official and unofficial accountability. I believe we can follow the unreconstructed liberals and call the usual realms of life "private," so long as we understand that people are and should be legally, morally, and socially accountable for many of the activities that go on in those realms. This book is an effort to elaborate on and evaluate common understandings of why "None of your business!" is sometimes the decidedly incorrect response to others who scrutinize our private lives. My chapters are essays that undertake to illuminate pervasive forms of accountability in and for private life, and why they are deemed acceptable and unacceptable. My chapters will explore some of the key respects in which, for better or worse, we are all held accountable to our families, our friends, our ethno-racial groups, our employers, the press, and the general public with respect to sex, marriage, child rearing, and health.

FILLING A GAP

This book fills a gap in the philosophical and legal literature for discussions that focus explicitly and comprehensively on personal accountability in interpersonal realms.[21] Much of the existing explicit, policy-oriented literature on accountability deals with just a few subjects. These are chiefly, corporate accountability, criminal accountability, and government accountability. The central question within corporate accountability is the extent to which individual managers, auditors, employees, and shareholders can be held to account for the decisions, failures, and misdeeds of the corporate entity. The Enron debacle and the subsequently uncovered corporate accounting fraud reveal that meaningful corporate accountability sometimes comes too late. The central question within criminal accountability is under what circumstances and in what way a person should be held legally responsible for conduct. Criminal answerability for sex-related conduct, a well-studied topic, is a subject on which I will not dwell. The central question within government accountability is what structures, institutions, and practices can make government—including its officials and employees—optimally answerable to citizen constituencies. The accountability of public school educators for student achievement, for instance, has become a major issue in local and national politics.[22] Educator accountability for pupil performance falls outside the scope of my study, but the problem of the accountability of public officials for sexual conduct and misconduct falls squarely within.

THINGS TO COME

This book will freshly emphasize the centrality of accountability in ordinary personal life while promoting ideals of accountability and privacy that I believe are consistent with contemporary reconstructions of liberalism.[23] Chapter 1 will be an introduction to the theory and practice of personal accountability. We are accountable for private life to many other people and entities, in many different ways. To elaborate this deceptively simple observation, I begin by distinguishing diverse forms and functions of accountability. What does it mean to be accountable for conduct? Who can be held accountable? What forms of accountability are reciprocal? What bearing do specific roles, professions, hierarchies, and cultural identities have on the nature and extent of one's accountability to others? What are the grounds of accountability in private life? Feminism has been blamed in the popular press for fostering excessive accountability for private life. I explain why, and consider the broad parameters of a normative theory of accountability that might be thought to issue from the insights of contemporary feminist theory.

With chapters 2, 3, and 4, I take a topical turn. Chapter 2 studies the question of to whom one is accountable for personal life; chapters 3 and 4, for what personal matters one is accountable. In chapter 2, I will examine accountability to family and race for decisions basic to contemporary family life: whom we marry (or the equivalent), how our children will be raised, and whether we use drugs. I begin with accountability for drug use as an instance of arguably "self-regarding" high-risk conduct that can breach intrafamilial accountability imperatives. I will continue by discussing the emerging expectation that adoptive families will form ongoing relationships with birth families as an instance of shifting norms toward greater accountability for family life. The "open adoption" movement calls on the parties of adoption to engage in an exchange of information and dialogue prior to and after the placement of the child in a new home. Several feminist lawyers and legal philosophers have voiced support for open-adoption practices as a way of (1) empowering birth mothers to care for their offspring and (2) binding adopted children to their biological families and communities of origin. Adoptive families have always been more accountable than other families to third parties. Open-adoption practices make adoptive parents more accountable still, by requiring information sharing and dialogue with biological parents to an extent unheard of in traditional adoptions. I endorse common pre-placement accountability practices and accountability to the state of all parents, biological and adoptive, for child protection. However, I suggest that certain postadoption accountability practices that give birth families and other third parties a say in child rearing may make adoption a less attractive option for prospective adoptive parents who want families of their own.

"Transracial" adoption is a growing trend. The popularity of open adoption stems in part from the belief that children adopted outside their own racial group need access to that group to ensure that the child will develop an "appropriate" racialized identity. Concerns about the racial identities of children have been a part of discussions about "transracial" adoption and "interracial" marriage. Liberal moral and political theories seldom acknowledge the special, group-specific accountability norms recognized by members of minority groups. Yet, despite the diminishing socioeconomic significance of race and the stark biological evidence that race is a myth, Americans commonly experience a need to reckon with others of their own perceived kind. Focusing on African Americans' moral objections to exogamy, I describe modes of explanation, justification, and punishment-oriented accountability for interracial intimacy that have persisted decades after the great era of civil rights in which the Supreme Court's decision in *Loving v. Virginia* (1967) struck down state laws banning miscegenation.[24]

In chapter 3, I will examine accountability to others for health information. Most discussions of health information depict it as a confidential product of the physician-patient relationship, a confidential product whose disclosure to third parties could expose patients to the sting of indignity, embarrassment, and discrimination. I will stress, however, that health information exists prior to the physician-patient relationship or any record created in the context of the physician-patient relationship. Because we must often reckon with our families, friends, and even law enforcement officials about our health concerns and secrets, significant accountability imperatives for information, explanations, justifications, and sanctions can exist prior to any contact with medical professionals. Meeting the imperatives of accountability for health requires a learned understanding of the subtle demands of context and relationships. I will describe health accountability imperatives, in an effort to illuminate them and a seemingly inconsistent cultural trend: greater openness about health matters and increased popular demand for strong medical privacy laws.

In chapter 4, I address accountability for sex. Starting with accountability to employers, I examine gender-related conduct at work, in business, and in professional relationships. Some civil libertarians, privacy advocates, and feminists believe contemporary employers have grown unduly intrusive. Employers monitor employee email, prohibit dating between co-workers, and punish jovial sex talk among peers. Some employee monitoring is designed to promote performance and productivity, or to deter theft of business property. Other monitoring, though, is specifically designed to satisfy the perceived demands of Title VII of the Civil Rights Act of 1964.[25] Under judicial and Equal Employment Opportunity Commission interpretations of Title VII, employers are liable for discrimination based on sex, defined to include sexual harassment and maintaining a hostile work environment. Civil libertarians characterize the conduct some employers try to prevent in the name of Title VII as lawful employee exercises of free speech or mere breaches of etiquette. I stress reasons for believing that continued punitive accountability for sexual harassment and sexually demeaning expression in business and professional relations will further equal employment opportunities for women.

I continue the theme of accountability for sex by turning my attention to the accountability of employees who work for us all, our public officials. Today journalists freely disclose intimate facts about public figures. They employ covert and high-pressure tactics for acquiring personal information and explanations for conduct. Coverage of some officials and public figures has been condemned as excessive, even cruel. Officials have been more accountable to the public than they needed to be in recent decades, with costly consequences for the public fisc, individual lives, and public character. Excessive accountability constrains reasonable freedoms and fosters deception among honest people. However, regulating sexual intimacy is unavoidable. Accountability for sex is called for in a range of situations. I attempt to characterize two such circumstances: first, when officials knowingly and avoidably commingle private intimacies with official duties; and second, when there is a high probability that serious, distinct harm to rights or official duties will result from secrecy about personal affairs.

This book is a response to the old accountability on the occasion of the New Accountability. Under the old accountability, accountability for personal life was pervasive. For example, in important respects, workers were accountable to their bosses, and husbands to wives. Today, however, quoting a newspaper headline, "Companies Dig Deeper into Executives' Pasts."[26] The New Accountability means that when a person applies for a managerial position with a large corporation, the company may hire a private investigator to do "everything short of 24-hour surveillance" to "find out if they did drugs, with whom, and what, [and] if they had an affair."[27] Today, "U.S. Agents Arrest Dozens of Fathers in Support Cases."[28] The New Accountability means that if Bob has failed to pay child support to Linda, Linda can make a highly publicized federal case out of it. It is not a purely personal or local matter.

The chapters of this book ponder how a preeminently liberal, democratic society accommodates the competing demands of vital privacy and vital accountability.[29] Other scholars conclude that the United States is a privacy-obsessed nation whose laws and policies overvalue privacy at great cost to the common good.[30] My conclusion is quite different. Privacy is not an overprivileged value in practice. In practice, privacy interests are balanced against interests in safety, welfare, public health, national security, and efficiency.[31] Private life is far from a sacred, obsessive zone of immunity in America, by custom or by law. The United States is a diverse and evolving society in which accountability for personal life is pervasive and genuinely paramount both for intimacy and social control. We have not evolved into a society with perfect, consistent accountability norms.[32] In some respects, extant accountability norms are too weak, impairing legitimate calls to government and private actors for more protection and equality. As feminists have emphasized, accountability for domestic violence has lagged behind accountability for violence generally. In other respects, however, extant accountability norms are too strong. Not only are individuals still subjected to criminal sanction for consensual adult sex, but a New Accountability has created novel expectations of disclosure and answerability whose risks and consequences are not well understood. Already underway, accountability reforms are needed to further core liberal democratic values.

NOTES

1. Richard McKeon, "The Ethics of International Influence," *Ethics* 120, no. 3 (1960): 187–203.

2. For example, see, Mark Bovens, *The Quest for Responsibility: Accountability and Citizenship in Complex Organizations* (Cambridge, U.K.: Cambridge University Press, 1998); Peter French, *Collective and Corporate Responsibility* (New York: Columbia University Press, 1984); Scott Greer, Roland D. Hedlund, and James L. Gibson, eds., *Accountability in Urban Society: Public Agencies under Fire* (Beverly Hills, Calif. and London: Sage Publications, 1978); Joseph McCahery, Sol Picciotto, and Colin Scot, eds., *Corporate Control and Accountability* (Oxford: Clarendon Press, 1993); and Robert B. Wagner, *Accountability in Education* (New York and London: Routledge, 1989).

3. G. R. Semin and A. S. R. Manstead, "The Accountability of Conduct: A Social Psychological Analysis," *European Monographs in Social Psychology* 33 (1983): 32–185.

4. Vincent J. Samar, "Gay-Rights as a Particular Instantiation of Human Rights," *Albany Law Review* 64 (2001): 983–1030.

5. John Stuart Mill, *On Liberty* (London: J. W. Parker and Son, 1859). In the first paragraph of chapter 5 of *On Liberty*, Mill lays out the maxim I quote that "The individual is not accountable to society for his actions, in so far as these concern the interests of no person but himself."

6. *Poe v. Ullman,* 367 U.S. 497 (1961); *Griswold v. Connecticut,* 381 U.S. 479 (1965); *Roe v. Wade,* 410 U.S. 113 (1973).

7. Quoting the Justice in full: "In sum, even though the State has determined that the use of contraceptives is as iniquitous as any act of extra-marital sexual immorality, the intrusion of the whole machinery of the criminal law into the very heart of marital privacy, requiring husband and wife to render account before a criminal tribunal of their uses of that intimacy, is surely a very different thing indeed from punishing those who establish intimacies which the law has always forbidden and which can have no claim to social protection." *Poe v. Ullman,* 367 U.S. 497, 553 (1961), Harlan, J., dissenting. Harlan was not prepared in this case to extend the realm of nonaccountability to traditionally prohibited acts including adultery or homosexuality.

8. Mill, *On Liberty,* chapter 5, paragraph 2.

9. Andreas Schedler, "Conceptualizing Accountability," in *The Self-Restraining State,* ed. Andreas Schedler, Larry Diamond, and Marc F. Plattner (London: Lynne Rienner, 1999), 2.

10. Cf. Ellen Frankel Paul, Fred D. Miller Jr., and Jeffrey Paul, *Responsibility* (Cambridge, U.K.: Cambridge University Press, 1999).

11. Paul Laurence Dunbar, "Accountability," in *The Complete Poems of Paul Laurence Dunbar* (New York: Dodd, Mead & Company, 1976), 6–7. The narrator makes a case both for toleration and divine intent: "When you come to think about it, how it's all planned out it's splendid. / Nuthin's done er evah happen, 'dout hit's somefin' dat's intended; / Don't keer whut you does, you has to, an hit sholy beats de dicken,– / Viney go put on de kittle, i got one o'mastah's chickens" (Dunbar, 7). Dunbar's invented African American dialect was more popular with his white critics than with Dunbar himself. See Eleanor Alexander, *Lyrics of Sunshine and Shadow* (New York: NYU Press, 2001), 37–40.

12. A rational slaveholder who wanted to reduce the likelihood of losing food to rational underfed unpaid labor would have to increase surveillance or increase the penalty of detection.

13. See, for example, Amitai Etzioni, *The Limits of Privacy* (New York: Basic Books, 1999).

14. See, for example, Michael Sandel, *Democracy's Discontent: America in Search of a Public Philosophy* (Cambridge, Mass.: Harvard University Press, 1996).

15. See, for example, Charles J. Sykes, *The End of Privacy* (New York: St. Martin's Press, 1999); and Jerry Kang, "Information Privacy in Cyberspace Transactions," *Stanford Law Review* 50 (1998): 1193–1294.

16. Anita L. Allen, "Coercing Privacy," *William and Mary Law Review* 40 (1999): 723–57.

17. I discuss privacy sympathetically in a number of articles and two books: Richard Turkington and Anita L. Allen, *Privacy Law,* 2nd ed. (Minneapolis: West Publishing Co., 2002); and Anita L. Allen, *Uneasy Access: Privacy for Women in a Free Society* (Totowa, N.J.: Rowman & Littlefield, 1988). My survey articles include: "Privacy as a Practical Value," in *Oxford Handbook of Practical Ethics*, ed. Hugh LaFollett (in press, Oxford: Oxford University Press, 2002); "Privacy" in *A Companion to Feminist Philosophy,* ed. Iris Marion Young and Alison M. Jaggar (Oxford, U.K.: Blackwell, 1998), 456–65; "Genetic Privacy: Emerging Concepts and Values," in *Genetic Secrets,* ed. Mark Rothstein (New Haven, Conn.: Yale University Press,

1997); "The Jurispolitics of Privacy," in *Reconstructing Political Theory*, ed. Uma Narayan and Mary Lyndon Shanley (Cambridge, U.K.: Polity Press, 1996), 68–83; "Constitutional Privacy," in *A Companion to Philosophy of Law and Legal Theory*, ed. Dennis Patterson (Oxford, U.K.: Blackwell, 1996), 139–55.

Other privacy-related articles include, "Minor Distractions: Children, Privacy, and E-Commerce," *Houston Law Review* 38 (2001): 751–56; "Gender and Privacy in Cyberspace," *Stanford Law Review* 52, no. 2 (May 2000): 1175–1200; "The Public Right to Know," in *The Encyclopedia of Ethical Issues in Politics and the Media*, ed. Ruth Chadwick (San Diego, Calif.: Academic Press, 2000): 251–62; "Privacy as Data Control: Conceptual, Practical, and Moral Limits of the Paradigm, *Connecticut Law Review* 32 (2000): 861–75; "Coercing Privacy," *William and Mary Law Review* 40 (1999): 723–57; "Moral Multiculturalism, Childbearing, and AIDS," in *HIV, AIDS, and Childbearing: Public Policy, Private Lives*, ed. Ruth Faden and Nancy Kass, (New York: Oxford University Press, 1996), 367–407; "Privacy in Health Care," in *Encyclopedia of Bioethics*, rev. ed., ed. Warren T. Reich, (New York: MacMillan, 1995), 2064–73; "The Proposed Equal Protection Fix for Abortion Law: Reflections on Citizenship, Gender, and the Constitution," *Harvard Journal of Law and Public Policy* 18 (1995): 419–55; "Autonomy's Magic Wand: Abortion Law and Constitutional Interpretation," *Boston University Law Review* 472 (1992): 693–98 ; "Tribe's Judicious Feminism," *Stanford Law Review* 44 (1991): 179–203; "Legal Issues in Non-Voluntary HIV Testing," in *AIDS and the Next Generation*, ed. Ruth Faden et al. (New York: Oxford University Press, 1991), 166–200; "The Power of Private Facts," *Case Western Reserve Law Review* 41, no. 3 (1991): 757–67; Anita L. Allen and Erin Mack, "How Privacy Got Its Gender," *Northern Illinois Law Review* 10 (1991): 441–78; "Privacy, Surrogacy, and the *Baby M* Case," *Georgetown Law Journal* 76 (1988): 1759–92; "Taking Liberties: Privacy, Private Choice, and Social Contract Theory," *Cincinnati Law Review* 56 (1987): 461–91; "Rethinking the Rule against Corporate Privacy: Some Conceptual Quandaries for the Common Law," *John Marshall Law Review* 20 (1987): 607–39.

Some of my publications reflect concern for privacy policies and accountability practices. These publications began as lectures or symposia talks and are the basis of sections of chapter 2 and chapter 4 of this book. They are: "The Wanted Gaze: Accountability for Privacy Invasions at Work," *Georgetown Law Review* 89 (2001): 2013–28; "Privacy and the Public Official: Talking about Sex as a Dilemma for Democracy," *George Washington Law Review* 67, no. 5/6, (1999): 1165–82; and "Lying to Protect Privacy," *Villanova Law Review* 44 (1999): 161–88.

18. *The Gramm-Leach-Bliley Financial Services Modernization Act*, Public Law 102, 106th Cong., 1st sess. (6 May 1999), 113 Stat. 1338, requires financial institutions to protect the security and confidentiality of customers' nonpublic personal information. *The Health Insurance Portability and Accountability Act of 1996*, Public Law 191, 104th Cong., 2d sess. (21 August 1996), 110 Stat. 1936, sets standards for security of confidentiality of health information and medical records. *The Children's Online Privacy Protection Act*, U.S. Code, vol. 16, sec. 6501 (1998), requires commercial websites to refrain from collecting personal data from children under age thirteen without parental consent.

19. *Uniting and Strengthening America by Providing Appropriate Tools Required to Intercept and Obstruct Terrorism Act of 2001 (USA PATRIOT ACT)*, Public Law 56, 107th Cong., 1st sess. (24 October 2001), 115 Stat. 272.

20. Debra Morris, "Privacy, Privation, Perversity: Toward New Representation of the Personal," *Signs* 25 (2000): 323–52.

21. But see Eric A. Posner, *Law and Social Norms* (Cambridge, Mass.: Harvard University Press, 2002). Posner's book focuses on nonlegal mechanisms of social control. He does not explicitly discuss the concept of accountability. However, his game theoretic perspectives on compliance with "social norms" as "signaling" are illuminating for anyone interested in why people answer to some and avoid answering to others.

22. Robert Wagner, *Accountability in Education: A Philosophical Inquiry* (New York: Routledge, 1989), 55–56. Although it ultimately focuses closely on the specialized subject matter of education, this book contains the single most lucid philosophical analysis of accountability that I have uncovered.

23. Martha Nussbaum, "The Feminist Critique of Liberalism," in *Sex and Social Justice* (New York: Oxford University Press, 1999), 55–80.

24. *Loving v. Virginia*, 388 U.S. 1 (1967).

25. Civil Rights Act of 1964, Title VII, 42 U.S.C. 2000e, P.L. 88–352, 1st sess. (2 July 1964).

26. Alex Kuczynski, "Companies Dig Deeper into Executives' Pasts," *The New York Times*, 19 August 2002, 1.

27. Kuczynski, "Companies Dig Deeper," 1.

28. Robert Pear, "U.S. Agents Arrest Dozens of Fathers in Support Cases," *The New York Times*, 19 August 2002, 1.

29. American society is all at once, to use Philip Pettit's terminology, populist, republican, left of center liberal, libertarian, communitarian, and so on. See Philip Pettit, *Republicanism; A Theory of Freedom and Government* (Oxford, U.K.: Oxford University Press, 1997). Varied strands of western political thought can be observed. Public discourse is dominated, though, by ideas and ideals of noninterference, tempered by frequent appeals to equality, nonsubordination, welfare, and community.

30. Etzioni, *Limits of Privacy*.

31. One way to judge whether privacy is a privileged value in the United States is to look at how courts treat privacy claims. If your first encounter with privacy law is the Supreme Court's famous search and seizure or reproductive rights cases from the 1960s and 1970s, you could easily walk away thinking that American law privileges privacy. However, a closer look at the great sweep of privacy law—tracking court cases brought under state and federal constitutions, tort law, and state and federal statutes—reveals that balancing privacy interests against other competing interests is the general practice. Privacy claims fall easily in the face of claims about, for example, public health and safety, national security, military need, law enforcement, freedom of speech and press, and the public right to know. See Richard Turkington and Anita L. Allen, *Privacy Law*, 2nd ed. (Minneapolis: West Publishing Co., 2002).

32. I use "norm" here, as philosophers typically do, to refer to values and practices of all sorts; among legal economists, the fashion is a narrower use, under which norm is contrasted to law. I try to make it clear when I am talking about laws, as opposed to other sorts of norms.

Chapter One

The Theory and Practice
of Accountability

Accountability for private life is pervasive, wide-ranging, and essential. Individuals are accountable for their private lives to the extent that they are obligated or impelled, whether by internal or external norms, to perform acts of reckoning with respect to nominally personal matters. This compact characterization of accountability for private life requires elaboration. To start, I will distinguish several different modes of answerability, that is, modes of reckoning with or accounting to others. A distinct sense of accountability attaches to each. In our society, moral, ethical, legal, and other imperatives require that individuals not only reckon or account in the senses of (1) reporting, (2) explaining, and (3) justifying acts and omissions, but also that they (4) submit to sanctions and (5) maintain reliable patterns of behavior. In making these distinctions, I build on conceptual understandings of accountability found in the modest philosophical literature on the subject. My aims are pragmatic. I will make no claim to have hit upon the "essence" of accountability. Distinguishing types of accountability up front will facilitate later efforts in subsequent chapters to explain the ways in which I maintain we are or should be accountable to others, using a consistent, reasonably precise vocabulary.

In addition to elaborating a general characterization of accountability for purposes of a thesis about accountability for private life, I will also offer a series of observations about the grounds, functions, and contours of accountability practices in American society.

Accountability for private life has become a salient feature of contemporary American culture. The New Accountability is bold, democratic, and superpowered by technology. Yet much accountability to the state and private sectors for personal life has been the historic rule. Accountability for personal matters is older than feminism, Anita Hill, cell phones, and reality television. The organization of American society has always featured diverse requirements that individuals report, explain, justify, face sanctions for, and routinize their private lives. The breadth of accountability for personal life that emerged in the United States in the late twentieth century is nonetheless remarkable. As American culture has evolved, the contours of accountability for private life have also evolved. Notably, accountability norms have become more democratic as slavery, Jim Crow, and patriarchy have given way to greater equality for women and racial minorities. Individual actors and the state commonly find themselves answerable to formerly marginalized minority groups and popular media.

The New Accountability reflects overdue public response to the social consequences of harmful conduct in nominally private spheres of sex, family, and health. After 1980, concerns about rampant domestic violence, sex crimes, and gender inequality intensified accountability demands. Over the ensuing decades, changes in American legal doctrines, law enforcement policies, and the judiciary met some of the pleas for fair intervention and sanctions made by feminists and others.[1] In the wake of the AIDS epidemic, new levels of accountability between sexual partners gained public acceptance.[2] At the same time that this public health crisis intensified, government and celebrity sex scandals erupted. The media signaled in response that political leaders and the public would now openly demand accountability for sexual misconduct. A president accused of sexual harassment and adultery would not be sheltered from exposure.[3] Adding to the mix, a popular culture of self-disclosure emerged. Individuals from all walks of life now believe that speaking openly about intimacies is socially permissible and even advantageous, if not an outright imperative of responsible family ties, friendship, and citizenship.[4] Broad accountability for private life is often the result of voluntary choices.

FIVE FORMS OF ACCOUNTABILITY

According to Andreas Schedler: "*A* is accountable to *B* when *A* is obliged to inform *B* about *A*'s (past or future) actions and decisions, to justify them, and to suffer punishment in the case of eventual misconduct."[5] He adds: "In experiences of political accountability, usually all three dimensions—information, justification, and punishment—are present."[6] The same is probably true of moral and social accountability as well. Following Schedler and adapting his understandings to the subject matter at hand, accountability for private life would entail (1) obligations to report or to provide others with information about private life, that is, accountability in an information-emphatic sense; (2) obligations to provide others with a narrative justification for acts and omissions relating to private life, that is, accountability in a justification-emphatic sense; and (3) obligations to face punishment from others for conduct in one's private life, that is, accountability in a punishment-emphatic or sanction-emphatic sense. Schedler characterized accountability as a matter of obligation. Accountability can be a matter of obligation, but also of duty or responsibility.[7] I will ultimately characterize accountability broadly as a matter of actual and felt imperatives, including obligations, duties, and responsibilities.

Other theorists have recognized essentially the same three senses of accountability that Schedler recognized, though sometimes under an alternative nomenclature. Thus Nicolas Haines distinguished accountability as explanation or "explicability," which seems to combine what Schedler called "information" and "justification"; from accountability as "liability" or "punishments, penalties and indemnities," embracing what Schedler termed "punishment."[8] Haines seems correct when he notes that the "explicability" and "liability" meanings of accountability "are not, of course, even in ordinary usage, kept apart."[9] The "explicability" meaning of accountability may have especially deep etymological roots, as Haines suggests.[10] Although, as Robert Wagner urges,[11] ultimate linguistic history in no way delegitimates further, expanded meanings in current usage.

Inform, Explain, and Justify: an Illustration

It proves helpful, for closer understandings of the accountability demands confronted in ordinary life, to distinguish an explanation-emphatic sense of accountability from a stronger, justification-emphatic sense. An example from real life will make the intended distinction plain. In January 2000, newspapers reported that the Reverend Jesse Jackson, a married Christian minister, civil rights leader, and one-time presidential candidate, had fathered a child by a woman not his wife. His lover worked for Jackson's civil rights organization. Some people responded to the news with calls that Jackson be "held accountable" for his private conduct. Among them was Clarence Page, Pulitzer Prize-winning reporter for the *Chicago Tribune*. Claiming special ambivalence about holding others accountable for their personal lives, Mr. Page told a *Columbia Journalism Review* interviewer:

> We will always be aggressive in looking for accountability of public figures. I was one of the first reporters to report on the questions surrounding Jackson's operation Push for Excellence and their expenditures of federal funds back in 1980. Jackson doesn't like accountability. But that hasn't stopped us. When it gets into private life, I know I am less aggressive in pursuing those stories. . . . When it comes to the private life of any official, you approach it with ambivalence. But my philosophy is, when in doubt, let it out. Our impulse should be in favor of releasing information to the public, not suppressing it. . . . As an

African-American who has been covering the Reverend Jackson and other civil rights figures for over thirty years, I particularly feel that it is my responsibility to be as aggressive as possible. . . . I am very concerned about leadership in general and about the quality of black leadership. And he is the most widely known and respected black leader. I feel obliged to be more aggressive because I feel a special responsibility to African-Americans and others in Jesse Jackson's constituency to hold him accountable. Like a sort of consumer advocate.[12]

People who agreed with Page that Jackson should be held accountable could have disagreed about what forms of accountability were appropriate.

When the reports of a "love child" hit the newsstands, some people thought it would be sufficient for Reverend Jackson to confirm or deny what newspapers were reporting. They thought it would suffice for Reverend Jackson to say publicly something akin to this: "I had a sexual relationship with Ms. So and So, an employee of my organization, and fathered a daughter, to whom I provide this and that type of support from monies earned in this and that way."

After Reverend Jackson provided the basic facts, though, some members of the public and the media were still not satisfied. They seemed to think the Reverend owed the public, or at least *his* public, an explanation of the facts and circumstances of the affair: "Although I was married at the time, and although I profess that adultery is a sin, I faltered; I had a sexual relationship with Ms. So and So, an unmarried employee of my organization, with whom I had enjoyed working for many years. I fathered a daughter and assumed financial responsibility for her care. I know that I have caused my wife and children pain and disappointed loyal supporters." Others seemed to want even more from Reverend Jackson. They seemed to want an explanation that included an earnest effort at justification. The most complete explanations are both explanations *that* and explanations *why*. Justifications are explanations *why*. They explain, for example, why a person's conduct seemed acceptable or was acceptable under the circumstances: "I was very lonely and feeling the emotional stress and isolation of long days and nights away from my wife, necessitated by my civil rights mission; I was overcome by Ms. So and So's kindness and devotion to her work; I believed I was in love with her; I ignored the call of conscience and betrayed my faith; I am a sinner, we are all sinners, but I have asked for and received forgiveness; I am providing financial support for my daughter using only my own personal financial resources, not those of any organization."

A few people seemed to want yet more from Reverend Jackson. Beyond the information, the explanations, the justifications, they wanted his head. They wanted to bring the big guy down. They wanted him punished with moral censure, ostracization, and any criminal or civil liability appropriate for adultery and hypocrisy. They wanted accountability in the punishment-emphatic sense.

Liability to Punishment

The call for punishment can be regretful or gleeful.[13] Opponents of the sometimes-sanctimonious Reverend Jackson were gleeful in the belief that he, of all people, was guilty of major moral error. The gleeful, with a taste for the prurient, relished an excuse to demand salacious detail from Jackson, of the sort demanded of Monica Lewinsky, President William Jefferson Clinton's White-House lover. Fallen preachers and fallen women potentially face harsh forms of what has been called "negative accountancy." Negative accountancy "involves attitudes and practices such as condemnation, blame, punishment and the like," whereas "positive accountancy" includes "attitudes and practices such as praise, gratitude and admiration."[14]

Homosexuals face negative accountancy, too. Homosexuals in the United States military face peculiar demands of privacy and accountability. On the one hand they are coerced into secrecy about their personal lives. That is the point of the Don't Ask, Don't Tell policy adopted during the Clinton presidency. On the other hand, service members suspected of homosexuality can be coerced into accountability. Upon suspicion of gay or lesbian sexual orientations, homosexual service members are held accountable in both information-emphatic and punishment-emphatic senses. Consider the fate of Timothy R. McVeigh. McVeigh was a successful naval officer with a good heart and a privacy-insensitive Internet service provider. As reported in *McVeigh v. Cohen* (1998), a fellow officer's wife reported suspicions of McVeigh's homosexuality to her husband after receiving email signed "Tim" offering to help with a base charity drive.[15] "Tim" gave no last name but used the moniker "boysrch" and seemed to have a naval affiliation. McVeigh faced military discipline when AOL.com revealed his identity and sexual orientation to a Navy paralegal investigating whether he was the "Tim" who had sent the email.

Further Illustrations

Other examples from real life will help to make the basic abstract distinctions drawn thus far concrete. A few years ago, the Coca-Cola Company discovered that an employee in a managerial position had posted nude photos of himself on the Internet. In an unrelated incident, police officials discovered that a female officer had posed nude for *Playboy* magazine during her tenure on the force. In both instances embarrassed employers pondered whether their employees should be held accountable for their after-hours private conduct, and if so, how accountable. Perhaps one could expect workers in certain "role model" jobs to tell employers about what they do after hours. Neither the manager nor the police officer had felt an obligation to give prior notice and seek permission, though both occupied role model positions.

If the Coca-Cola Company and police officials believed the offending employees had the duty to reveal the facts of their provocative activities, and if they had expectations to that effect, I would say that the employees were accountable in the information-emphatic sense of owing another information. If, in addition, the employers expected their employees to explain or justify their sexy pictures, I would say the employees were accountable also in the explanation-emphatic and justification-emphatic senses. Employers in a disciplinary proceeding might well expect proffers of explanatory detail, reasons, and special circumstances. If, with information, explanation, and attempted justification in hand, the employers sought to impose discipline, I would say that the employees were accountable to their employers in the punishment-emphatic sense of being subject to punishment or other negative sanction.

Reliability

In addition to the information, explanation, justification, and punishment-emphatic senses of accountability just illustrated, I will distinguish one more. There is a reliability-emphatic sense of accountability, accountability in the sense of being predictable and compliant.[16] An employee who arrives at work at the same time every day and completes the same quantum of work is accountable to her employer because she does what is expected of her, not because she directly provides factual information, explanations, justifications, or is subject to sanction. She is accountable because of her regularity. She is always, as they used to say in the military, "present and accounted for." A spouse who returns home from work every night at six o'clock is accountable to her partner in the reliability-emphatic sense. This sort of accountability can be crucial for security and trust in personal relationships. Economists make a related point. Some forms of accountability signal to others a person's willingness to behave cooperatively. Accountability is an effective signaling strategy for rational, self-interested actors. If I routinize my conduct, I signal that it is safe to be my friend, lover, or partner. Having successfully evidenced the intent to cooperate, individuals can reap the benefits of appearing to be desirable partners in cooperative endeavors.[17]

A FULLER DEFINITION

The preceding set of five basic distinctions suggests a fuller definition of accountability for private life than the one with which this chapter began, as follows. Individuals are accountable for aspects of their lives considered personal, to the extent of being obligated or impelled, whether by internal or external norms, (1) to provide information to others; (2) to explain themselves; (3) to justify themselves; (4) to face positive or negative sanctions; and/or (5) to maintain a predictable pattern of conduct on which others can reasonably rely. We are accountable for private matters when we are bound by obligation, duty, or responsibility—or motivated by a sense of obligation, duty, or responsibility—to reckon with others. We reckon by supplying them with personal information, explanations, justifications, sanctions, or reliability. When I say in the discussions that follow that individuals are accountable for private life, I mean to make only the descriptive observation that they or others judge them to be morally, legally, or otherwise accountable. As an empirical matter, Jesse Jackson was morally accountable and held accountable to the public for his extramarital affair. One can acknowledge the fact of his accountability even if, from one's own point of view or the point of view of an ideal moral or ethical theory, he was not morally accountable and ought not to have been subject to account.

Correspondence, Disconnect, and the Grounds of Accountability

Because of widely shared values, when others consider a person accountable, the person is likely to agree that he or she is accountable. I call this unity of belief *correspondence*. Correspondence can obtain where the person deemed accountable is unenthusiastic about being accountable, as well as where the person is sanguine or enthusiastic. For example, Dan and Lou are domestic partners. They embrace standard promise-keeping and family accountability norms. Dan happily promised Lou to make supper for the two of them by six o'clock on weekdays. Lou believes Dan should make supper or reckon with him, and Dan believes that he should make supper by six or reckon with Lou. There is correspondence, and would still be correspondence even if Dan grew tired of the kitchen. If Dan failed to make supper on a Tuesday night, he would know that neither "None of your business!" nor "I hate cooking!" would be an adequate response to Lou's "Why didn't you make dinner?" The response "None of your business!" would be an inapposite response in view of moral accountability. "I hate cooking!" could be construed as an attempt to give account with an explanation, but the selfishness of the explanation implies disrespect for the grounds of accountability.

The Grounds of Accountability

What, though, are the grounds of accountability? By virtue of what is anyone accountable to anyone else for anything? One observed ground for accountability is especially comfortable to liberals: consent. If individuals contract, agree, promise, vow, pledge, or commit themselves to carry out a specific performance, then they are often held accountable for that reason.[18] Another observed ground of accountability is reliance. If others are relying on an individual and an individual knows it, he or she may be accountable for that reason. The case for reliance-based accountability is especially strong in our society when an individual does something to induce reliance to another's detriment. For example, Bill wants to befriend Jill. Every day for a month he shows up at her bus stop and offers her a ride home from work. On the thirty-second day of free rides, Jill allows her bus to pass and waits for Bill, who never shows up. She has to shell out thirty dollars for a cab—ten times the price of a bus ride. Bill owes Jill an explanation, even though he never promised to pick her up.

Forming families, marriages, partnerships, and close friendships signals conferring a right to rely and induces reliance. It therefore is plausible to understand the existence of certain intimate relationships as itself a ground of accountability. Jill expects to have sex with her husband Bill. If he suddenly chooses to make himself unavailable to her, she is owed an accounting. The accounting imperative could be characterized as a responsibility, duty, or obligation of the marital relationship. Reciprocal reliance is often a feature of intimate sexual relationships. Relationships (such as marriage) in which mutuality and reciprocity of expectations play a role are the relationships most often deemed to give rise to accountability. Contract, reliance, and relationship thus provide alternative explanations for accountability. The basis for Bill's being bound to account to Jill regarding sex could be explained by direct appeal to relevant marriage vows; or, in the nonexclusive alternative, by appeal to the fact that Bill is Jill's husband, or that Jill has relied on Bill for sex, forgoing other opportunities for physical intimacy in the interest of their relationship. Dependency is another common ground for accountability. Reliance is a kind of dependency. However, a Jill who only depends upon a Bill for rides home or for sex is not dependent in the comprehensive way that, say, a blind paraplegic is dependent upon his or her caretakers. An infant is comprehensively dependent on a parent, and an elderly parent is comprehensively dependent on an adult child. Dependency can mean that a global set of important emotional and physical needs of one person are the responsibility of another. Accountability obtains when individuals have vital needs for which they depend upon particular, responsible others, who are then answerable to the dependent person (and perhaps third parties) for care.

A further, recognized ground of accountability is public need. This is an expansive category. People are accountable to the government for terrorist plots transmitted over the Internet because the government is obligated to thwart credible threats to public safety and national security. People are accountable to public health authorities for tuberculosis or AIDS because the government is obligated to contain highly contagious diseases. People are accountable for plans to kill lovers revealed to psychiatrists because the courts say that the duty to protect human life is more important than the duty of medical confidentiality.[19] People are accountable to law enforcement for selling cocaine on school property to minors because society has a compelling interest in the health and education of its youth.

A recognized but controversial category of public need is the enforcement of morals. Social conservatives wholeheartedly support controversial moral and legal requirements that aim at improving the moral tone of society by prohibiting such actions as oral sex, the use of pornography and drugs, prostitution, homosexuality, and adultery. Controversy about the accountability that is justified by appeal to morality stems from the fact that some admittedly immoral conduct arguably harms no one, or only the people who engage in it. Other controversy relates to the fact that people disagree about what is morally right and wrong in the first place.

Disconnect

Despite the social origins of most accountability norms, a disconnect of accountability can occur. A person is held accountable by someone but does not judge himself to be accountable. An overly conscientious person believes she is accountable, but no one considers her accountable. When members of the same society share many beliefs, values, and circumstances in common, profound disconnects are few and correspondence is typical. But disconnects are not at all rare, as children and parents, men and women, quarreling lovers, employers and employees, and liberal politicians and conservative politicians disagree about accountability. Lou could feel entitled to a reckoning concerning a dinner Dan failed to prepare, long after preparing suppers at home has become a meaningless ritual for Dan because Lou works late and eats out most nights.

The possibility of a disconnect helps to explain why theorists have said that accountability can be measured from both "internal" and "external" perspectives.[20] Viewed from an external perspective, accountability entails strictures that others' expectations (shaped by their beliefs, values, and circumstances) impose on us, including "negative restraint on action imposed by law and punishment."[21] We may be motivated—impelled—by others' strictures. We may feel obliged to heed them, even when our own ideals dictate otherwise. In the internal sense, moral accountability, for example, depends upon our own genuine sense of obligation, responsibility, duty, or restraint. Viewed in its internal dimension, accountability is a manifestation of the accountable person's own values. In the internal sense, accountability "depends on the moral judgment of the individual rather than on [for example] the prohibition of law, and it becomes a manifestation rather than a restraint of freedom in the pursuit of recognized values."[22] Yet, because the moral values of the individual are influenced by social experience, feeling accountable, like being held accountable by others, is rooted in the social.

One of the purposes of moral and civic education has been to teach youth to internalize the "right" externally imposed conventional accountability rules. Educators aim to teach children that genuine friends share personal information on a confidential basis, hoping that the children will grow to expect intimate data sharing of others and feel internally obligated to do it. Internalization of values is more difficult after childhood. Law and business schools despair of teaching accountability values in the internal sense. Educators present young lawyers the proscription against commingling client funds and hope they adhere to it whether or not they actually agree that the rule is essential for financial accountability. Prudent awareness and external acceptance of applicable rules of accountability are sometimes good enough.

Prima Facie Imperatives

Accountability ascriptions entail prima facie imperatives of the sort that we commonly term obligations, responsibilities, and duties. The accountability of a child to her parent entails an obligation to keep her parent informed as to her whereabouts. English speakers can comfortably term such an obligation a responsibility or duty of the child. The accountability of a public official to the media entails an obligation to meet with the press and answer questions forthrightly. The obligations of accountability are only prima facie obligations, however. A newspaper that has once again recklessly printed libelous stories about officials may not be owed what responsible media are owed. The father who has molested his daughter is no longer entitled to the previous levels of accountability from her.

Legal responsibility, that is, being subject to civil or criminal sanctions, is one important category of accountability. It does not follow from this that "accountable" is just another word for "responsible." It seems more accurate to say that responsibility and accountability are closely related but not synonymous concepts.[23] Responsibilities can imply accountability to others for conduct relating to the discharge of duties. Conversely, accountability can imply responsibilities for management and care. It is noteworthy that we sometimes ascribe responsibility to mark a terrain of prerogative and limited accountability to others: "normally, parental latitude in the raising of children is considerable" and government agencies and corporations "enjoy considerable discretion."[24] And then again, we sometimes ascribe responsibility to convey expectations of heightened accountability for conduct. For example, parents and corporations have significant spheres of unaccountability to the public, coupled with special social responsibility. With many types of legal powers and privileges come obligations of informational accountability. In order to issue certain stock, companies must file with the Securities and Exchange Commission. In order to practice medicine, physicians must report the names of patients with certain contagious diseases.

Performative and Communicative

By their very logic, the imperatives of accountability are performative and, largely, communicative. Nonaccountable persons are immune from communicative requirements. Personal accountability in the information-emphatic sense requires that the person communicate facts to one or more others. To satisfy the accountability debt, one must tell something by, for example, saying, writing, or signing it. In the explanation and justification-emphatic senses, accountability can require distinctly dialogic modes of communication. That is because, in order to explain or justify, one may need to engage others, as interlocutors, in a conversation, discussion, or even debate.[25] Reliability-emphatic accountability is more performative than communicative, requiring that one behave or act in a certain routine way rather than that one report or converse. Punishment/sanction-emphatic accountability may call upon a person to tell (as in a confession), dialogue (as in submitting to examination by a judge in a sentencing hearing), or perform (as in making an apology, rendering community service, serving time in jail).

Accountability to Oneself

Personal accountability appears to include accountability to oneself.[26] Journalists held Jessie Jackson accountable, and Jackson probably felt accountable. But did he feel accountable to himself as much as to others? Did he think he owed it to himself to confront the truth of his conduct, fighting against denial and self-deception? Did he think he owed himself carefully formulated explanations and justifications for his extramarital affair or failure to use adequate contraception? Did he probe his conscience and render self-judgment? I suspect Jackson is the sort of man who would do some of this moral work. Unfortunately, the demands of public life can easily rob public officials, public figures, and celebrities of the solitude and inner lives required for meaningful and productive accountability to oneself. Self-judgment carries notable risks. People may be too hard on themselves. Whole classes of people may grow to be too hard on themselves because their conduct is unfairly blamed and condemned by society over a long period of time.

SOME FUNCTIONS OF ACCOUNTABILITY

Accountability as I have defined it can have any of a number of functions. By "functions" I mean to include implicit operations as well as explicit goals, purposes, and motives. A comprehensive theory of accountability must recognize the plurality of its functions. Here, I point out that accountability functions, among other things, to enable and limit power, to enable and limit responsibility, and to foster intimacy and solidarity.

Power

One function of accountability relates to the management of power. Accountability can be used to disable power and, conversely, to enable it. Anyone owed accountability, like anyone able to extract it, has social power over others. Government maintains its power over citizens by holding them legally accountable. Like government, private actors with the ability to extract information, explanations, justifications, punishment, and routine out of others on a nonreciprocal basis can control and dominate. Much of the control government effects via accountability is the kind of control on which safe, healthy societies vitally depend. For example, informational accountability to public health agencies for infectious diseases and to the police for violent crime is highly beneficial. In the world of gender relations, men's power over women has included nonreciprocal accountability obligations requiring women to report, explain, and justify conduct for which men were not held similarly accountable. Under slavery, the slaveholder's power over the slave included nonreciprocal accountability obligations. The house slave was legally accountable to the master for the fate of the master's children, but the master was not legally accountable to the slave for the fate of the slave's children. Ten years ago, a scowling stranger on a Berlin subway walked up to sociologist Norman Birnbaum and asked, "Are you a Jew?" The stranger was attempting to reassert the power non-Jewish Germans once exercised over German Jews by demanding informational accountability.

Democratic and egalitarian societies fear the abuse of power. They employ mechanisms designed to encourage and compel accountability of power holders. The need to constrain power is a central rationale for two major forms of accountability in our society: government accountability and corporate accountability to the public. For example, state power is safe and palatable because of state accountability. Mechanisms of state accountability, such as freedom of information laws and open meeting rules, render the activities of government more transparent and accessible. All five types of reckoning are employed in tandem in public administration to deter, check, and punish abuses of power by government. Although accountability can be a way of taming power, it is also a way of unleashing power. By holding another accountable in information and punishment-emphatic senses, one can ensure the flow of information and threaten negative sanctions needed to achieve and sustain dominance.

Responsibility

Regulating responsibility is a second function of accountability. Accountability serves to monitor persons and entities charged with important responsibilities for others. Failures of responsibility can be detected, criticized, and repaired if accountability mechanisms are in place. Accountability can also function to fortify or enable responsibility. Parents are able to perform their responsibilities toward children in large measure because the former grow to feel accountable. Men's socially assigned responsibilities for women in an early era were thought to justify the nonreciprocal accountability obligations of wives and daughters. Men were accountable to women, socially and by law, for economic support and affection, but they enjoyed customary social freedoms women did not enjoy. Physicians and lawyers cannot demand accountability of patients and clients. However, feeling accountable to the professionals we pay to help us with medical and legal needs impels many people to yield information and explanations that facilitate the performance of contractual professional responsibilities.

Trust

Accountability can function to induce desirable forms of reliance and create trust. This is a third function of accountability. Friendships, for example, are built on trust. Friendships are greatly helped by the expectations and feelings of mutual accountability. Accountability also has value for relationships that lack the intimacy and depth of the best friendships. I only trust you as far as I can throw you, goes the saying. The point is that with key bits of information about others, we can trust them not to hurt us. With the ability to expect—or extract—key bits of information as a result of accountability norms, we can trust others not to injure our interests. Likewise, if others maintain regular, predictable patterns of behavior respecting us, we can grow to trust and rely on them. Returning to an earlier example, by showing up every day to take Jill home after work, Bill induces her reliance and warm regard, and he ultimately wins her trust.

Solidarity

A fourth function of accountability is that it can enhance group solidarity, creating incentives for loyalty and conformity to group norms. The obligation to reveal information, explain, and justify conduct can function to restrain conduct that the group might disapprove of and even punish. If I want to belong to a religious group that permits only heterosexual marriage to other group members, I may avoid a marriage outside of my faith or a same-sex relationship for which I would have to answer to group leaders. Grooming is a personal matter, but if my peer group dictates denim pants and long hair, I may wear jeans and avoid the salon just to avoid the punishment-emphatic accountability that results from nonconformity. The obligation to explain myself may deter conduct I do not care to explain, even if I did not expect to be punished.

Accountability as Self-Reinforcing

Accountability facilitates accountability. Some forms of accountability make other, more onerous kinds of accountability possible. Suppose Rex is an anxious, controlling working parent and wants to be able to sanction (reprimand or fire) a nanny who does not strictly follow his instructions. Rex can make the nanny informationally accountable to him by installing a series of video cameras in his home that he can monitor from his office via the Internet. The information-emphatic accountability Rex establishes is but a means to an end. It is a tool enabling sanction-emphatic accountability. If I want the capacity to shame someone for deviant conduct, then I want the means to find out that they have engaged in deviant conduct. If I ascribe obligations of informational accountability to prospective deviants, I might get what I need for punitive, shaming, negative accountability. If you explain yourself to someone, you risk being called upon to try to justify yourself to him or her as well. And then you face the risk of sanctions that may flow from inadequate justification.

CULTURAL CONTOURS

Accountability for private life is a cultural fact, a complex set of social norms and practices. To be sure, details about our friendships, sex lives, health, and finances are generally considered appropriately private matters. Yet we often believe we are morally, ethically, or legally obligated to reveal otherwise private matters that we would prefer to keep to ourselves. Moreover, we sometimes feel obliged or obligated to explain or justify our otherwise private conduct, if not to strangers, at least to people with whom we have intimate bonds. I have already identified commonplace grounds for accountability: contract, reliance, relationships, dependency, and public need. These same general grounds potentially apply to accountability for personal life.

Accountability norms and associated practices are discovered, learned, and taught. Mastering the contours of accountability for personal matters is a part of mastering the cultural universe. Social competence means knowing when accountability obtains, that is, when the grounds of accountability are satisfied. Knowing whether the grounds of accountability are satisfied requires knowing who is a qualified agent of accountability, which accountability norms are reciprocal, and what roles, relationships, professions, or identity groups give rise to special accountability demands. The diverse, evolving, and nonauthoritarian complexion of American society makes dissent and disagreement about accountability norms difficult to avoid.

Who Is Considered Competent for Accountability?

One contour of accountability to master is the classes of persons to whom accountability norms of particular sorts apply. Who is a competent agent of accountability? Some classes of people are excused from some classes of accountability. Young children and mentally disabled adults are typically excused from the high level of accountability imposed on adults. This is true in morality and to some extent in law. Controversies over the move to prosecute even the youngest violent felons as adults reflect disagreement about who is a competent agent of accountability. The Supreme Court held in 2002 that mentally retarded adults convicted of heinous crimes could not be executed, on the ground that the death penalty was unconstitutionally "cruel and unusual" punishment for persons of pervasively diminished intellectual capacity.[27]

A caretaker could not fairly expect a man with Alzheimer's disease who has wandered away from home to justify or explain his whereabouts. Justification-emphatic accountability may be out of place and very limited information-emphatic accountability reasonable. According to Jay Wallace, "[t]he community of morally accountable agents is thus the set of people who are capable of successfully exchanging moral criticism and justification: grasping the reasons behind moral criticism, and responding constructively on the basis of such reasons."[28] Young people and persons with mental or severe emotional disabilities will be unable to stand up to the full burden of across-the-board accountability in all of its varied informational, explanatory, justificatory, punitive, and reliability senses.

Who Is Considered Accountable to Whom?

Another major contour to master is who can make accountability demands on whom, reciprocal or otherwise. Accountability demands concerning private life may come from one's government, one's political community, one's employer, one's family, and even one's ethnic, racial, or religious group. Thus, sometimes people are held accountable, or feel accountable, because of who and what they are. Identity matters. When and why identity-indexed, nonuniversal accountability demands seem to possess legitimacy are questions of great importance taken up later in this book.

Which Accountability Norms Are Reciprocal?

Some ideals of what it means to be a responsible moral agent participating in a moral community place mutuality at the core. Yet, society is not organized so simplistically that all accountability demands for competent adults are mutual or identical. In hierarchical social organizations, lower-status persons are easily more accountable to higher-status persons than higher-status persons are to them.[29] As previously noted, accountability enables power, and nonreciprocal accountability norms reinforce lopsided power arrangements. A nineteenth-century black slave was legally accountable to his master for appropriating food, but a master was not legally accountable to his slave for appropriating his labor. A hundred years ago, men enjoyed a higher status than women. Male heads of households were less accountable to wives and daughters than wives and daughters were to them. Today, though, men and women are approaching social equality and have similar expectations of accountability. For example, spouses feel reciprocally obliged to reveal and justify extramarital sex.[30] Mainstream contemporary marriages are egalitarian in ways families with children are not. In the hierarchy of the family, parents can come and go as they please, but children face accountings. In the hierarchy of the prison, the clock-punching prison guards are not accountable to the inmates whose body cavities and cells the guards can search virtually at will.

A modern employee is accountable to his employers, and employers are accountable to employees under wage, benefit, civil rights, and labor laws. Employees, though, are subject on a nonreciprocal basis to concerted monitoring and discipline. In a traditional workplace, hourly employees who "punch the clock" are accountable to salaried managers for their work schedules, but the reverse is not true. Beginning in the 1980s, workers in the United States found that accountability to their employers did not simply mean showing up at work on time and putting in a day's labor. Much more than reliability-emphatic forms of accountability were expected. The demand for information increased with the availability of techniques and technologies for gathering it. Workers were asked to submit to unwanted drug, alcohol, and HIV/AIDS testing. In the 1990s, accountability at work came to mean tolerating surveillance by video cameras and submitting to telephone and email monitoring. In addition, concerns about the enforcement of Title VII and liability for sexual harassment have led some employers to demand high levels of employee accountability for potentially offensive workplace speech and conduct. Employers who prohibit co-worker dating, employee smoking, and "vices" outside of work are being criticized for seeking too much accountability from their workforce.

Nonreciprocal Accountability

Lack of reciprocity is one thing; domination, another. Although employers once exercised near-complete dominion over employees, by the middle of the past century most workers could effect personal lives beyond the scrutiny of employers. Many, though, could not. Some who still cannot are military service members on active duty and dependent migrant farm workers crowded in shabby housing provided by farming enterprises. Men and women in the military have consistently faced very high expectations of accountability. Officers still face punishment for marital infidelity. As noted earlier, gay and lesbian service members' accountability for their sexual orientation was scarcely abated by the supposedly ameliorating Don't Ask, Don't Tell policy adopted in 1993. The military is one of the few employers that can categorically demand HIV/AIDS testing and genetic testing of its employees. Several years ago two Marines, fearful of the Department of Defense's DNA databanking program to facilitate the identification of battlefield remains, refused to participate and promptly faced discharge.[31]

Government, public officials, and large commercial institutions are accountable to the general public in respects that are not strictly reciprocal. Subject to important exceptions, the secrecy preferences of these actors easily yield to the public's demand for accountability. Corporate and government accountability "expresses the continuing concern for checks and oversight, for surveillance and institutional constraints of the exercise of power."[32] The accountability of public officials is often a way of controlling, regulating, and managing the power won by politics.[33] Hence, at a press conference the candidate for mayor must answer questions about personal health, family, and finances that he could not ask in good taste of any individual member of the press corps.

The special accountability demands that the public makes of public officials and public figures have been subject to wide discussion in the past few decades. The phenomenon is not limited to the United States. In October 2002, a reporter asked the fifty-five-year-old president of the Philippines, Gloria Macapagal-Arroyo, if she still had sex, prompting her to answer that she still had plenty, and that sex in marriage is a sacrament. Just how accountable should an official, public figure, or celebrity be? And in what senses and to whom? As a practical matter, high-ranking public officials rarely enjoy the physical and informational privacy others enjoy. Nor should they, when it comes to private lives needlessly intermixed with the discharge of their duties.

(I am thinking of episodes in the White House Oval Office in which President Clinton engaged in sex with Monica Lewinsky while talking on the telephone to his advisors.) The distinctly personal, unofficial conduct of the president, members of Congress, federal judges, and mayors can become public business, too. Officials suspected or accused of illicit sex, sexual harassment, drug use, viewing pornography, offensive speech, and medical problems that may bear on fitness for office have found themselves under a microscope.

Journalist Clarence Page, whom I mentioned earlier in connection with Jesse Jackson, leans on the concept of "the public's right to know" to justify investigation and reporting about the personal lives of public officials and public figures. For obvious reasons, Vice President Richard Cheney is accountable in the information-emphatic sense to the public for his life-threatening heart troubles, notwithstanding the general norm of medical privacy. The public has a need, and for that reason, a right to know. Other defenses of accountability are routinely cited. I will mention three that will be aired more fully in chapter 4. First, it is commonly argued that public figures and celebrities in the limelight implicitly waive their privacy interests and thereby make themselves fully accountable, in effect by consent. Second, it is also argued that citizen trust of government demands transparency and accountability of public officials. A third argument for the accountability of public officials and public figures—like the second, a public need argument—is the relevance of their lives to public issues and debates.

On the basis of public need, a pop diva can be accountable for health information, no less than a vice president. The secreted personal truth that Ofra Haza had died of AIDS was finally reported a week after her death. Out of respect for Ms. Haza's medical privacy, the press initially kept the cause of the popular entertainer's death secret. A week after she died, citing the need to replace pervasive, feverish rumor with truth, the daily newspaper *Ha'aretz* reported that Ms. Haza had died of complications of AIDS. Disclosures about the deceased diva's AIDS were prompted by the press's sense that people whose actions are of consequence to public debate are informationally accountable to the public. Some thought the entertainer made herself accountable when she sought treatment in the emergency room of a public hospital.

Apparently, the Japanese people believe they can make legitimate demands on a celebrity for information and explanations about her marital woes. If the demands are not met, sanctions may follow. Here the ground of accountability seems to be the perceived public need for the enforcement of morality. In 1999, Ayumi Kuroda was forced to leave her job as a popular television talk show host when it was learned that she had divorced her husband without informing the viewing public. A common, though by no means universal, sentiment in Japan is that professional women are accountable to the public for information and explanations about developments in their private lives.

Relational Accountability

The contours of intrafamilial and intra-ethic accountability, explored in chapter 2, merit initial notice here. Accountability demands attach to the roles of spouse, parent, dependent child, and sibling. One can think of these as *sui generis* status-based demands. However, because denominate roles and relationships are capable of self-definition and redefinition in a liberal realm, it is useful to stress the underlying norms at play. Promise, reliance, and dependency are at the root of most seemingly status-based familial accountability.

We worry that "tweens" and teenagers who are not held strictly accountable are among those most likely to fall prey to sociopathologies and criminality, but we worry too about whether youth should be expected to cooperatively yield to their parents' random drug tests and electronic eavesdropping. The husband/wife and parent/child dyads are not the only kinship ties that generate *sui generis* expectations for accountability. Sibling relationships can also carry specific expectations of accountability. In sibling relationships, along with expectations of mutual aid and support come obligations of accountability in every sense—information, explanation, justification, punishment, and reliability. An unemployed man with a secret drug addiction who approaches his brother for financial help should not be surprised that his brother may inquire about suspicions of narcotic dependency, rejecting "None of your business!" and "It's my body!" as appropriate answers.

In our individualistic society many people nonetheless face expectations and feelings of accountability based on common membership in particular identity groups. Identity groups are also, to borrow a phrase from Allan F. Gibbard, "communities of judgment."[34] Indeed, accountability, like political responsibility, "is a relation of citizen and political community; but the citizen is a member of many cultural communities–determined by religion, education, taste, ethnical derivation, economic situation, occupation, and many other factors."[35] Many people belong to professions and religious organizations whose norms encourage, permit, even require scrutiny of what might otherwise be personal conduct and choices. Thus the psychologist who has sex with a client is accountable to the profession. A practicing Catholic who wishes to marry a non-Catholic is accountable to the church. Of interest to me here, along with concerns about accountability to one's family, employer, and the public, are concerns about accountability to ethno-racial groups. These groups commonly demand accountability for personal grooming (as in the case of the Black Muslims), sex, marriage, and child-rearing practices.

Intragroup accountability for private life has special contours in the case of public figures. Recall Clarence Page's remarks in conjunction with Jesse Jackson. Page said that as an African American journalist he held African American leaders to a higher standard of accountability than leaders of other races. A public figure may be accountable in one sense and to some degree to the general public, but in further senses and to further degrees to members of his or her identity group. The late Supreme Court Justice Thurgood Marshall was accountable for his personal life, not simply to the public, but also, and critically, to his African American public. Vivian "Buster" Burey Marshall, Marshall's first wife of twenty-five years, died in 1955. That same year he married his second wife, Cecilia Suyat, who was not, in the parlance of the day, a "Negro." The victorious attorney in *Brown v. Board of Education*, Marshall was one of the most influential men in the United States.[36] Known to have had a large ego, Marshall enjoyed his stature as a voice of leadership within the NAACP. One might guess that in mid-twentieth century America, such a man could marry whomever he wanted, no questions asked. But that was far from the truth in the decade before *Loving v. Virginia*.[37] Marshall's closest advisors knew that questions would be asked about his motives for out-marriage and his intentions about continuing at the forefront of the fight for black civil rights. Marshall's second marriage threatened to be a political liability for the NAACP. His personal choice could have cost the organization money and support at a critical juncture. Showing both moral sensitivity and political savvy, NAACP leaders successfully urged Marshall to hold a press conference in which he graciously introduced his bride and affirmed his commitments to civil rights work.

More than a half century later, accountability for out-marriage remains on the moral landscape. Only about ten percent of black men marry women who are not black. Blacks are the most endogamous of the major "racial" groups in the country. Among African Americans, those who out-marry still face a surprising degree of negative accountancy premised on feelings of betrayal. African Americans are not the only minority group whose members often feel accountable to the group for personal choices.

Problems of intragroup accountability exist in the world of child rearing and adoption too. Native American women seeking to place their children for adoption are accountable to tribal authorities for adoption decisions. Although one might think that a parent's decision to place his or her child for adoption is a personal one, a 1978 federal law, the Indian Child Welfare Act, gives Native tribes the right to veto the placement of a Native child with a non-Native family. In a related context, advocates of "open adoption" advise adoptive families that they have obligations that I characterize in chapter 2 as accountability obligations, obligations to communicate with the biological families of their adoptive children. Information-emphatic accountability norms are now pervasive in the world of domestic adoption. Adoptive families are expected to provide photographs, narratives, and even visitation privileges to biological parents. Some open-adoption practices have been prompted by the sense that respect for adopted children's and birth parents' common genetic, cultural, or family identities requires continuing ties.

TOO MUCH ACCOUNTABILITY?

It is one thing to know the contours of accountability in one's society and something else to approve of them. Since the 1980s the press and public have lavished attention on the personal lives of public figures and officials. A hundred years ago, the public might have learned in time that a great man had had an extramarital affair. Today we learn not only that a man has had an affair, but precisely what sex acts were performed, when, where, with whom, and what she was wearing. Exquisite details issue from the national Congress rather than the *National Enquirer* alone. Extensive involuntary accountability for private life such as this has come under fire as prurient and demeaning.

Websites and public access television that reveal the identities of patients and physicians create an unwanted, dangerous level of accountability for abortion.[38] Others invite voluntary educative accountability for women who agree to, for example, webcast childbirth and mastectomy.[39] But voluntary accountability has come under fire, too, lambasted as degrading exhibitionism. The number of television and Web forums in which ordinary people are invited to disclose their personal and intimate lives to the general public has mushroomed in recent years. Not all of this is pure exhibitionism or is bad. To the extent, though, that accountability for private life in the United States seems excessive, who or what is to be blamed?

About forty years ago feminists began to frame problems of gender subordination, domestic violence, and sex crimes as political problems for a democratic society. Prior to that time, a beating or rape might pass as a purely personal matter best left unreported to family, friends, or law enforcement authorities. Household offenders were not significantly accountable and could easily escape moral censure. The eventual politicization of the personal was warranted because, as Jennifer Nedelsky explains, privately perpetuated violence "was an essential part of a social and political system in which one group was kept subordinate."[40] Nedelsky's "relational feminism" is a reconstructed liberalism that prioritizes rights framed in response to visions of cruelty-free, accountable relationships rather than the prerogatives of isolated agents.

Because vocal feminists called for making traditionally private matters political, some observers blamed feminists for the New Accountability— especially the humiliating level of highly public attention paid to other people's personal lives after the 1980s. Critics in the popular press perceived a feminist influence in the bitter controversies about public accountability for sex and sexual harassment that dominated Washington following Supreme Court Justice Clarence Thomas' Senate confirmation hearings and President William Jefferson Clinton's impeachment. They blamed feminists for creating an overall climate in American life in which the public would accept lurid disclosure as legitimate and would freely publicize sexual intimacies for political gain.[41] Are feminists culpable?

Accountability in Fiction and Fact

Highly public accountability for sex and sexual misconduct preceded the feminism and feminists who got stuck with the blame. Accountability for private life antedates contemporary feminism, Betty Freidan, and the sexual revolution of the 1960s. A classic literary depiction of accountability for private life stands as a reminder—Nathaniel Hawthorne's novel, *The Scarlet Letter.* The hypocritical New England society depicted in the story strikes readers as unjust. Civic authorities subjected Hester to punishment-emphatic accountability for normal, illicit sex. Even though she was punished, the man who impregnated her was not. The manner of punishment was cruel. Hester's punishment enacted and perpetuated society's accountability demands. Forced to wear the "A," Hester continuously confessed her adultery and continuously received punishment. Hester achieved heroism by resisting one accountability demand (naming her lover) and by capitalizing on the other, embroidering "A" after "A" of extraordinary artistic beauty.

Public accountability for sex has long been a part of American fact as well as fiction. It is admittedly possible to cite historical examples of nonaccountability for matters deemed private. For example, no early American state or federal laws criminalized birth control or abortion. Married people did not have to account to public authorities, anyway, for the uses of intimacy to control fertility until well into the nineteenth century. Moreover, ideals of female modesty entailed privileges of nonaccountability for women. A good example from the law books is *Botsford v. Union Pacific Railway,*[42] a case from the late nineteenth century with little value as precedent but one that is frequently cited by privacy scholars. Today, plaintiffs of both sexes routinely submit to compelled medical examination, as a matter of basic fairness, to verify injuries alleged in their suits. However, in *Botsford,* the Supreme Court held that a female plaintiff claiming to have been injured aboard a train could not be expected to submit to the examination of a physician at the request of the defendant, a rail company seeking verification of injury. Modesty ruled over accountability, fairness, and common sense.

But one can find historical examples in which modesty counts for nothing in the courtroom and in which extremes of accountability for intimacies govern. The rediscovered Rhinelander case is illustrative.[43] Eighty years ago a wealthy New York man, Leonard "Kip" Rhinelander, sued to have his marriage annulled. The peculiar ground for annulment was that his wife, Alice Jones Rhinelander, had deceived him as to her race. The legal proceedings and journalistic frenzy that followed led to expectations of accountability for the most intimate aspects of the young couple's lives. The courtroom drama that ensued demanded the ultimate in accountability of the information-emphatic and explanation-emphatic sorts. Mr. Rhinelander endured opposing counsel's reading aloud in court his sexually explicit love letters to his future bride. His wife's lawyers hoped to brand him in the minds of the jury as a perverted and unmanly seducer. Attorneys asked Mr. Rhinelander to explain intimacies (possibly, oral sex) referred to obliquely in intimate correspondence. Alice Rhinelander was the eventual victor in the case. However, after listening to her premarital trysts with her husband detailed in court, her own lawyer insisted, with the approval of the judge in the case, that she bare her "dusky" naked breasts and legs to the jury to prove that her lover-turned-husband had to have known she was "colored" when he married her. Bizarrely, the famous black-face entertainer Al Jolson was dragged into court to deny an affair with Mrs. Rhinelander, solely because she once mentioned in a letter that someone she met at work called "Al Jolson" was a flirt. That a perfect stranger to the litigants was held accountable for his sex life, too, is evidence of the sweeping character of private life accountability at the time.

In light of the Rhinelander case, blaming feminism for Anita Hill's or Monica Lewinsky's frank testimony looks like fallacious post hoc reasoning. Accusing feminists who supported sexual harassment laws of hypocrisy for not siding with Paula Jones and Independent Counsel Kenneth Starr flowed from a rational failure of another dimension. As a feminist, one could certainly advocate accountability for workplace sexual harassment and consistently condemn both Paula Jones' apparent political partisanship and the insensitive methods of the investigations that led to President Clinton's impeachment trial and acquittal.

Expanded Accountability

Feminist theory has made major contributions to ethics, political philosophy, and epistemology. Recent feminism has characteristically called for

knowing and being known; for mutual obligations of deliberation and dialogue; for personal narrative and empathy; for expanded and blended families; and for a willingness to recognize and punish injuries to women, children, and other traditionally vulnerable or subordinate groups. One finds no
chapter entitled "Accountability" in the books of leading feminists. However, there are ways in which the very soul of recent feminist moral, political, and legal theory has been an effort to fortify anemic conceptual paradigms of accountability for private life. Concern about accountability for
private life is plainly at play in the critique and reconstruction of liberal autonomy and the public-private distinction that have been emblematic of academic feminist theory.[44] Feminists seeking to explicate the value of controlling one's own body and living one's own life for the sake of agency,
equality, or autonomy nevertheless stress that "social relationships and in-
terdependencies are necessary" for their realization.[45] Accountability is entailed by safety, emotional-health, and other necessitities.

"Feminist ethics has made its most important contribution to the ethic of
responsibility," according to Larry May,[46] aptly citing the contributions
of Nel Nodding, Diana Meyers, Margaret Walker, Sara Ruddick, and others.[47]
The ethic of responsibility holds important implications for how we should
conceive moral accountability for personal matters. The need to address competing paradigms of social "difference" has been central in feminist political
theory.[48] However, the need to address competing paradigms of accountability within society is the implicit common impetus behind feminist articula-
tions of moral obligation and ethics of care. It has been implicit, too, in
feminists' theories of intimacy, community, and democracy. These theories
propose expanded agency and responsibility in private life.

The political accountability for private life that popular feminists advocated after the 1960s was never a *per se* rejection of the concept of having a
personal life. "The personal is political" was a slogan, like "Just do it" is
a slogan. Feminists have wanted to sell policy makers on moving ahead on issues key to women's lives, and the Nike corporation has wanted to sell us all
on wearing their brand of athletic gear. "The personal is political" no more
called for the obliteration of intimacy and privacy than "Just do it!" calls for
the obliteration of deliberative judgment about the limits of physical exertion.
Legal feminist Catharine MacKinnon is notable for work in the 1980s that
condemned privacy categorically as a pernicious concept, ideology, and jurisprudence, seemingly to demand complete accountability for conduct. I argued then and subsequently that she cannot have meant what she said.[49] Even
she has admitted that she cannot have meant what she said.[50] She accepts that
the experience of privacy of the sort that is protected by tort law can have
value for women. In fact, many contemporary theorists embrace the critique

of privacy while also embracing opportunities for solitude, intimacy, the exercise of agency relating to one's own body, and identity.[51] The point is not to eliminate experiences of privacy but to "socialize and democratize our conceptions of privacy."[52]

Modes of privacy and private choice make us all—male and female—morally and psychologically more fit for responsible social participation.[53] Patricia Boling agrees. She has argued that protecting "politicalness" and privacy are "important parts of the process of nurturing democratic citizens."[54] Judith Wagner DeCew offers a different point against MacKinnon-style feminist critiques of privacy, echoing Jed Rubenfeld's antitotalitarian defense of privacy laws, published on the eve of the centennial of Samuel Warren and Louis Brandeis' seminal call in the *Harvard Law Review* for legal recognition of privacy rights.[55] If privacy is valueless, nothing holds back government control over all dimensions of our lives, DeCew fears. Accountability, even if newly, justifiably expanded, must be bounded.

Feminist Approaches to Accountability

Feminist theorists have implicitly said that we are broadly accountable for what we do as citizens, family members, intimates, and workers. Feminist activists have celebrated modes of collective action, concern, dialogue, and involvement premised on mutual accountability. Feminist lawyers and legal theorists have surely played a material role in decreasing individual accountability to the state for contraception and abortion while increasing punishment-emphatic forms of legal accountability for violent and coercive sex.[56] Still, as an empirical matter, the precise role recent feminist theory or politics has played in shaping the New Accountability for private life is unclear. The full story has yet to be told.

Beyond the empirical question of the impact feminism and feminists have had on public accountability for private conduct is this one: what specific accountability norms and practices would a society adopt to honor the insights of late twentieth and early twenty-first century feminist theories? What would a normative approach to accountability for private life look like, if informed by the concerns and insights of feminism? Everything depends, of course, on what one takes to be the concerns and insights of feminism, a decentralized body of interpretation, criticisms, and proposals, ranging from the reactionary to the postmodern. Plainly, there can be a plurality of feminist approaches to accountability norms. Relational feminists, neorepublican feminists, communitarian feminists, care-ethic feminists, Christian feminists, lesbian feminists[57], postmodernist feminists, and so on will have their own takes. A postmodern feminist might ask, "Which accountability is available to feminists working outside the reference to a universal, coherent, and stable self and yet still committed to agency, the empowerment of women, and to theoretical and methodological accuracy?"[58] A liberal feminist might focus on allocating once male-only rights to women or applying a more egalitarian or relational account of rights to the battle against female subordination and exclusion.[59] A lesbian feminist might argue for skeptical regard toward ideals of accountability that could fuel repressive, homophobic moralism.

Jennifer Nedelsky demonstrated an understanding of the visceral fear that accompanies the very idea of reforms that would expand accountability, especially by increasing legal sanctions for "private" behavior. Nedelsky imagines the critic of relational feminism, asking her:

> Will not the magnitude of responsibility implicit in my approach be overwhelming, personally, psychologically, and socially? Will it not end up erasing the divisions of rights, boundaries, and limits that have made freedom and security possible? Doesn't it invite vast intrusion at a collective level?"[60]

With accountability, what happens to difference, deviance, peace of mind? What happens to rights? In short, won't expanded accountability make it harder for a person to feel secure, whether he is a thief or a property owner? Behind the problems of thievery and ownership are structural problems of inequality and subordination that feminist reforms seek to address.

Recent feminist theory, particularly feminist legal theory, has been distinctly egalitarian, antiformalist, and antilibertarian. With appropriate caveats against overgeneralization and vagueness, I would like to suggest that, whatever the particulars, a normative approach to accountability inspired by recent liberal and progressive feminist theory would likely be (1) premised on progressive claims about gender equality, (2) antiformalist, and (3) antilibertarian. The approach I take in the next three chapters of this book reflects those very premises.

Progressive Equality

One defining concern of Anglo-American feminist theory has been gender equality—the equality under the law and in social life of men and women. Feminists could be expected to cast a skeptical eye on a normative theory of moral or legal accountability that merely represented "in abstract and idealized forms, aspects of the *actual* positions and relations of some people in a certain kind of social order . . . where the typicality of these positions depends on gender, age, economic status, race and other factors that distribute powers and forms of recognition differentially and hierarchically."[61] Women deserve no fewer of the substantive political, economic, employment, educational, and social opportunities than are accorded men.

As accountability can function to enable power, including the social power of one sex over another, ideal accountability practices would be mindful of the implications of accountability ascriptions for gender equality. Accountability is both a burden (because it can limit privacy and freedom) and a benefit (because it is a by-product of wanted intimacy, responsibility, and power). Equality of accountability means that the benefits and burdens of accountability should be equally distributed among men and women. This will require, *inter alia*, that roles, occupations, and offices in the society are genuinely open and attractive to both sexes. If this condition is not met, individuals wind up with obligations, duties, responsibilities, and attendant modes of accountability that they do not much want.[62]

Currently, many occupations are segregated by sex. A male blue-collar worker who is the sole support for a family is more accountable to his employer and his family for his whereabouts during the business day than a pregnant homemaker, whose responsibilities allow her more flexibility and less immediate accountability to others for her whereabouts. Gay or straight men in egalitarian relationships who "stay home rather than work" enjoy similar conditions of reduced accountability. Women who work in blue-collar jobs face similar accountability demands from employers as men in blue-collar jobs. Women in "pink-collar" office jobs and nursing positions are among the most accountable employees of all. The woman who cleans houses is more accountable than the man who mows lawns, even if they are paid the same wage, because of the nature of the tasks they are required to perform. Equal accountability will require economic arrangements that fairly distribute opportunities for the desirable forms of accountability.

Equality of accountability will also require that when men and women engage in the same activities, women are neither more nor less accountable than male counterparts. Accountability functions to enable the discharge of responsibilities. A male lover, parent, or schoolteacher should not be able to expect more from partners, teenagers, or pupils than a woman lover, parent, or teacher. Men and women in similar roles should benefit from the same accountability norms. Equality of accountability cannot mean, though, that, without regard to actual capacities and roles, individual men and women should be accountable in precisely the same ways to precisely the same people. The criminal or civil accountability that might be appropriate for a nursing mother who knowingly consumes dangerous drugs that will be delivered to her infant through breast milk is not appropriate for the father of the infant who consumes those same drugs. Criminal or civil accountability could be appropriate, though, for a father who knowingly consumed drugs that clouded his judgment and led him to neglect his helpless infant.

To achieve equality of accountability, men may need to be, on the whole and compared to fifty years ago, more accountable to their families and to society, and women may need to be less accountable to their families and society. Late twentieth-century feminism is associated with an argument for greater state and personal accountability, implicit in the familiar feminist critique of privacy as the condition of female subordination, domestic violence, and societal neglect of welfare interests; *and* with an argument for less accountability, implicit in the feminist call for reproductive freedom and for gender equality under law as well as in social institutions and practices. Under fading regimes of patriarchy, privacy is the place where men lord over women and is the excuse that the state uses to justify letting them do it. The proposed cure for the injustice of privacy so conceived has been for men to be more accountable to the state and for women to be less accountable to men. For example, men who beat women should be accountable to the police and the law courts. Women who want independence should not be utterly accountable to their fathers, spouses, or lovers for their decisions or conduct. This understanding of the requirements of equality sits easily with progressive western liberalism, less easily with conservative, fundamentalist, and traditionalist perspectives that understand respecting human equality as being equally respectful of women's properly subordinate roles and men's properly dominate or paternalistic roles in their families and communities.

Contextualism

A report of accountability informed by feminism would have a nonformalist, contextual quality to it. Formalism, conceived as a vice, is the tendency to treat matters of substance as decidable by straightforward acts of conceptual categorization. Eschewing formalism, one would not say, "people should not be accountable for sexuality (or medical decisions, finances, etc.) because they are private." One would instead remain open to asking what ought to be afforded privacy in particular cases and contexts. "Personal," "family," "private," "sexual," and "religious" are not words of exclusion that mark fixed realms of unaccountability unamenable to revision and political negotiation.[63] It has proven harmful to treat "privacy" as a mantra of exclusion—a magic word to utter as justification for keeping people and the state out of one's life.

Accountability norms for private life are highly context-specific in practice.[64] So although spouses are usually accountable to one another for sexual conduct, they may not be accountable in specific circumstances. It is easy to imagine situations in which spouses should not be obligated to reveal adultery to one another, such as in cases of long-term estrangement. And although unmarried couples may by express agreement or implied understandings be less accountable to one another than married couples, prevailing norms and practices would suggest that domestic partners and other unmarried couples expect a high degree of accountability for sexual intimacy.

Accountability for private life is context-specific in another respect as well. We are accountable to different categories of people in different ways. What we are obligated to reveal about sexual conduct to spouses, domestic partners, and live-in lovers we rarely are expected to reveal to neighbors, casual friends, employers, or professionals. What we are expected to reveal about our feelings and perspectives to our closest friends we are not expected to reveal in similar detail to our employers. What we are expected to reveal to our employers about debilitating medical problems or to explain to our lawyers or accountants about irregular financial transactions we are not expected to reveal to our neighbors.

Forged in the context of evaluating the ethics of technology, Gary Marx's views about distinguishing public and private are highly consistent with my expectations of a theory of accountability for private life that would issue from feminism. Noting a Chinese proverb that "Clean water kills the fish," Marx suggests that we begin thinking more clearly about appropriate boundaries between selves and others by taking into account the potential relevance of legal norms regarding public and private places and accessible and inaccessible information; customs, manners, expectations, and practices regarding public and private; the actual accessibility of information and the public knowledge; and finally, social status, roles, and personal traits. To take all of this into account is to forego the search for a simple rule, principle, or definition to delineate public or private. He wrote:

> I argue that rather than approaching the public and private as uni-dimensional, rigidly dichotomous and absolute, fixed and universal concepts, whose meaning is determined by the objective content of behavior, they are best conceptualized as multi-dimensional, with dimensions sometimes overlapping or blurred and at other times cross cutting or oppositional, continuous and relative, fluid and situational or contextual, whose meaning lies in how they are interpreted and framed. [65]

This approach may lead to more tentative, less sweeping generalizations but also to a greater appreciation for actual complexity.[66] Legal scholar Paul M. Schwartz has urged contextualism in thinking about public and private as well. A contextual approach to the norms of public and private favored by so many legal scholars and philosophers today implies a contextual approach to the norms of accountability for private life.

To say that accountability is a matter of context might be thought to imply that any effort to think systematically about accountability norms is futile, that there can be no rules or even principles of accountability to guide us. My essays are designed to reveal the challenge of both discerning *de facto* accountability norms from cultural norms and practices, and of formulating ideal, *de jure* accountability norms to guide practice and policy. Yet I do believe certain goals, including moral dignity and autonomy, inclusive workplaces, public safety, effective leadership, happy families, and a pluralistic society, will point us away from certain specific accountability practices and toward others, for defensible reasons that can be straightforwardly explained. (Jean L. Cohen demonstrates this for legal institutions that require judges to rationalize decisions regulating the intimate realm.[67]) For example, if, as I will argue in the next chapter, adoptive parents should not be broadly accountable to birth parents, the reason is not to be found in a definition of family or privacy or accountability, but in an assessment of the impact of being expected to report, explain, and justify parenting decisions on incentives to rear young children, and on the capacity to live emotionally secure and satisfying lives.

Relationships

Finally, I suggest that a normative theory of accountability informed by feminism would have an antilibertarian quality to its recommendations. Libertarians sometimes rely upon John Stuart Mill's formulation of public and private. John Stuart Mill's principle of liberty rejected accountability to the state for "self-regarding" conduct. Persons are not answerable to the community for conduct that is truly self-regarding; that is, not significantly harmful or injurious to others. Our Supreme Court has sometimes cited Mill's formulation with approval. Mill and the Supreme Court each have advanced idiosyncratic notions about what is self-regarding and what is not. Bearing and begetting children, sacred private turf for the Court in its child rearing, sterilization, and birth control cases, was not so for Mill, who placed child welfare above parental autonomy.

Feminists reject libertarianism's thin vision of accountability.[68] Feminists are among those who are skeptical about the existence of realms of action and conduct without significant, relevant impact on others. Purely self-regarding conduct is, indeed, a myth. Our lives are importantly interconnected and interdependent. If I use cocaine, whip my children, gamble, have unprotected sex, or drive a gas-guzzling, flip-over-prone SUV, my choices affect others. It is for this reason that Nedelsky theorizes appeals to rights as occasions for examining the relationships with others affected by their ascription.

Feminist liberals accept the ideals of tolerance and civic freedom implicit in John Stuart Mill's classic argument that government should leave alone people who are not plainly hurting others. Yet liberal feminists sometimes disagree with other liberals about when conduct is hurtful to others, by locating meaningful externalities where libertarians find none. A strong libertarian, the philosopher Jan Narveson construes narcotic drug use as purely self-regarding conduct. He has argued that drug use is unjustly subject to state prohibition, because the person who takes drugs introduces them into her own body and assumes all the risks. Although they respect the sanctity and separateness of the individual's body, liberals can easily reject the idea that the ingestion of substances that incite violence, induce crime, destroy families, cloud intellects, and undermine public health is self-regarding conduct.

A more radical libertarian than Mill might condemn both government and nongovernment interference with self-regarding conduct. An opponent of accountability to the state for personal matters, Mill was not as forceful an opponent of moral and ethical accountability to the private sector. Mill did not propose to restrict family, friendly, and neighborly interference with others. His main object of attack was coercive, moralistic government interference. Suppose you know someone who spends his time in bars and on the beach. He is wasting his life, you conclude. He is irresponsible, you believe. These are good reasons for, in Mill's words, "remonstrating with him, or reasoning with him, or persuading him, or entreating him."[69] A stronger libertarian than Mill might take the view that both coercive government restraint and what philosophers sometimes call "moral suasion" are wrong. People should be let alone. If she isn't hurting anyone but herself, how a person spends her time is none of anyone else's business. Let her prefer club and casino to church and college. I believe many feminists would endorse moral suasion and the deliberative, explicative, and justificatory accountability it presupposes, subject to frank concern about hegemonic uses of morality.

However, not all feminists endorse moral suasion. Consider the broad brush of Sarah Hoagland's rejection of blame and accountability in her lesbian ethical theory.[70] Hoagland presents what I would term nonreciprocal justification-emphatic accountability as the special burden that traditional ethical theories wrongly place on the shoulders of lesbians and other marginalized, oppressed groups. As Barbara Houston notes, Hoagland decries "pointing a blaming finger," "nailing so-and-so to the wall for a given act and holding her up before the community for condemnation," "the obsession with confession and absolution before the community," and "trying to make another admit she was mean and nasty."[71]

Lesbians face both legal coercion and moral suasion aimed at deterring and punishing same-sex lifestyles. Both similarly subject lesbians to shame, guilt, and secrecy. According to Hoagland, oppressed groups (women, Jews, slaves, lesbians, gay men) generally find themselves blamed for their oppression and victimization, as if the injury others do them were their choice. Hence, "[m]oral accountability as we understand it . . . does not present us with a viable concept of choice under oppression." This observation leads Hoagland to reject the institution of moral blame altogether. Rather than have people blaming one another and justifying themselves to others, she urges instead an ethic of intelligibility wherein persons would seek to understand others' needs and values even when they clash with their own.

Hoagland's theory suffers from a lack of clarity about the forms of accountability and blame she seeks to condemn. As we have seen in this chapter, there are at least five distinguishable senses of accountability, and not all of them reduce conceptually or functionally to blame. The institution of blame, Hoagland stresses, casts an onus of self-justification on targets of disapprobation. Yet, as we have seen, justification is not the only form of accountability, and not all forms of justification merit condemnation. Indeed, the most serious problem with Hoagland's ethic of intelligibility is that it is a perfect instance of tossing the baby out with the bathwater. The bathwater is oppressive, self-serving moralism. The baby is justification-emphatic accountability and the information and explanation-emphatic accountability it presupposes. Barbara Houston effectively rescues the baby in her sensitive reply to Hoagland. Accountability is something moral agents can badly want because it implies their status as agents. "I recall occasions," Houston writes, "on which I desperately wanted to be held accountable when it seemed others were refusing to blame me out of a sense of the futility of it."[72] Others withhold accountability when they believe an individual is incompetent to deliver the performances of answerability or when they believe an individual is competent but unimportant. Drawing on P. F. Strawson's account of expressive responsibility, Houston continues, "[f]or me to be good, to *be* a moral agent just *is* to (want to) be the subject of responses to others that express normative expectations. I cannot imagine myself as an agent without also imagining myself being held to some standard and being regarded as a disappointment when I fail to live up to it."[73] Paul Benson makes a similar point when he argues that responsibility presupposes there "being others who could morally criticize us and expect us to answer for our actions."[74]

Part of what it means to live cooperatively in relation to others is to live with a degree of answerability, accountability, and blame. The cooperative person is willing to expose himself or herself to others' emotions and judgment, and to enjoy a correlative sense of entitlement to expose others to his or her own emotions and judgments. There are limits, of course, on extremes of emotion and judgment. The bipolar rage attack and the delusory dogma do not merit accommodation in the same way as the ordinary range of emotions and belief. Holding others mutually and reciprocally accountable implies recognition of their moral equality. It also implies their membership in a common "community of judgment."[75] The reason Barbara Houston has on occasion wanted so badly to be held accountable is to avoid the pain of felt inequality and exclusion. Hoagland is right that accountability can be a weapon of oppressive inequality and exclusion, but Houston is also right that equal, mutual accountability is presupposed by moral agency. The African American who believes that the white man shines too bright a light of accountability on him and his kind compared to the light shone on fellow whites has a complaint. The complaint, though, is about the wattage, not the light. It would be a mistake to read even a long history of accountability abuses as a sign that there is something per se wrong with social accountability. The lesbian's just complaint against heterosexual oppressors is wattage, too.

NOTES

1. See, for example, Stephen J. Schulhofer, *Unwanted Sex: The Culture of Intimidation and the Failure of Law* (Cambridge, U.K.: Harvard University Press, 1998).

2. For a discussion of privacy and accountability concerns in the United States raised by the AIDS epidemic in its early days, see generally Ronald Bayer, *Private Acts, Social Consequences: AIDS and the Politics of Public Health* (New York: The Free Press, 1989); and Amitai Etzioni, *The Limits of Privacy* (New York: Basic Books, 1999).

3. Jeffrey Rosen, *The Unwanted Gaze: The Destruction of Privacy in America* (New York: Random House, 2000).

4. Anita L. Allen, "Coercing Privacy," *William and Mary Law Review* 40 (1999): 723–57.

5. Andreas Schedler, "Conceptualizing Accountability," in *The Self-Restraining State*, ed. Andreas Schedler, Larry Diamond, and Marc F. Plattner (London: Lynne Rienner, 1999), 7.

6. Schedler, "Conceptualizing Accountability," 17.

7. See generally, for example, Robert B. Wagner, *Accountability in Education* (New York and London: Routledge, 1989).

8. Nicolas Haines, "Responsibility and Accountability," *Philosophy* 30 (1955): 142–43.

9. Haines, "Responsibilty," 144.

10. Haines, "Responsibilty," 7, 8.

11. "If it is fairly representative of common usage to hold that being accountable means, among other things, being obligated or subject to giving account, then in saying that a particular agent is accountable we could imply that he is obligated to give report, relation, description, explanation, justifying analysis, or some form of exposition. For we have observed that from an etymological standpoint the term account has come to mean all of the above." Wagner, *Accountability in Education*, 8–9.

12. I quote here an interview with Clarence Page concerning Jesse Jackson, *Columbia Journalism Review* (March/April 2001), http://www.cjr.org/year/01/2/qanda.asp.

13. That gleeful affects are possible in this context was suggested to me by Professor James Whitman.

14. Saul Smilansky, "Moral Accountancy and Moral Worth," *Metaphilosophy* 28, nos. 1–2, (1997): 124.

15. *McVeigh v. Cohen*, 983 F. Supp. 215 (Dist. Ct. D.C. 1998).

16. Peter Schönbach, *Account Episodes: The Management or Escalation of Conflict* (Cambridge, U.K.: Cambridge University Press, 1990), 4.

17. Eric A. Posner, *Law and Social Norms* (Cambridge, Mass.: Harvard University Press, 2002), 5.

18. Cf. James J. Van Patten, "Reflections on Accountability," *Journal of Thought* 7, no. 2 (April 1972): 112.

19. *Tarasoff v. Regents of the University of California*, 551 P. 2d 334 (Cal. 1976).

20. Richard McKeon, "The Ethics of International Influence," *Ethics* 120, no. 3 (1960): 187–203.

21. Richard McKeon, "The Development and the Significance of the Concept of Responsibility," *Revue International de Philosophie* no. 39 (1957): 26.

22. McKeon, "Development and Significance," 26.

23. Wagner, *Accountability in Education*, 55–56.

24. Patricia H. Werhane, "Formal Organizations, Economic Freedom, and Moral Agency," *Journal of Value Inquiry* 14, no. 1 (Spring 1980): 43.

25. R. Jay Wallace, *Responsibility and the Moral Sentiments* (Cambridge, Mass.: Harvard University Press, 1994), 165.

26. I am indebted to Anthony Kronman for underscoring the importance of accountability to oneself.

27. *Atkins v. Virginia*, 536 U.S. 122 S. Ct. 2242 (2002).

28. Wallace, *Responsibility*, 164.

29. Peter A. French, "'Senses of 'Blame',"" *Southern Journal of Philosophy* 14, no. 4 (Winter 1976): 448; Gerry Gaden, "Rehabilitating Responsibility," *Journal of Philosophy of Education* 24, no. 1 (1990): 28–9.

30. A. I. Melden, *Rights and Persons* (Berkeley: University of California Press, 1997), 32.

31. *Mayfield v. Dalton*, 109 F. 3d 1423 (9th Cir. 1997).

32. Schedler, "Conceptualizing Accountability," 13.

33. Schedler, "Conceptualizing Accountability," 13.

34. Allan F. Gibbard, *Wise Choices, Apt Feelings* (Cambridge, Mass.: Harvard University Press, 1990). Compare Michael J. Sandel, *Democracy's Discontent: America in Search of a Public Philosophy* (Cambridge, Mass.: Harvard University Press, 1996).

35. McKeon, "Development and Significance," 25.

36. *Brown v. Board of Education*, 349 U.S. 294 (1955). See Juan Williams, *Thurgood Marshall: American Revolutionary* (New York: Times Books, 1998).

37. *Loving v. Virginia*, 388 U.S. 1967.

38. In the spring of 2002, a federal appeals court held that the so-called "Nuremberg Files" website constituted an illegal threat to abortion providers in view of the murders of several abortion doctors. See *Planned Parenthood of the Colom./Willamette, Inc. v. Am. Coalition of Life Activists*, 290 F. 3d 1058 (9th Cir. 2002).

39. For the details of "Patti's" mastectomy and "Elizabeth's" delivery, see my article "Gender and Privacy in Cyberspace," *Stanford Law Review* 52, no. 2 (May 2000): 1188–90.

40. Jennifer Nedelsky, "Violence against Women: Challenges to the Liberal State and Relational Feminism," in *Political Order: Nomos XXXVIII*, ed. Ian Shapiro and Russell Hardin (New York: NYU Press, 1996), 472.

41. See, for example, Juliette Cutler Page, "Why Do Feminists Support Clinton?" *Feminista* 2, no. 1 (1998), also available at www.feminista.com/v2n11/clinton.html (accessed 29 October 2002).

42. *Botsford v. Union Pacific Railway*, 141 U.S. 250 (1891).

43. Earl Lewis and Heidi Ardizzone, *Love on Trial: An American Scandal in Black and White* (New York: W. W. Norton & Co., 2002).

44. Marilyn Friedman, "Feminism in Ethics: Conceptions of Autonomy," in *The Cambridge Companion to Feminism in Philosophy,* ed. Miranda Fricker and Jennifer Hornsby (Cambridge, U.K.: Cambridge University Press, 2000), 210–220. Also, see generally the following edited collections of diverse feminist perspectives: Fricker and Hornsby, *Cambridge Companion to Feminism in Philosophy* ; Carol Gould, ed., *Gender: Key Concepts in Critical Theory* (Atlantic Highlands, N.J.: Humanities Press, 1997); Nancy J. Hirshmann and Christine DiStefano, eds., *Revisioning the Political: Feminist Reconstructions of Traditional Concepts in Western Political Theory* (New York: Westview, 1996), 181–91; Dana E. Bushnell, ed., *Nagging Questions: Feminist Ethics in Everyday Life* (Lanham, Md.: Rowman and Littlefield, 1995); and Mary Lyndon Shanley and Uma Narayan, eds., *Reconstructing Political Theory* (Cambridge, U.K.: Polity Press, 1995).

45. Friedman, "Feminism in Ethics," 216–17.

46. Larry May, *The Socially Responsive Self: Social Theory and Professional Ethics* (Chicago and London: University of Chicago Press, 1996), 98.

47. See Nel Nodding, *Caring: A Feminine Approach to Ethics and Moral Education* (Berkeley: University of California Press, 1984); Diana Meyers, "The Socialized Individual and Individual Autonomy," in *Women and Moral Theory*, ed. Eva Feder Kittay and Diana T. Meyers (Totowa, N.J.: Rowman and Littlefield, 1987), 151; Diana Meyers, *Self, Society, and Personal Choice* (New York: Columbia University Press, 1989); Margaret Urban Walker, "Feminism, Ethics, and the Question of Theory," *Hypatia* 7, no. 3 (summer 1992): 23–38; and Sara Ruddick, *Maternal Thinking: Toward a Politics of Peace* (New York: Ballantine, 1989).

48. Diemut Bubeck, "Women's Difference," in Fricker and Hornsby, *Feminism in Philosophy*, 185–204.

49. See my book, *Uneasy Access* (Totowa, N.J.: Rowman & Littlefield, 1988), 43–53. Privacy furthers personal and group goods. Privacy makes us more fit for social participation and contributions to society up to our capacities.

50. See Catharine MacKinnon, "Reflections on Sex Equality under the Law," *Yale Law Journal* 100 (1991): 1311. MacKinnon acknowledges that the invasion of privacy concept found, for example, in tort law, has worth in our legal system, even if constitutional privacy discourse in connection with abortion rights does not.

For a discussion of legal feminists' objections to privacy see my article "The Proposed Equal Protection Fix for Abortion Law: Reflections on Citizenship, Gender, and the Constitution," *Harvard Journal of Law and Public Policy* 18 (1995): 419–55.

51. According to Robert E. Goodin, the two worlds of relational feminism and liberalism do not look so different. See his "Structures of Political Order: The Relational Feminist Alternative," in Shaprio and Hardin, *Political Order*, 514.

52. Zillah Eisenstein, "Equalizing Privacy and Specifying Equality," in Hirshmann and DiStefano, *Revisioning the Political*, 181–91.

53. See my book, *Uneasy Access*, 51, 70–75 (discussion of feminist critiques of privacy, including MacKinnon). I will not repeat here the analyses of feminist critiques of privacy in my "Privacy," in *A Companion to Feminist Philosophy*, ed. Alison M. Jaggar and Iris Marion Young (Oxford, U.K.: Blackwell, 1998), 463–65; and my "The Jurispolitics of Privacy," in *Reconstructing Political Theory*, ed. Uma Narayan and Mary Lyndon Shanley (Cambridge, U.K.: Polity Press, 1996), 68–83.

54. Patricia Boling, "Why the Personal is Not Always Political," chapter 1 in her *Privacy and the Politics of Intimate Life* (Ithaca, N.Y.: Cornell University Press, 1996), 36.

55. See Jed Rubenfeld, "The Right of Privacy," *Harvard Law Review* 102, no. 4 (1989): 737–807 and Samuel Warren and Louis Brandeis, "The Right to Privacy," *Harvard Law Review* 4 (1890): 193–220. See also Judith Wagner DeCew, "The Feminist Critique of Privacy," chapter 5 in her *In Pursuit of Privacy: Law, Ethics, and the Rise of Technology* (Ithaca, N.Y.: Cornell University Press, 1997), 81–94. She worries about "granting excessive power to the state."

56. See Tracy E. Higgins, "Reviving the Public/Private Distinction in Feminist Theorizing," *Chicago-Kent Law Review* 75 (2000): 847–867.

57. For overviews of various feminist approaches, see works cited in notes 44 and 55. See also Sarah Hoagland, *Lesbian Ethics: Toward a New Value* (Palo Alto, Calif.: Institute of Lesbian Studies, 1988); Catriona MacKenzie and Natalie Stoljar, eds., *Relational Autonomy: Feminist Perspectives on Autonomy, Agency, and the Social Self*, ed. (New York: Oxford, 2000); and Diana Tietjens, ed., *Feminist Social Thought: A Reader* (New York: Routledge, 1997).

58. Rosi Braidotti, "Sexual Difference Theory," in Jagger and Young, *Companion to Feminist Philosophy*, 305.

59. "Every time a right is invoked, a full scale inquiry into the relations at stake will have to follow it . . . . The relational approach does not offer pat answers, but a framework to analyze the problem in ways that can facilitate the necessary change so urgently required" (Nedelsky, "Violence against Women," 488).

60. Nedelsky, "Violence against Women," 457.

61. Margaret Urban Walker, "Moral Epistemology," in Jagger and Young, *Companion to Feminist Philosophy*, 365.

62. See Nancy J. Hirshmann, "Rethinking Obligation for Feminism," in Hirshmann and DiStefano, *Revisioning the Political*, 168.

63. Martha A. Ackelsberg and Mary Lyndon Shanley, "Privacy, Publicity, and Power: A Feminist Rethinking of the Public-Private Distinction," in Hirshmann and DiStefano, *Revisioning the Political*, 213.

64. This is one of the reasons Jean Cohen urges a new "reflective" paradigm for legal decision making relating to the intimate sphere. She writes: "I believe that the reflexive paradigm provides the most appropriate perspective for dealing with such issues [contraception, abortion, surrogacy, marital rape, sexual harassment]. This paradigm presupposes the decentered character of contemporary society and a nuanced relationship between the state and civil institutions. It enables one to acknowledge contextual differences and ethical multiplicity in modes of intimacy, as well as the plurality of possible legal approaches. It thus allows for a reflexive choice among forms of regulation and an intelligent combination among these." See Jean L. Cohen, *Regulating Intimacy: A New Legal Paradigm* (Princeton, N.J.: Princeton University Press, 2002), 151.

65. Gary Marx, "Murky Conceptual Waters: The Public and Private," *Ethics and Information Technology* 3 (2001): 157–69.

66. Marx, "Murky Conceptual Waters," 168.

67. Cohen, *Regulating Intimacy.*

68. See Marilyn Friedman, in Fricker and Hornsby, *Feminism in Philosophy,* 205–20.

69. John Stuart Mill, *On Liberty* (London: J.W. Parker and Son, 1859). In chapter 1, Mill wrote: "the only purpose for which power can be rightfully exercised over any member of a civilized community against his will is to prevent harm to others. His own good, either physical or moral, is not a sufficient warrant. He cannot rightfully be compelled to do or to forbear because it will be better for him to do so, because it will make him happier, because in the opinions of others to do so would be wise or even right. These are good reasons for remonstrating with him, or reasoning with him, or persuading him, or entreating him, but not for compelling him, or visiting him with any evil in case he do otherwise. To justify that, the conduct from which it is desired to deter him must be calculated to produce evil to someone else."

70. Hoagland, *Lesbian Ethics,* 215–221.

71. Barbara Houston, "In Praise of Blame," *Hypatia* 7, no. 4 (fall 1992): 128–147, 131.

72. Houston, "Praise of Blame," 132.

73. Houston, "Praise of Blame," 134–55.

74. Paul Benson, "'Feeling Crazy,' Self-Worth, and the Social Character of Responsibility," in MacKenzie and Stoljar, *Relational Autonomy,* 72–93. Compare Wallace, *Responsibility and the Moral Sentiments,* asserting that a person is accountable if she possesses the powers of reflective self-control.

75. I am again citing Allan F. Gibbard's phrase. See note 34.

Chapter Two

Accountability to Family and Race

Genuine intimacy is a treasure. Accountability is its price. Intimacy and accountability go hand in hand. The intimacy of which I speak is the intimacy of friendship and kinship. Among intimates, accountability for personal thoughts, feelings, and conduct is normal, expected, and often valued. This is as it should be.

FRIENDSHIP

Friendship is a form of intimacy. I prefer as close friends people who can give me love and accept love; trust and be trusted; respect and be respected; enjoy and be enjoyed. My ideal friends are not simply capable of loving, trusting, respecting, and enjoying. They are all of those things in relation to *me*. My friends participate in my personal world. We are bound together, companionate. The imperatives of accountability are welcome burdens when they function well to foster meaningful ties. I prefer as close friends people with whom mutual accountability for private life works. Accordingly, I want friends who are competent at eliciting accountability from me: friends with whom I can communicate my innermost beliefs, from whom I can accept constructive criticism, and on whom I can rely, come what may. Friendship is a two-way street. I therefore want friends who invite me into their worlds on a mutual, reciprocal basis; friends who communicate back, accept my constructive criticism, and can rely on me in a range of circumstances. Moving about the world, I note who has what conception of commitment, reliance, dependency, and need. I try to surround myself with people whose substantive moral values suit me. They may be people I meet at school; they may be the parents of my children's friends; they may be members of my family. My friendships work best with people with whom I have compatible accountability styles. I choose to be with Lucy over Linda because Lucy is more open and less judgmental. Or Linda over Lucy because Linda is less dramatic and a tougher critic. A shared ethic and style of accountability is only a part of what friendship is about, but it is an important part.

Like an eagerness to share secrets, eagerness to answer to another about personal matters can be an important sign that friendship has been achieved. It feels good to be *involved* with someone. Purposeful acts of reporting, explanation, justification, and judgment within a framework of shared values is a distinctly human form of social involvement. Reckoning with loving friends is among the most engaging, satisfying forms of human interaction. On the one hand, that I am at all impelled to explain and justify myself to someone could be a sign that I regard him or her as special. On the other hand, I often feel obliged to answer to people who are not close to me. I feel obliged to explain personal matters to strangers I meet on airplanes and high school classmates reencountered on the Internet. Impulsion to account *per se* does not entail genuine intimacy, but reflects the reality of social connections as generic as common humanity and fellow alumnae.

KINSHIP

Like friendships, family ties can be intimate bonds, too, although they do not have to be. Commonly, however, the closest ties people have are ties to spouses, parents, grandparents, children, aunts, cousins, and other kin. Family can be friends and friends, family. Among African Americans, the distinction between friends and family is notoriously blurred, as girlfriends become sisters, kindly adult role models morph into "play aunts," and peers of nearly any sort, from fellow church members to neighbors to strangers, earn the label "brother." Interdependence blended with identification is the essence of family. I view the African American tendency to convert everyone into family as a recognition of the general truth that interdependence and identification are at home in, but by no means limited to, families.

With respect to families, we sometimes speak and act as if accountability for private life exists principally by virtue of roles that define the parameters of familial duty. We presume that accountability for private life comes with the territory of certain roles. Viewed in this way, reckoning imperatives obtain among kin because accountability is constitutive of certain kinship roles. "You are my husband," I say, "and so you have got to explain why in the world you would. . . ." Or, "I am your mother," I plead, "I need to know whether you. . . ." One could approach accountability in families from an affective rather than a status or relational, role-based perspective. Indeed, family members sometimes feel bound to account because of emotional ties rather than because of formal relational categories that they occupy in one another's lives. I love, I care, and so I account. I have loved, I have cared, and so I expect an accounting. Yet, the act of playing certain family roles or participating in certain family relationships makes both affection and accountability for private life more likely. In fact, we seek out the form—the role—hoping to experience emotional connection in the exercise of conventional kinship status prerogatives. I adopt a girl in order to have a daughter. I expect to love her as mothers love daughters and to be loved by her as daughters love mothers. I marry a man in order to have a husband. (Perhaps in vain) I am seeking all that the identities and roles of daughter and husband signify to me about vows, reliance, and dependencies, or other grounds of personal accountability in private life.

It pays for interdependent kin to share values and styles of accountability. When they do, intrafamilial accountability can be a satisfying experience. Substantial communication over the norms of accountability is a boon to family life. Few circumstances can make families more miserable than disconnection, because family ties resist severance. The stranger on the airplane, the high school classmate—these people one can escape with minimal cost. The sister, the grandparent, the spouse—these are linked by law, love, friendship, need, responsibility, and shared identities.

Moral accountability in and for private life can be a matter of considerable choice—products of contract, promise, commitment, invitation, inducement. To a large degree, I have chosen my friends by making myself more available to certain people than to others and by pursuing certain people more than others. Moral accountability is a function of choice and chance, however. Moral luck is a determinant of who we are, what we need, and what we can be. I chose my spouse, but not my biological aunts. I chose my adopted daughter in a way that I did not choose my biological son. I didn't choose my older sister and great aunts at all. Intrafamilial accountability is thus not well understood simply as a matter of freely chosen commitments or promises. It is not a domain of contract alone. Anyone dealt a familial role could wind up with mutual accountability obligations that are distinctly unwanted. Like it or not, in our society, playing certain roles and having certain categories of responsibility both induces reasonable reliance and forecloses other options in our society.

In practice, intrafamilial accountability is a massively complex phenomenon. It is hard to describe the expectations, the avoidance, the information flows, the variation in degrees and styles of explanation and justification, the forms of censure. I can think of no better way to convey some of the complexity than by illustrating it. To illustrate accountability to family for personal conduct, to problematize it, and to defend it, I offer a story of narcotic drug addiction. Taking drugs is one of those personal decisions sometimes labeled as "self-regarding" choices. However, my story shows drug use in another aspect, as causing harm to others, moral complicity, and a failure of ideal accountability to family, race, and community.

ACCOUNTABILITY IN THE FAMILY: AN ILLUSTRATION

In his arresting book *Rosa Lee*, Pulitzer Prize–winning journalist Leon Dash narrated the devastation of drugs, violence, theft, sex crimes, and drug abuse among four generations of a poor, African American family in Washington, D.C.[1] My personal experience instantiates the proposition that drug use can take its toll on families that are not poor as well, introducing violence, theft, sex crimes, and child abuse into the homes of comfortable white-, pink-, and khaki-collar families for the first time. Experiences like my middle-class family's and Rosa Lee's impoverished one should be essential food for thought for moralists advancing visions of personal accountability. Against the background of my experience, I shall outline what I have come to think of as meaningful moral considerations against recreational drug use.[2] They are considerations about accountability, too.

"Self-Regarding" Disasters

I lived in Ann Arbor between 1974 and 1978, when the local penalty for possession of small quantities of marijuana was a mere five-dollar fine, seldom levied. I attended the University of Michigan, where it seemed that just about everyone used drugs. There was even an annual drug festival on campus each April 1, known as the "Hash-Bash." Hundreds of people congregated in the center of campus and openly consumed pot and more exotic drugs. As a scholarship student on a tight budget, I could not afford to buy drugs at any price. But I was introduced to marijuana free of charge in the homes of young professors with whom we graduate students were friendly. After leaving Ann Arbor, the culture of drugs and issues relating to drug use soon left my radar screen. A dozen years later, drugs were once again in the picture. This is why.

In 1987, when I lived in Washington, D.C., my sister Gwen suddenly began telephoning me to ask for money. (I have fictionalized the names used here.) Until that time, Gwen and her husband Dave had seemed to live well on a $60,000 income in an inexpensive region of the country. In her calls, Gwen represented that Dave had stopped paying his half of the bills and that their marriage was in trouble. She said she was considering divorce but feared its impact on their son Tommy. I gave Gwen what money I could, mainly for the sake of my nephew and godson, Tommy. My willingness to lend my sister money became a source of discord in my marriage. I soon had to stop.

When I could not or would not help Gwen, someone else in the family generally stepped in. I have a total of five brothers and sisters, scattered all over the east coast. For several years, we all lent Gwen money for car payments, rent, school clothes, and medical care. We lent a hundred here, a few hundred there, according to our means as members of the middle and upper middle classes. My older sister Debra even took out a bank loan of several thousands of dollars and gave Gwen the proceeds. Loans to Gwen became gifts. She was rarely able to pay anyone back.

Early in 1991, Gwen told me that she was in danger of losing the secretarial job she had held for a dozen years. Gwen was thirty-five years old and a civil servant. Gwen said her secretarial job was at risk because she was often absent from work. She said she had gynecological problems. She had used up her paid sick leave and vacation time, but took additional time off as needed. When Gwen missed work, her boss docked her pay. Her paychecks were getting smaller and smaller. She could barely meet expenses.

There was more. Gwen's job required a top-secret military security clearance. Her security clearance depended upon good credit, but her credit was bad. She said it had been ruined both by her recent inability to pay bills on time with dwindling paychecks and by her husband's spendthrift habits. She began to describe her husband as an alcoholic and as physically abusive. In June 1991, Gwen called to say that she and Tommy had had to flee their home. She said Tommy had challenged Dave to a knife fight. In response, Dave had flung his sixty-pound son into a wall and dared him to stab first. Stunned, I invited Gwen and Tommy to spend time with me while Gwen plotted her next move. She declined to come but agreed that I should come and get Tommy for a two-week visit while she began to get her life in order. I boarded an airplane, flew to a distant city, met my nephew at the airport, and turned around and flew with him back home to Washington. Tommy arrived with a fresh haircut and handsome luggage filled with a wardrobe of neatly folded, fashionable new clothes. And he looked adorable and untraumatized, like a product of the practically perfect families one sees on prime-time television. Only later would I learn that Gwen had informed Tommy before dropping him off at the airport that he might have to live with me forever.

Prior to that summer, I had seen Gwen and Tommy about twice per year for several years. Tommy, who had been diagnosed with behavioral and neurological disorders, had always seemed normal to me. This time he seemed disturbed. He talked incessantly, usually about violence, adult movies, rap music, food, and certain fashionable items of clothing. He could not sit or stand still for even a moment, unless he was watching television. Sometimes he would dash away for no apparent reason. He said odd things. Once he warned that some little boys of eight or nine whom we passed on the street were going to rape me. He was as thin as a rail but would indiscriminately eat anything and everything placed before him. In a Chinese restaurant he ate the head of a fish, relishing the eyes. He also had a strange habit: for days, whenever we walked down the street, he spat every three or four feet, leaving a trail of quarter-sized wet spots on the pavement in his wake.

Tommy wanted to go to every tourist attraction in town, but could bear to remain nowhere for very long. At the end of each exhausting day he joyfully called his father to tell him what he had done and seen. These calls made me nervous. Oddly, he seemed less interested in calling his mother, whom we were never able to reach by phone, anyway. After less than a week of caring for Tommy full-time, my husband and I were tired and bewildered. For a change of scenery and to get some help, I flew with Tommy to my parents' house (they lived a couple hours' drive from Gwen). I shared my concerns about Tommy's mental health with my parents, who knew him well. We speculated for several days about where my sister was and why her son was so troubled. We asked Debra for clues, as she lived in Gwen's neighborhood. Debra provided shocking clues. Debra said it was rumored that Gwen had begun showing up at work in skimpy evening attire. She also said she had heard from cousins who used crack that Gwen used crack, too.

By the time my two weeks with Tommy were near their end, everyone agreed that someone in the family should confront Gwen about the possibility of drug use. The day Gwen was supposed to come to get Tommy, she called in tears saying she was having financial troubles that she needed to work out with her employer before she could meet us at my parents' house and take Tommy home. I sensed that she was making excuses and that she did not want to come for Tommy at all. When Gwen finally arrived the next day, she was well-groomed and calm. She behaved indifferently toward her son, pushing him away when he rushed to show her the souvenirs of his vacation, including a genuine photograph taken of himself arm in arm with Senator Robert Dole.

I reluctantly asked Gwen in a private conversation whether she used drugs. She denied drug use. She attributed her problems to the stresses of her job, poor health, and a bad marriage. I was reluctant to leave Tommy with Gwen, but decided to return home. I did not have a car at my parents' house, so Gwen drove me to the airport on her way home. Our conversation along the way to the airport was sisterly and upbeat. I half decided the crack suspicions had to be wrong, despite some cocky behavior: Gwen drove down the highway toward the airport with one foot propped atop the dashboard and wearing only one contact lens.

A few weeks later, my parents and some of my siblings conferred by telephone. We decided that we had to find out for sure whether Gwen was a drug addict. Our decision was made after my parents learned from Debra of Gwen's arrest for passing a bad check. They also learned from Debra that Gwen sometimes left Tommy alone at home and abandoned him to friends overnight. Before confronting Gwen again, we confronted Dave. At first, Dave said he was not sure whether Gwen used drugs. He admitted, however, that she habitually left home in the late evenings and did not return until four or five o'clock in the morning.

My mother, then fifty-eight years old, and my brother Jim, a thirty-year-old lawyer, were central to the plan we devised to discover the truth about Gwen. Jim flew down from New York to help. He picked up my mother, and they drove from my parents' home to Gwen's home a hundred miles away. They parked outside Gwen's apartment all night, which was no small feat for my mother, frail with lung cancer. When Gwen arrived home in the wee hours of the morning, my mother and brother surprised her. They sat her down inside her apartment on her bed and forced a confession. They threatened to have her institutionalized against her will if she did not confess. Gwen begrudgingly admitted to drug use. She admitted that she was addicted to crack cocaine, having become a progressively more frequent user. Lately, she said, she had spent every night at a certain crack house, risking arrest and violence, enjoying the protection of a powerful dealer, and offering sex to bare acquaintances when she needed to earn money for drugs. She had spent the entire two weeks that I had cared for Tommy in the crack house.

We moved quickly to intervene. We spent the next few weeks trying to persuade Gwen to get medical help. We also spent a good deal of time trying to adjust to the unbelievable truth that one of *us* could be an addict, a profoundly neglectful mother, a liar, and a thief. Our crisis was primarily a crisis of identity, not morality. My parents knew their children had tried marijuana as young adults in the 1970s. But ours was not a family with a drug problem. We were surprised by Gwen's downfall into addiction. Nothing would have predicted it. Our sister/daughter so nice, proper, and vain, now a denizen of the drug world, glad to be some macho pimp crack dealer's "Miss It," crouched in the dark closets of a dilapidated house listening to rats in the walls and her heart racing. This could not be true, and yet it was true.

I helped to arrange for Gwen to enter a reputable rehabilitation program. This required some days of negotiating with the civil service, various private hospitals, and Gwen. The price tag for the twenty-eight-day program we finally selected was $20,000, half of which was waived because of Gwen's affiliation with the federal government. I made up half the difference after getting a promise of repayment from Gwen's husband. He never paid me back.

Gwen executed a note for the rest, a debt partly repaid by the family and partly discharged in bankruptcy.

Since her hospitalization, Gwen has remained drug- and alcohol-free. Once trim and athletic, she has put on weight and has intransigent health problems. She goes to Narcotics Anonymous (NA) meetings religiously. She tries to understand why her life took the turn it did and how to avoid a relapse. Part of her recovery has been to speak openly about her past and share her experience with others who might benefit from it. I tell her story today, with her permission, comforted by the knowledge that she has become a new person. But the first five years of her recovery were difficult. Her problems, which initially included depression and, in my judgment, cognitive impairment, taxed the resources of our family.

We joined the miserable ranks of the crack families. Issues relating to the allocation of responsibility for Gwen (sick and unemployed) and Tommy (neglected and traumatized) threatened to demoralize and divide our family. My mother died fearing that someone in the family had sexually assaulted Gwen, because Gwen kept alluding to awful secrets that she had discussed with her drug counselors but could never tell the family. Some of us resented other family members' unwillingness to contribute financially and emotionally to Gwen's recovery. Some of us felt shame about our previously cavalier attitude about drugs and our failure to comprehend our individual and collective vulnerability.

Gwen was frank about preferring her drug-recovery friends to family members, whom she felt judged her and could not comprehend what she had gone through. The talks Gwen and I have had since her recovery have been among the most open and honest of our lives. But in the early years of her recovery, our honesty was selective and manipulative. We spoke the truth, not because of our love, but because of guilt, caution, and the teachings of Twelve-Step Programs. Rightly or wrongly, I missed the days when naïve pride and trust were more alive between us.

Things were especially bad for Gwen during the fourth year of her recovery. Before she recaptured the focus and prudence she needed to secure and sustain full-time employment, Gwen ran out of unemployment compensation, retirement savings, and people to give her money. I will never forget the predicament she presented to me one day and the fact that, at the time, she could only see her situation as a predicament. On the day in question, Gwen phoned me to say she needed a loan, a gift, a job, or welfare. She said she was too proud to ask family and friends for money. She said had no right to expect gifts after tricking the family into indirectly supporting her drug habit. She could not find suitable work. It was hard to look for a job, she said, because she was worried, depressed, and did not have a working automobile. Her car was parked in her driveway, needing a new transmission. When the transmission had blown months earlier, she could not afford to have it fixed, so she put a quart of transmission fluid into the car every day; eventually, because she forgot to put oil in the tank, the car just died. Gwen could not afford to buy a new car; she had no job and no credit. There is no convenient public transportation serving Gwen's neighborhood. She said that she had had to turn down an offer of employment because the job required khaki pants and a white shirt; she owned the required items of clothing, but they were too small. She could not afford new clothes because, of course, she was jobless.

But other dimensions to Gwen's predicament emerged that day. Gwen did not want to apply for welfare because the application process was demeaning. Moreover, she probably could not qualify for welfare because she and Dave were still married. She said she could not ask Dave for more money because he might expect sex in return. Besides, Dave had just had a heart attack (at age forty) and was living with a new girlfriend now, his former girlfriend having recently died of cancer. Gwen's boyfriend, whom she met at an NA meeting, was in the hospital with AIDS. Gwen feared that when he got out of the hospital, he would need help. She believed she was one of the few people he could rely on, but she felt unequal to the task. Her boyfriend had a daughter. But this pregnant teenager lived thousands of miles away, the only guardian of her half-sisters while her mother and stepfather served jail terms.

Our conversation continued. Gwen complained that she could not see well; she owned only one contact lens. She said that a while back she had forgotten to soak her lenses in fluid; the next day she found them cracked into three pieces. So she dug out a cloudy old lens. She used to have glasses—in fact, one of our brothers had purchased them for her after she left the drug treatment hospital—but she sat on her glasses and broke them. Glue and tape worked for a while to hold them together. Eventually glue got on the lenses, and the lenses would not stay in the frames. How could she get a secretarial job if she could not see, she wondered?

Gwen related that she had had two car accidents, both while driving without adequate eyewear and without liability insurance. One of the men with whom she collided was trying to sue her. Gwen described herself as depressed. She did not want to take an antidepressant because she was afraid she might get addicted. She was sick with "female troubles" for which her physician had recommended surgery, but if she were stuck at home recovering from surgery, she could not look for a job; and if she had a job she could not take time off for surgery, so she felt she had to suffer in pain.

A final element in the story: Tommy's behavior worsened. Prior to drug treatment, Gwen had herself abusively consumed the Ritalin prescribed by Tommy's doctors. Medication might have helped Tommy, but Gwen refused to allow him medication to control his behavior. Tommy was expelled from the main track of his public school for spraying his classmates with urine pumped from a stolen "super soaker" water gun. He now attended a special education middle school. He often ran away from home and school. He stole. He lied. He swore at his teachers. From time to time Gwen would say that she ought to move into a cheaper apartment to save money but that cheaper housing was in "bad" neighborhoods where kids Tommy's age routinely confront drugs and violence. Already Tommy had threatened to alleviate the awful poverty brought on by his mother's drug use by (what else?) selling drugs. Tommy has not become a drug dealer, however. Hard work on his part and a number of financial and legal interventions by the family have placed him on track for a decent life.

Making Connections

I would like to contrast two broadly drawn normative perspectives on the morality of drug use. I will refer to them as the "pro-privacy" and the "pro-accountability" perspectives. The primary concern of the pro-privacy perspective is unwanted intervention in the lives of adult individuals who choose to use drugs. The primary concern of the pro-accountability perspective is unwanted *failures* of intervention in the lives of individuals, families, and communities affected by drugs.

By construing drug use as an independent exercise of taste and essentially "self-regarding" conduct, the pro-privacy perspective understates the social character and some of the risks of illegal drug use. A response to the casualties of the "war on drugs" and the "Age of Crack," the pro-accountability perspective is not without difficulties of its own.[3] It pushes the boundaries of the self, positing contexts for virtue and unassumed obligations of care for self and others. Philosophers Douglas N. Husak and Jan Narveson are my exemplars of the pro-privacy perspective on the morality of drug use. Their reflections on drug use focus on public policy but include thoughts about personal morality, too.

Narveson opposes tagging drug use as "immoral." I am sympathetic to those who oppose tagging illegal drug use as "immoral" when addiction is a public health problem and when drugs function as self-medication. But Narveson's objection has nothing to do with health. He contends that drug use by one person does not typically affect other people at all, and, when it does affect others, it affects them insufficiently seriously, adversely, or directly. Narveson describes drug use as "self-regarding" conduct defined, after the fashion of John Stuart Mill, as conduct that does not much affect or harm other people. Narveson argued that drug use is not only self-regarding conduct, but also is "essentially" so.[4] Narveson labels as arrogant authoritarianism the notion that someone other than the individual drug taker is best able to assess whether taking drugs makes him or her better off than not taking drugs. To show that drug taking is "essentially" self-regarding, Narveson argues that it is only the person who chooses to take drugs who "gets high"; it is only the person who takes drugs who gets "into a certain state of mind, or feeling or sensation known as 'getting high.'"[5]

In *Drugs and Rights,* Douglas N. Husak took criminal drug laws to task, defending what he termed a "moral right of adults to use drugs for recreational purposes."[6] Husak compared adult drug users to "women and blacks," a class of people whose moral rights against subordinating governmental authority were once "greeted with disdain and ridicule."[7] Husak urged the intellectual community to take the rights of drug users seriously, responding with overdue sympathy to what he thinks could very well be "the greatest [injustice] in American history."[8] While positing no specific moral right to use drugs, liberal legal philosophers Samuel Freeman and Michael Moore concur with Husak's basic point that respect for individual liberty limits the power of government to criminalize consensual adult drug use. The common implication of these philosophers' views is that rationales for existing drug laws, whether premised on paternalistic considerations of the best interests of would-be users or on public safety considerations about the best interests of society, are inadequate unless they can be squared with the just demands of personal liberty. Freeman argues that government is morally permitted to ban only those drugs whose use impairs rational judgment to such an extent that participation in liberal governance is undermined.[9] Liberal societies may employ coercion when needed to preserve their citizens' cognitive abilities to act as citizens in their own interests.

Husak is intentionally vague about the exact foundations of his moral rights claims. In fact, he boldly asserts that metaethical niceties are irrelevant. He argues that the reasons policymakers offer for their laws against drugs are so bad, on so many grounds, that philosophers with divergent moral theories can join hands to reject them. Clearly, though, Husak assumes a strong principle of human liberty, according to which people generally have a moral right to do certain things and that no one has a right to bar them from doing these things. Narveson is overtly libertarian; Husak effectively so.

Qua libertarians, Husak and Narveson bring spoken and unspoken Kantian and utilitarian assumptions to their normative analyses of drug use. A familiar Kantian conception of morality understands the moral agent as a metaphysically free individual with a capacity for moral autonomy. Moral autonomy, the capacity for rational self-legislation, in turn gives rise to a moral right of individuals to employ judgment and suffer the moral and legal penalties of their errors. To intercept opportunities for effective right and wrong judgment is to show moral disrespect.

Civil libertarians inspired by Mill's utilitarianism sometimes contend that through their free acts, moral agents rationally pursue their own good (utility), thereby expressing and defining themselves as individuals. The classic civil libertarian will claim for individuals a hefty package of moral rights (good against governments and private persons) to formulate and live out their own conceptions of a good life. For many libertarians, the right to speak one's mind, practice a religion, choose a spouse, pursue a vocation, select a mate, bear children—these are sacrosanct modes of self-expression and self-definition. Libertarians, however, understand that a moral right to pursue utility (or categorical Kantian goods) through such activities cannot be absolute. They concede that many people are apt to violate others' rights to, for example, bodily integrity and property. With Mill, some libertarians concede that activities that sufficiently harm others' important interests or rights fall outside the domain of morally permissible conduct, but they assert that moral agents may permissibly engage in activities that either harm no one or that are what John Stuart Mill called "self-regarding" and that harm only the moral agent herself.

Two issues dominate Narveson's and Husak's analyses of drug norms. The first issue is whether illegal drug use is harmful to the people who engage in it. They conclude based on a variety of empirical considerations and statistics that many illegal drugs, including marijuana, are not especially harmful to users, especially when compared to the health effects of alcohol, cigarettes, caffeine, and other legal drugs. Whether or not this conclusion is correct, the *user's* health, mental state, and likelihood to stair-step to riskier behavior are not the only factors relevant to a moral assessment of a drug's use. A person concerned about the personal morality of drug use has much to consider. He or she should give attention to considerations of his or her own risks, to be sure, but also to whether violence, corruption, neglect, or exploitation have contributed to producing his or her supply of drugs and to whether any person, group, or community is placed significantly at peril by virtue of his or her use of a drug. Drug users have hedonic and dignitarian interests at stake, but so do others.

Appropriately, then, the second issue that dominates Narveson's and Husak's analyses is whether drug use by one individual is harmful to others. They answer that drug use has limited negative externalities and is rarely itself the direct cause of serious injury or death. From these considerations they conclude that there can be no general duty or obligation to self or others militating against the use of a number of popular illegal drugs. They seem further to conclude that there are no obvious virtues that militate against drug use. Husak does suggest that virtue-based arguments against purely recreational drug use "might have merit," though we cannot be sure until "some philosopher attempts" to make the argument.[10] I will later mention a line of plausible virtue-based moral arguments, along with obligation-based moral arguments, against the use of popular illegal drugs.

Although Husak made an arguably provocative case for a "moral right of adults to use drugs," he offered the important concession that "[p]erhaps all recreational drug use, legal and illegal, is morally tainted":

> The conclusion that the adult use of recreational drugs is protected by a moral right does not entail that drug use is beyond moral reproach. The exercise of a moral right may be subject to criticism.[11]

Husak's concession that recreational drug use may not be beyond moral reproach came at the end of his 250-page argument that criminal laws against drugs violate moral rights. The structure of his argument is familiar to liberal theorists and their critics. It is common to argue with respect to abortion, for example, that government is not entitled to criminalize abortions because of women's rights, but then to concede that certain of the appropriately legal abortions women choose are (or may be) morally objectionable. The operative principle is that in a just liberal society, persons will be free to impose certain costs on others in order to exercise their most basic moral rights and live out their private conceptions of the good life. Drug use may violate no moral obligations that correlate to moral rights, and yet be morally objectionable on other grounds.

Does all so-called recreational drug use bear a moral taint? To this extent, I believe all illegal drug use does: in the present setting, consideration of the preconditions and the adverse consequences of drug use can turn a rational, thoughtful moralist—one with typical concerns about benefits and burdens, respect for persons, caretaking, character, and community responsibility—against some or all drug use. The preconditions and adverse consequences I have in mind are injuries to body, mind, and relationships suffered by the direct consumers of drugs, by their families, and by strangers in and beyond their immediate communities engaged in or affected by drug commerce.

Nonphilosophers may find baffling conceptions of rights and obligations that lead to conclusions like "people may be morally reproachable for exercising their moral rights" and "people do not always have a moral right to exercise their moral rights." Such axiological conundrums are familiar to philosophy, and I will not take the time to elaborate them greatly here. Suffice it to say that moral duties and virtues may call upon us to refrain from exercising our *prima facie* moral rights. For example, individuals may have a moral right to free speech and religious expression. But these rights do not give parents a moral right to leave their helpless infants at home without supervision while they attend political rallies and church services. Nor would these rights entail the conclusion that a person's decision to devote all of his or her time to politics and street-corner preaching is morally optimal or virtuous. Plainly, even if there were an abstract moral right to use illegal drugs, there could be contextual moral reasons not to use drugs in the world as we find it. Individuals may be supposed to have a right to rebel against seriously unjust laws, such as laws validating slavery and unfair drug laws. But, surely there are special situations when, because standing on one's moral rights would harm others or be injurious, one ought not to violate a bad law.

Externalities

To say, as with Narveson, that drug use "essentially" affects only drug users is to opt for rhetoric that distorts the social and biological dimensions of drug use. I believe it follows from the considerations I am about to raise that pro-privacy perspectives cannot establish, in any nontrivial sense, that drug use "essentially" affects only users.[12]

First, so-called "contact highs" and respiratory effects are reported among nonsmokers who breathe drug-permeated air. "Contact highs" and respiratory distress are experienced by the companions—friends, roommates, spouses, and children—of drug users whose drug delivery systems are based on the inhalation of smoke. Perinatal transmission of cocaine and heroin to fetuses in utero by pregnant women can result in infants born drug-addicted and underweight.

Drug use affects others in an important social sense, in addition to the biological senses just noted. Drug consumption is an overwhelmingly social and socially mediated activity. This point merits special emphasis. Contemporary American patterns of drug use are not individual. Most people do not spontaneously go out alone into nature or cultivated fields to gather and consume illegal drugs. A person generally becomes a user following initial exposures to drugs by other people. Other people who use or deal provide or impose sampling opportunities. Other people model drug use behaviors. Other people provide a context of encouragement or pressure in which the techniques of getting high and enjoying it can be taught and learned. Other people provide shelter (e.g., the "crack house" and the "freak house"), companionship, conversation, needles, pipes, sex, weapons, and protection. A young person may come to smoke marijuana because his university professors smoke marijuana. A woman may try powdered cocaine because her spouse brings the drug into their home. My sister Gwen believes she became a crack addict because another nonaddict family member's initial passion for the drug and willingness to purchase it kept crack smoking an integral part of their intimate relationship as kin. The highly social character of drug use is in certain cases tied to its illegality. Some people rarely use drugs alone because they never acquire their own private "stash." These parasite-style users depend on others' willingness to participate in illegal markets or assume the risks of drug ownership. In the 1980s, Gwen used to offer her apartment to soldiers from a nearby military base who needed a place to conceal their illegal drugs. (Their barracks were subject to search.) Gwen pinched enough of her depositors' marijuana to maintain a high all day. At noontime and after hours, her living room was a popular gathering place.

But drug use is highly social for another reason, unrelated to the stigma and risks of illegality. People enjoy letting their hair down together, and drug consumption is one way of doing it. Like alcohol, drugs can function as social lubricants and icebreakers. For some people, drugs function as stimulants, facilitating efficiency at work and masking depression that can make one miserable and an unfit personal companion or professional colleague.

Legal or illegal, drug use and, in particular, irresponsible drug use and addiction, can adversely affect one's employer, friends, and family. The effect of drug use on interdependent family members is strong. Whole family systems can be affected by the drug user's use of drugs, both during the period of addiction and long after. Leon Dash's friend Rosa Lee employed her son to sell drugs and her daughter to inject her with drugs. Later, Rosa's young daughter persuaded her mother to give her drugs. The members of Rosa Lee's family who did not use drugs suffered drug-related emotional, educational, and financial strains.

Fraudulent Externalities?

Husak, Narveson, and others are persuaded that drug use has few bad consequences or negative externalities of the sort that justify censure or criminalization. These philosophers view a number of claims about the negative effects of drug use as "fraudulent," arguing that certain harms that flow from our legal regime ("war on drugs") are assigned to drug use itself. They believe recreational drug use and users have been stuck with a moral rap that they do not deserve. Drugs do not cause violence, prostitution, and HIV; people do—the people behind the public law that creates the wrong rational incentives.

Let us suppose, for the sake of argument, that the use of marijuana, cocaine, and heroin would not be associated with social evils if these drugs were decriminalized. Let us further suppose that many criminal drug laws and enforcement, prosecution, and sentencing policies are unjust, as indeed I believe they are. Would it follow that your illegal drug use or mine is morally acceptable behavior? I do not think so. Morality assesses conduct in the world as we find it, not in the worlds to which we aspire. Gwen stole to buy drugs. Gwen traded sex and performed favors for dealer-thugs. Gwen exposed herself and others to HIV/AIDS. Under today's legal regime, illegal drug use is made possible by crime and degradation. We know this. People who use the relevant drugs knowing this are knowingly imposing risks on others. They are complicit in Gwen's addiction and Tommy's near abandonment. Considerations like these lead moralists plausibly to classify as "wrong" the use of marijuana, crack cocaine, cocaine, LSD, heroin, and popular party drugs.

The case for the moral wrongness of drug use has three main dimensions, one global, one local, and one personal. First, the global: Those who use illegal drugs contribute directly to a corrupt market. They participate in a form of social and economic intercourse with deadly consequences for the well being of millions of the nation's least fortunate residents. Human misery is the predicate of drug use. It may be literally true, for example, that Dr. Smith or Lawyer Chen is able to enjoy an evening's worth of cocaine only because Luke, an anonymous stranger across town or in another part of the country or world, faces ill health, violent wounding, legal prosecution, or death under a regime of unfair laws. The successful downtown professor who sometimes uses cocaine or crack is complicit in the drug deaths of uptown teenagers. In the realm of tort law it is said that a person cannot be blamed for the consequences of his or her conduct, except where those consequences are reasonably foreseeable and proximate. But we are not talking about an explosive in a plain wrapper here. The extremely violent nature of the drug market, along with the health and social risks of addiction, are no secret to the educated, affluent people who use popular illegal drugs. I am not convinced that applications of the tort principle should immunize the downtown drug user from culpability or responsibility for uptown tragedies.

It might be argued that flouting unjust laws is a moral good. If otherwise respectable people do drugs, the government will have to legalize them, one argument goes. I would reply that it matters very much whether the means one takes to flout the law imposes too high a cost. If a Washington, D.C., professor wants to flout antimarijuana laws, perhaps he should do it by turning his garden into a marijuana field rather than by purchasing drugs from a ruthless dealer.

Second, the local dimension: Those who use drugs assume the risk of failing to perform their most basic responsibilities to others. Some drug users—a very small minority—inadvertently become drug abusers and addicts; some—perhaps a great many more—inadvertently become inadequate role models, parents, and caretakers; some become less productive workers and public servants. All of these things unexpectedly happened to Gwen.

It is impossible to know for sure in advance whether one will be a casualty of the drugs with which one "experiments." Self-deception, bravado, weakness of will, and physiology may overcome conscious will. To conclude from this that drug avoidance is the only morally acceptable alternative seems admittedly severe. The following principle may be less objectionable: the heavier a person's palette of obligations to others (in number or kind), the less acceptable it is to engage in risky behavior. But now suppose that most of us have a heavier load of obligations than we have been taught to recognize or take seriously?

Third, the personal dimension: As Sam Freeman (see page 108 note 9, this chapter) plausibly demonstrates, drug use may be morally problematic because of its impairment of individual capacities for independent judgment. This effect is extremely important. Judgment is important for participation in one's social roles in a liberal society or any other type. If one is cognitively impaired, others will have to let one harm oneself or will have to take over as one's guardian, much as I and others functioned for a while as *de facto* guardians of Gwen. Finally, excessive drug use offends conceptions of temperance and prudence relevant to some types of virtue-based moral assessments of drug use. Virtue-based moral arguments that may be promising are those that stress character traits akin to courage and altruism (as opposed to temperance and prudence). It reflects altruism to give up drugs because of their global and local affects on others, when one very much enjoys them. It takes courage to buck fads and fend off the social pressure that often moves people to use drugs.

Identity and Coercive Redefinition

Using drugs is one of the ways some young adults define themselves. Clothing, hairstyles, tattoos, body piercings, religious practices, and gang membership are also channels of self-definition. Conduct of self-definition is arguably a kind of conduct that one should be at liberty to perform, again, unless others are directly, seriously, and adversely harmed. In "Liberty and Drugs," Michael Moore properly asks whether self-definition is always morally important.[13] Like Moore, I believe that self-definition is never unimportant. However, self-definition has individual and collective dimensions relevant to the moral evaluation of recreational drug use.

Conventional morality accepts that parents have the power to define the identities of their children by choosing their religions, schools, and neighborhoods. Through drug use, a teen or even an adult child can require new self-concepts, roles, and affiliations from their parents that redefine their identities. The parents, siblings, and children of a drug user may find that the user's acts of supposed individual self-definition coercively redefine their collective identities, too. Gwen's drug use helped her to establish her identity outside the family as "Miss It," an exciting and popular risk taker. For more than thirty years my parents took special pride in rearing six African American children, three sons and three daughters, none of whom ever "got into trouble." As parents, they were role models for other parents and often offered advice and comfort to friends and colleagues whose children experienced addiction, teen pregnancy, violence, arrests, and unemployment. Gwen's crisis of addiction forced my parents to abandon the false belief that they had managed to rear the rare Teflon brood of children. For my father, a military man, who had spent many years as

a successful father figure both to his own children and to countless army recruits, Gwen's fall was especially unwelcome. It came after his identity as a
preeminently successful parent among peers in his community of origin had
been cemented: "Why did she wait until she was thirty-six years old to get involved in something like this?" Some of my siblings and I felt a good deal of
this sentiment too. Gwen's drug problems led Tommy to redefine himself. His
mother's drug past caused him shame. It led him to understand himself as a victim of drug culture, no different from the "bad" kids in "the ghetto" from whom
he had been urged to distinguish himself.

With new obligations came new identities. With the abandonment of our
cocky self-identities as the ones who got away, came new duties tied to Gwen's
recovery. I found myself changed, identifying with other crack families and taking previously silly-seeming Twelve-Step Programs seriously, for example.

Alcohol Parity

Critics of the "war on drugs" frequently cite alcohol use and the history of
Prohibition. They cite alcohol use to suggest the injustice of allowing one person her poison (alcohol) and disallowing another hers (cocaine). Critics argue, too, that marijuana and certain other drugs may be safer to use than
alcohol. Alcohol products are legal despite their association with a variety of
health, economic, and social ills. The Prohibition Era proved that violent
crime follows trade in illegal intoxicants, but not legal ones. Yet the alcohol
parity argument is unlikely to lead U.S. policymakers to give up on drug regulation anytime soon.

One of the positive effects of having a member of my family fall prey to
crack cocaine was to draw attention to the unacknowledged problem of alcohol abuse in our family. After her hospitalization for crack addiction, Gwen
gave up drugs and alcohol simultaneously. She quite sensibly asked why our
interventionist family had never attempted to intervene on behalf of our heavy
drinkers. Her question was interesting in light of Narveson's statement: "One
can blame alcohol for very much more evil than all of the known drugs."[14]

I speculate that my family's lack of will to aggressively fight alcoholism
has had to do with the legal status of alcohol. It has also had to do with sex
bias and the family status of a patriarchal family's worst alcohol offenders.
My crack-addicted sister was, in relational terms, a mother, a wife, the
youngest of three daughters, the cherished baby sister. Our heaviest drinker
was a father, a husband, a grandfather, a great-grandfather, a veteran of two
wars. He was in charge of us, not we of him. In addition, to the members of
my family, crack appeared more debilitating than alcohol. Crack addiction
eventually caused my sister to abandon her responsibilities. Despite heavy

drinking, and with the help of a stay-at-home wife, our worst alcoholic kept a large family financially afloat, often working two or three jobs. He would have been a better husband and father had he not abused liquor, but he managed to perform his core duties as society defines them. This is also true of one of the female alcoholics in my extended family.

Gwen's good example eventually emboldened her siblings to propose to one member of our family that he enter an alcohol treatment facility. He (graciously) declined, but in response to our concerted solicitude dramatically cut back on alcohol consumption and began to take better care of himself. What combination of criminal punishment, product regulation, taxes, licenses, education, and/or social services is best for abusers of alcohol, narcotics, stimulants, etc. is not a question for armchair philosophy, but for social scientists and public health experts, eyes open, sleeves rolled up.

The Age of Crack

There is a striking discrepancy between the way mainstream philosophers have talked about drug use and the way prominent African American intellectuals have talked about it. The former have spoken of "moral rights" to use drugs and of drugs as "recreation." The latter speak of drug use as a moral problem and a plague on the community. Recall, Husak asserted that the "war on drugs" may be the greatest injustice in American history. Drug users, he said, are like blacks and women—victims of unjust laws who are due sympathy and political recognition. To be the greatest injustice in American history—or even among the greatest—an injustice would have to be very great indeed. The injustice done to drug users as a class compares unfavorably to the injustice done to, for example, the Native North American tribes. Moreover, it may be less telling to observe that drug users are like blacks and women in deserving our sympathy than to observe that many of those who have been harmed by the adverse consequences of restrictive drug laws *are* blacks and women.

Husak is far from alone in his intellectual battle against the "war on drugs" or in his sympathy for the "plight of drug users who are prosecuted and convicted."[15] Some notable minority culture critics, policymakers, and public officials share Husak's skepticism about the wisdom of continuing to criminalize serious drug use. The government has spent an estimated $40 billion on the drug war, but drugs are cheap, pure, and easy for children to get.[16] A very significant percentage of the most direct victims of current drug policies and practices are nonwhite Americans who live in minority neighborhoods. Some poor, urban minority communities have been overtaken by the drug trade and the culture it creates. The persistence of the drug culture may suggest a lack of social will to combat it, a reluctance inseparable from the historic lack of respect for poor black, brown, yellow, and red peoples. Although I do not, many blacks do believe there is evidence of Central Intelligence Agency responsibility for introducing crack cocaine into poor minority neighborhoods in California.[17]

The pervasiveness of the legal, medical, and social problems associated with drug use in minority communities earned the final decades of the twentieth century the ignoble moniker "The Age of Crack." A dozen years ago, a Boston minister by the name of Eugene Rivers opened up a debate on the pages of the *Boston Review* about the responsibilities of intellectuals, and in particular African American intellectuals, in the Age of Crack.[18] Participants in the debates included Glen Loury, feminist author bell hooks, and law professors Randall Kennedy and Regina Austin. Rivers portrayed drug use as a social evil by virtue of the devastating role it has played in the demise of low-income neighborhoods. Peak use of crack cocaine may have subsided, but the Age of Crack problems persist, in the form of whole urban communities demoralized by poor health, truncated educations, violence, poverty, child neglect, and family decay. The Age of Crack is also an age of heroin, powder cocaine, marijuana, LSD, and many other drugs, the use of which is reportedly on the rise in some segments of the population when compared to the previous decade.[19]

African American boys and men are being arrested, prosecuted, and jailed for drug offenses in record numbers. (The same is true of Hispanic men.) Although 72 percent of drug users are white, African Americans are 72 percent of those sentenced to prison for possessory drug offenses. About 54 percent of crack users are white; 38 percent are African American, and yet 88 percent of those *sentenced* for crack offenses are African American, and only 4 percent are white. Because of drugs, blacks and their communities are losing the right to vote. About 14 percent of African American adult men are disenfranchised as a result of felony convictions, many tied to drugs. At one point in the early 1990s more than half of all black males in Washington, D.C., were under criminal supervision; at the same time the public school dropout rate for black boys was about 60 percent. Drugs are a major public health problem for blacks. African American users of injectable drugs are at a high risk of contracting AIDS, the leading cause of death among black men ages twenty-five to forty-four. (As needle sharing is more common among low-income drug users, the risk of HIV infection from injecting drugs is greater for low-income users than for high-income users.) Perinatal drug transmission reached epidemic proportions in the 1980s and 1990s. Pregnant black women have been ten times more likely than pregnant white women to be reported to child welfare authorities for prenatal child abuse and neglect offenses.[20]

Any solution to the problems associated with excessive drug use and drug commerce may require major innovations in government drug policy, community leadership, and private behavior. The prospects for government and community leadership are uncertain. The Age of Crack is an era in which many of the people making and enforcing punitive drug policies include some who now publicly disavow drug use but who once consumed illegal drugs.

For a short while it looked as though partisan politics would disqualify qualified men and women who used drugs from public service. A notorious admission of marijuana use thwarted Federal Court of Appeals Judge Douglas Ginsburg's bid to become a justice of the United States Supreme Court. Ginsburg admitted to drug use after an academic colleague told a reporter for National Public Radio that Ginsburg had smoked marijuana while a law professor at Harvard. But past drug use was not disqualifying for long.

First, prior to his election as president of the United States in 1992, William Jefferson ("Bill") Clinton admitted to smoking marijuana cigarettes as a young man, claiming not to have inhaled.[21] Second, in 1996, several members of Clinton's White House staff told the FBI that they had used marijuana, cocaine, and hallucinogens, some within five years of taking office.[22] Third, an admission of drug use did not keep Susan Molinari off the podium as a keynote speaker at the 1996 Republican National Convention. After an initial denial, Representative Molinari confessed that she had used drugs while a student in the early 1980s. Molinari's *mea culpa* to the *Washington Post* is typical:

> I did experiment with marijuana less than a handful of times. It was the wrong thing to do. . . If I knew then what I know now, I wouldn't have done it.[23]

As a last example, in 1996 the police department of Prince Georges County, Maryland, abandoned a standard against prior drug use, opening the door to police service to applicants who professed no drug use in the three years prior to application.[24] In Maryland and elsewhere, police officers responsible for arresting drug offenders may be fairly recent drug offenders themselves.

Judge Ginsburg, President Clinton, Representative Molinari, and the others used drugs without becoming addicted or getting swept up into an irresponsible or violent drug culture. They can be thought of as drug-use success stories. Yet their successes, when combined with their political ambitions, may do little to help them fully to empathize with addiction-riddled people, families, and neighborhoods. Many of our leaders must know from personal experience that moderate illegal drug consumption, like moderate alcohol consumption, can be safe and pleasant. Their own educational and professional successes prove that ruin of self and family is not the inevitable consequence of legally proscribed recreational drug use. Apparently, however, in their political judgment, their public roles require unqualified expressions of regret for past drug use— euphemistically termed "experimentation"—combined with general support for the concept of a criminalization strategy-based "war on drugs."

The "war on drugs" has bred extremes of injustice and overshadowed other policy options. President Clinton went to the White House while other men and women have gone to jail for years, serving mandatory sentences for possessing or importing small amounts of crack or marijuana. Gwen could easily have been jailed. A few months after she stopped going to her favorite crack den, it was shot up; her protector was killed and there were arrests. One of my black cousins made the law books after he was sent to federal prison for a term of years following his arrest in the Atlanta airport as he returned from the Bahamas with two female companions, one of whom was carrying cocaine in a handbag.[25] A less cynical view of the "war on drugs" waged by politicians moved to deny inhalation and confess the error of youthful experimentation is this: they genuinely believe severe criminal regulation is our salvation.

A recent Department of Justice study confirms an earlier study reporting that 85 percent of African American males are arrested and jailed by the time they reach age thirty-five.[26] Blacks are more likely to be arrested, prosecuted for, convicted of, and imprisoned for drug offenses than any other group of Americans.[27] Again, although about 54 percent of crack users are white, according to the National Institute on Drug Abuse figures, about 88 percent of those convicted of crack cocaine offenses are African Americans.[28] Congress has mandated especially severe jail terms for crack possession and trafficking, when compared to jail terms mandated for powder cocaine and other drugs. Because the law enforcement community appears to be so unfair to blacks, blacks would seem to have very strong prudential reasons to steer clear of drugs. And yet many blacks weigh the perceived risks of criminal sanction against the tangible benefits of drug-related income and choose the latter. I suspect many otherwise poor blacks also weigh the burdens of moral disapprobation (from self and other people) against the tangible economic benefits and choose the latter.

Ethno-Racial Accountability

Starting with the twin premises that one ought to combat social evils and that drug use has become part of a network of social evils, one could argue as follows: There are (a) obligations to refrain from illegal drug use, (b) obligations to do what one reasonably can to deter or prevent others, or certain others with whom one has special ties, from using drugs, and (c) obligations to respond with care and concern when others, or certain others with whom one has special ties, have been harmed by involvement with drugs. The main point, though, is a point about accountability rather than obligation. I have related a story of drug use to illustrate family interdependency and identity. For family members linked by identity and a sense of role- and emotion-related responsibility, accountability for "self-regarding" conduct like drug use is clear. I believe this story helps to explain why *de facto* moral accountability for private life is sometimes *de jure*.

If you use drugs, you owe your family an explanation and a justification for the risk. If you become an addict, you owe your family admissions and recovery. You may warrant their censure. If you do nothing in response to an addict's distress, you are accountable for that failure of engagement. Eugene Rivers suggested the argument, questioned by Randall Kennedy,[29] that African American intellectuals have a special obligation to put their minds and hearts to work on saving the black community from the scourge of drugs, one soul at a time, if necessary. Feminist bell hooks offered the perspective that the obligations of black intellectuals should not be seen primarily as heady obligations of formulating policy strategies.[30] Direct caretaking of family members, including those victimized by drugs, counts as the obligation of intellectuals as well.

I imagine that bell hooks would view what I did for Tommy and Gwen as the very least someone with my resources ought to have done. (Why didn't I do more? Why didn't I adopt Tommy?) Before I knew that there was a crack addict in my family, I came to know a Latino law student who was repeatedly summoned home by his parents to retrieve his heroin drug-addicted brother literally from the New York City gutters. The student's family had invested years and $100,000 in failed rehabilitation efforts. This law student felt as though he had no choice but to render what aid he felt he could to his brother, and our conversations educated me about some of the ways I might try to help Gwen. A second former Georgetown law student, an African American woman, has become the legal guardian of two of the six children of a drug-addicted ex-client; she has also adopted a third black child, born to a rape victim. This student already had a child when she took in her two foster children and adopted the fourth child. Neither student viewed these acts as heroic, but just as the right thing to do.

In the present context, use of popular illegal drugs is virtually always a moral problem, especially for those of us with meaningful options, and especially for African Americans in a position to serve as role models, caregivers, and community leaders. Drug use is also a moral problem for the people who turn to illegal drugs rather than legal medications to treat pain, depression, anxiety, and stress. They, too, ought to factor in the externalities of what they do and consider alternatives. The acquisition of many popular drugs is predicated on lethal violence and the social degradation of vulnerable people and their communities. Causally and symbolically, drug users are complicit in the social evils associated with drugs. Especially for African Americans, drug use carries significant health and legal risks for self, family, and group. It is difficult for a person contemplating drug use to know in advance whether he or she will be one of those people who will become an addict unable to act responsibly. When it comes to drugs, the fact of limited information about one's self and the world counsel prudence and perhaps risk aversion.[31] Moral character and accountability are required up front. There is little point to blaming, and expecting accountability of, addicts. Assessing drug use and policy as if drug users were wholly independent rather than profoundly interdependent is a mistake. There is no nontrivial aspect in which drug consumption affects and potentially harms only the consumer. In the case of drug addiction, family members are especially likely to be harmed and burdened by the addict's drug consumption. But there are worrisome nonfamilial victims of personal drug use as well. Although private choice in a number of contexts relating to how we use our bodies and minds is a good, I believe the social interdependence of individuals can bind persons of care, virtue, and self-respect to avoid certain attractive and meaningful risks.

Drug Policy Sidebar

I have been urging that at least some recreational drug use will be morally objectionable. As a general matter, not everything that is immoral is or should be deemed illegal. As I have tried to make clear, I do not think it follows that the government's "war on drugs" is a good and just policy simply because using drugs is morally objectionable. It does not follow that criminal laws or noncriminal regulations should be implemented in response to negative moral assessment.

Whether recreational drug use is one of those immoralities that should be illegal is a complex question.[32] We might want to retain the illegal status of recreational drugs to signal to young people that society thinks drug use is bad. The criminal drug laws could thus be put into the service of moral education. From her experiences, Gwen has come firmly to believe that decriminalization would increase the number of crack addicts and that criminalization is having a positive deterrence effect. But neither Gwen nor I is a social scientist. It may be, as many allege, that criminalizing drug commerce and usage makes recreational drug use more attractive to young people and adult nonconformers. Policymakers seeking to use law in the service of morality would have to take care that proscriptive policies did not backfire, enticing even larger numbers of young people into drug experimentation, use, and addiction.

In the literature on abortion, homosexuality, drugs, and prostitution, philosophers continually grapple with the question of whether it is just to use law as a handmaiden of morality. In a society as diverse as ours there is disagreement about what counts as morally correct behavior. Government, it is sometimes said, must be neutral. According to Narveson, through restrictive drug laws, the government expresses a non-neutral bias for some groups over others. Recall that Narveson claimed that (1) drug taking is essentially self-regarding, and that (2) drug taking lacks, on balance, serious genuine externalities. "We" want to criminalize drugs, Narveson suggests, because "we like chocolate and they (drug users) like vanilla."[33] We may want to criminalize at least some drug sales and drug possessions, I would suggest, because we like healthy, responsible, dignified lives, and they like to impose on themselves and others the risk of seriously unhealthy, irresponsible, and undignified lives.

It may be that some drug use should be legalized to save lives, liberties, and monies. But the reason to legalize drugs cannot be that liberty in the area of "essentially self-regarding" conduct requires it. Drug use is not essentially self-regarding conduct like, to use a trivial example, nail biting. The family welfare and public health consequences of drug use both undermine the good sense of describing it as self-regarding conduct and represent genuine externalities justifying limits on liberty. However much "fun" drug use is for some of us some of the time, it is hell for others of us, much of the time.

From a moral point of view, it seems reasonable to expect that optimal drug policy would meet three minimal requirements. First, it would be mindful of the importance of personal privacy and liberty. This first requirement calls upon policy to avoid unjustifiable paternalism and intolerance in the regulation of voluntary drug use by competent, knowing adults. If the use of a drug is criminalized when the usual justifications of criminalization are absent, there may be cause for moral concern. The usual justifications include harm caused to others and certain harms to self. If it were possible to bracket the problems of racial disparities raised earlier, we might be able to defend the basic direction of American drug policy, which has been to penalize "street" drug use. Drug policy is wracked with problems. But it is not a wholly arbitrary, intolerant deprivation of individual choice. It is a response to the harms and risks seemingly inherently associated with drug use. Drugs kill, but our law does not permit warrantless searches and commando raids to deal with the problem.

Second, optimal public policy would be respectful of interests in practical allocations of public revenues and resources. The second requirement demands that the use of resources garnered through public taxation or charity should be responsible rather than wasteful. This means public policies aimed at addressing the drug problem should be designed to succeed. Success, it seems fair to say, depends in part on whether a policy design takes into account what well-informed social scientists, and experienced social workers, families, and individuals know about drug use, addiction, and their consequences. I want to suggest that this will include due acknowledgment of the externalities of drug use.

Third, morally optimal public drug policy would be respectful of moral equality. Policymakers should distribute the benefits and burdens of regulation among individuals and social groupings in a way that avoids inequality and exacerbation of existing social inequalities, including patterns of subordination and disenfranchisement. Nearly every state and the District of Columbia has adopted laws that take away convicted criminals' right to vote. Fourteen percent of African Americans have lost the vote. Black men are losing the right to vote because of nonviolent drug offenses (and high rates of conviction for black-on-black violent crime). A 1998 Human Rights Watch Sentencing Project report predicted that racially disproportionate incarceration rates for African American men—3,098 per 100,000 versus 370 per 100,000 for white men—mean that 40 percent of the next generation of black men will be unable to vote.[34] Current restrictive drug policies disproportionately harm poor African Americans and Hispanics, yet decriminalization could sink poor racial minorities just that much further into the quagmire.

MY FAMILY, MY RACE

Empirically, family members are accountable to one another for their private lives. Prescriptively, they should be in a range of situations, concerning a range of matters. To ascribe accountability obligations to members of conventional nuclear families and first-degree kin is scarcely controversial. Feminists and other critical theorists caution, though, against safe-seeming accountability ascriptions concerning traditional families without attention to patterns of social power and subordination. Gender inequality and male domination can be observed in some conventional explications of the grounds of accountability and the accountability requirements of husbands, wives, children, and grandparents. In framing accountability ideals today, care must be taken to conceptualize the family so as to accord due agency and moral independence to wives, mothers, grandmothers, and daughters no less than male family members. Care should be taken not to stereotype men as emotionally independent in fact and ideal, cutting them off from the positive good of accountability for private life in affective relationships and familial roles.

Thinking about accountability in families holds the greatest challenge when one leaves the realm of the traditionally sanctioned nuclear, biological family. Consider prescriptive ascription of accountability obligations to members of just three sorts of less conventional families ("neo-families," I will call them)—same-sex-headed families, adoptive families, and multiracial families. How do we think about accountability for private life respecting gay and lesbian neo-families, ill-served by the vocabulary of husband, wife, and in-law? And how do we think about accountability for private life in adoptive neo-families, potentially with sets of every category of relation, one legal, the other biological? And what about multiracial families strained by conflicting cultural and racial demands?[35] What is the current accountability story in those domains? What should it be? I will focus on the two I know best, adoptive and multiracial families.

Families can be formed by adoption. Adopted kin also have biological kin. The controversies over open adoption are disagreements about how much accountability and other forms of inclusion are due birth families. Often framed in the feminist literature as disagreements about accountability to birth mothers, these controversies embed deeper ethical disagreements about what constitutes a family. The open adoption debates have an interesting relationship to controversies about "transracial" adoption, "interracial" intimacy, and accountability to race. One of the reasons some observers favor open adoption is that it allows adoptive families to adopt "transracially" without isolating adoptees from their racial, cultural, ethnic, or national communities of origin. Ties of this sort are thought to help adoptees develop strong, coherent, appropriate identities while ensuring the survival of vulnerable minority groups. Moral disapproval of exogamy is premised on the belief that intermarriage threatens the survival of vulnerable groups by assimilating their members and biracial offspring into the majority group. African Americans worry that children of African American ancestry reared in white homes and multiracial families will not develop an African American identity sufficient to participate in a distinctly African American culture. The accountability of nontraditional adoptive and interracial "neo-families" to birth families and demographic groups for choices about marriage and child-rearing practices is a controversial way of addressing the worry.

ACCOUNTABILITY TO BIRTH FAMILIES

For many adults, the goal of parenting is to have a family *of their own.* Having a family of one's own means being able to define the parameters of one's most intimate sphere and to make decisions about its course. People have and adopt children precisely to engage their intimacy-building, nurturing, and decisional capacities. Autonomy-related values support the right of adults to choose or refuse parenthood and, for those who choose it, to be permitted a degree of independence and agency within a framework of accountability to the state for child welfare protection. Beneficence and justice-related values require that society respond to the nesting and caretaking impulses of its citizens with care and fairness.

The parent-child family that experts say most children need and that many adults want for themselves has come to have constitutional dimensions. We speak of "family privacy" in the United States to suggest that a substantial degree of freedom from governmental and other outside interference is fitting for the parent-child unit.[36] Constitutional freedoms of association, marriage, parentage, religion, and education (along with a healthy dose of government welfare, protective services, and law enforcement) sustain private families of parents and children. The Supreme Court's decision in favor of the Amish in *Wisconsin v. Yoder*, 406 U.S. 205 (1972), affirmed the constitutionally protected status of the parent-child relationship and the nonconforming decisions parents may elect to make on behalf of their minor children.[37] Under our jurisprudence, not even grandparents are entitled to a relationship with children over the objections of parents.

As numerous feminist scholars have emphasized, "family privacy" can be taken to harmful extremes.[38] This was the painful lesson of *Deshaney v. Winnebago Department of Social Services* (1989).[39] In that case of gross parental abuse, the Court held that a state that fails to prevent child abuse called to its attention cannot be held civilly liable and thus accountable for the wrongdoing of a parent. Competent, consistent, accountable uses of government power to protect children from family violence and medical neglect are imperative limits on ideals of family privacy.

Adoption as a path to a family of one's own raises serious ethical concern because of its ability to forever sever the ties of adopted children and their biological kin. Feminist scholars have called particular attention to those concerns, advocating more "open" forms of adoption in which biological ties are not severed. Although greater openness in adoption has been a positive development, openness also represents difficult practical, ethical, and legal concerns. Many of these concerns boil down to concerns about accountability.

Open Adoption

"Open" adoption—also called "disclosed" and "cooperative" adoption—is gaining acceptance.[40] The adoptions between strangers that took place in the United States in the decades after World War II were unduly "closed." The parties were anonymous; the procedures were confidential; the official records were sealed. In addition, birth parents legally transferred all parental rights and responsibilities respecting their offspring. The experts of yesteryear maintained that closed adoption hastened the end of birth mothers' grief, spared them shame, enabled them to go on with their lives, and ensured that their offspring would grow up with secure identities. Experts also maintained that closed adoptions would allow adoptive parents to maintain secrecy and to bond more easily with their adopted children.[41]

A growing number of adoption professionals and legal experts now believe that the birth parents of children placed for adoption should not be forced out of sight and should strive to maintain a relationship with their offspring.[42] Although some birth parents prefer that the legal termination of parental rights and responsibilities also terminate their relationship with their offspring and the adopting families, other birth parents welcome postadoption contacts. Many adoptive parents reportedly value the information about their children's health and origins that contact with birth parents affords. Research by Drs. Harold D. Grotevant and Ruth G. McRoy discredits assumptions about the old, closed-adoption regime. Dozens of adoptive parents, birth parents, and adoptees interviewed over a period of years report good experiences with open adoptions, including what Grotevant and McRoy refer to as "time-limited" and agency "mediated" open adoptions.[43] "Time-limited" open adoptions are those in which the parties agree that for a limited time before and after birth, birth parents will have contact with the adoptive family. "Mediated" open adoptions are those in which the ongoing contact that birth parents have with the adoptive family is arranged or supervised by an adoption agency.

Domestic adoptions afford opportunities for one-time and ongoing interchange between birth and adoptive parents that international adoptions rarely do. In the case of international adoptions—that is, adoptions by United States citizens of infants or children who are foreign nationals—it is unusual for birth parents to have an opportunity to meet prospective adoptive parents. Postplacement contact of any type between, say, a Russian or Chinese birth parent and an American adoptive family is rare. In some cases, U.S. adoptive families maintain ties with adoption officials or others in their adopted children's community or country of origin. By contrast, in the case of domestic adoptions of infants in the United States, it is no longer unusual for birth parents to meet adoptive parents prior to or shortly after the birth of the child. In some instances these meetings are conducted semi-anonymously on a first-name-only basis and in the presence of an adoption professional. It is common for birth parents to request and receive letters, photographs, and videos concerning their offspring. Some birth parents share special holidays, events, and vacations with adoptive families. A few even enjoy the unrestrained spontaneous intimacy we associate with family or close friends.

In some instances of domestic adoption, the open relationships between birth parents and adoptive families are secured by oral understandings; in other instances, they are secured by written agreements setting forth the terms of post-adoption contacts (such as the frequency of letters). Relationships cemented by oral or written agreements may be mediated and monitored on an ongoing basis by adoption agency social workers. Although the parties to such agreements seldom intend to create legally binding contracts, the idea that oral or written agreements between birth parents and adoptive parents should be legally enforceable has adherents.[44]

Open-adoption practices have virtues and raise concerns. Legal concerns include whether open-adoption agreements should be legally enforceable and whether authorities should unseal adoption records. In legal debates, the sealed records issue gets framed mainly as a matter of privacy or confidentiality. But accountability concerns are evident, too, and often lurk behind what are framed as matters of privacy and confidentiality. Unsealed records mean that no-longer-anonymous birth parents may face unwanted, emotionally painful accountability demands from adoptees and intimate family and friends about secret events long past. What happened? Why did you do that? Why didn't you tell me; rely on me; trust me?

Practical concerns about open adoption include whether adoption agencies can effectively mediate contact and potential conflicts between birth and adoptive families. Some adoptive families resent the accountability demands implicit in the sustained relationships with adoption agencies and birth families entailed by popular and emerging open-adoption practices.

Ethical concerns include the limits of birth parents' responsibilities to provide information about their health, genes, and families to adoptive families. Information-emphatic accountability results from felt obligations to provide personal health and family history. One accountability-related ethical concern goes straight to the heart of the very idea of postplacement open-adoption arrangements in domestic adoptions: whether adoptive parents are ethically bound to include significantly birth parents in their lives, after an otherwise successful placement and termination of birth parents' legal rights.

Excluding Birth Parents

And what about those ethical concerns? The desire of adoptive parents to have families of their own, and the desire of birth parents for access to their own children, potentially are in tension. To address that tension, a number of theorists have begun to challenge the ideal of the nuclear family and propose in its place more inclusive notions of family.[45] For these theorists, adoption, and especially open adoption that reserves a place at the table for birth mothers, is an example of the reconceived, deprivatized family. The postnuclear family will have fluid, overlapping boundaries, not yet fully incorporated into law. Interestingly, though, opponents of the nuclear, private family ideal continue to press for a sphere of decisional authority for primary caretakers. Thus Alison Harvison Young argues for a "reconceptualization of the family which would (1) recognize the limitations of the ideology of the exclusive family and articulate a model that includes nontraditional family units as well as the range of roles potentially played by various actors in the life of a child, and yet (2) allocate the ultimate decision-making authority to a particular sphere, such as the primary caretaker or caretakers [i.e.,] the core family unit.[46] When adoptive parents have become the core family unit, should their moral powers include the power to substantially exclude birth parents, even kind and generous birth parents, from their daily lives? I believe they should."

I want to first baldly state my view and then, in subsequent sections, to offer philosophical and policy considerations in support of it. Adoptive parents are not ethically bound to include birth parents in their lives. Instead, adoptive parents are bound to do what they can do toward providing a good life for their children. The discharge of this obligation may or may not entail birth parent inclusion, depending upon individual circumstances. Of course, many adoptive parents will want to include birth parents significantly in their lives, and many will have good reasons to attempt even painful and inconvenient inclusion. For example, those who adopt older children with healthy ties with their birth families (and possibly foster families or others) are likely to have good reason to attempt to maintain those ties through some form of inclusion.

Adoptive families who prefer to end, limit, or forgo postadoption contact with birth parents should not be subjected to automatic moral condemnation, and, second, they should be supported in their good-faith decisions by adoption professionals and policymakers. Birth parents and their families do not have a *prima facie* moral right to maintain contact with adopted kin, because such an ascription of right would be inconsistent with adoptive parents' *prima facie* rights and responsibilities as caretakers. I expect that critics of the traditional, nuclear, privatized, and exclusive family will balk at the direction of my argument.[47] Yet even proponents of nontraditional, alternative models of the family and birth parent rights must recognize the importance to effective caretakers of secure spheres of agency, autonomy, and well being.

The preference for preserving closed adoption options is not a desire to return to the complete closed-adoption regime of the 1950s. A few short decades ago adoptive parents, adoption professionals, and the state collaborated to make it possible for adoptive parents to pretend that they were biological parents. Agencies placed children in families with whom the children bore physical resemblances. Adoptive parents often kept the fact of adoption a secret and passed adopted children off as their biological offspring. Having a family of one's own in the 1950s meant gaining social acceptance through a pretense of fertility and normalcy. Adoption was a secret kept from friends, neighbors, and even adopted children themselves. The state supported secrecy by issuing birth certificates naming the adoptive parents as the child's parents. Although some states still issue such certificates, they are intended to fool no one.

I know a lesbian couple in Washington whose adopted son was issued a birth certificate bearing the names of two female parents.

Today's adoptive families show little interest in secrecy and fictional birth parenthood. Families send out adoption announcements to proudly herald their adoptions. Adopted children know that they are adopted. They may be of a different race or ethnicity than their adoptive parents, and patently so. The contemporary adoptive parent's desire for a happy family of his or her own has nothing to do with secrecy and pretense, and everything to do with family privacy, intimacy, and the design of a healthy, workable private life. Not every prospective adoptive parent is prepared to meet or befriend birth parents. For this reason, a norm (or even a perceived norm) of open adoption could adversely reduce the size of the pool of prospective adoptive families, particularly for minority infants, who are not scarce compared to white infants. If open-adoption practices were to reduce the pool, America's most vulnerable children would pay the price. Children pay, too, if open adoption reluctantly undertaken makes the adoption process and postadoption family life significantly more taxing.

Legislators should not outlaw contact between birth and adoptive families, or even discourage it. But as a policy matter, I disagree with Annette Baran and Reuben Pannor's perspective that open adoption is morally obligatory because adoptive parents' relationship with their children should be understood, by contrast to biological parents' relationship with theirs, as merely "guardianship or stewardship."[48] Few practicing social workers explicitly portray adoptive parenting as mere "guardianship." But some social workers seem to believe that birth parents ought, in a moral sense, to have access to adopted children and adoptive families long after the judges' legal decrees are signed. Adoption can be thought, as this emerging perspective suggests, to enlarge the natural family to include birth parents and adoptive parents in a fused or blended family. But it remains plausible and morally legitimate to understand newborn adoption as configuring separate new families altogether.

Two Models of Adoption

I want to suggest two contrasting perspectives on the nature of adoption. We can think of adoption either as a way of *configuring* a new parent-child family, or as a way of *fusing* two or more existing families and making them into a larger one. Some of the most thoughtful defenders of open-adoption practices seem to urge that family fusion is a *fact* that adoptive parents must accept as part of the territory of adoption.[49] I believe family fusion is a *perspective* on adoption that need not be built into public policy and ethics. The two contrasting perspectives require elaboration.

Under the first, the configuration model, adoption takes individual adults and children who may have no preexisting biological or social ties to one another and establishes them as a new primary social unit. Under the configuration model, the primary social unit created by adoption is a family, consisting of one or two heterosexual or homosexual parents and one or more dependent children. The resulting family is "nuclear" in the sense of being small, distinct, and central to the lives of its members. It is not necessarily "nuclear" in the sense of being lorded over by a husband and father who provides economically for a dependent wife and mother who is responsible for day-to-day care of dependent children. From a traditional legal point of view it is easy to comprehend the sense in which adoption creates new families. On this view, adoption is an event or series of one-time events. The state issues new, fictitious birth certificates and reallocates actual rights and obligations for care. But from nonlegal, social, and emotional points of view as well, adoption can be thought to create new families. New, primary, caregiver/dependent relationships modify and supplant old ones. Adoption configures new families by reconfiguring established ones: one or more families essentially lose a member (if only temporarily until the child matures), and another family gains a member (it is hoped, for a lifetime). Whether the two or more families involved in an adoption ought to maintain some sort of contact after configuration and reconfiguration is an open question. It is conceivable, on the configuration model, that the adult parties to adoption are and remain practically strangers.

Under the competing fusion model, adoption takes individual adults and children who may have no preexisting ties to one another, plus those children's biological parents and perhaps other kin and ties, and establishes them as a new social unit. Under the family fusion model, the social unit created is also a family, but like a stepfamily, the adoptive family is not simply or aptly characterized as "nuclear." Under the fusion model, adopting parents gain family members, but birth parents do not lose family members. Whether adopting parents and birth parents ought to maintain contact is an open question under the fusion model, and yet because cooperative contact is normative for functional, loving families, cooperative contact might be viewed as a legitimate expectation for families fused by the adoption of a child.

Advocates of open adoption who think that all adoptive parents have presumptive obligations of birth parent inclusion may be relying on the family fusion model of adoption. It is theoretically possible that both models of adoption would lead adoption professionals who embraced them to advocate the same kinds of adoption policies and practices. I believe, however, that postplacement open adoption will seem rather more compelling to those who are strongly drawn to the fusion model than to those who are strongly drawn to the configuration model. That is because with open-adoption practices

come intimate exchanges of personal information, intergenerational displays
of emotion, and opportunities for relaxed, spontaneous physical contact most
closely associated in our society with functioning family units.

Fusion and Openness

From an ethical point of view, much can be said in favor of the family fusion
model of adoption and the open adoption practices for which it might be
thought to call. Open adoption policies will be especially attractive to anyone
who subscribes to the fusion model of adoption. In bioethics, practices facili-
tated and encouraged by the helping professions—including obstetricians, social workers, psychologists, psychiatrists, the clergy—are commonly assessed
by reference to whether they conform to recognized principles and ideals.[50] It
would be useful to consider what traditional principles, along with ideals of
care and agency that recent feminists stress, might suggest about adoption.[51] It
could be argued that the adoption-as-fusion model flows from and mandates a
profound understanding of the rights and needs of all of the parties to an adoption, including the informational needs of maximally effective adoptive parents and birth parents. It can be argued that adoption is best viewed as a
fusing or blending of families whose members subsequently acquire *prima facie* rights and obligations of intimate contact and disclosure. I will eventually
suggest, however, that attention to autonomy and beneficence countermands
an adoption regime in which adoptive parents are ascribed moral or legal obligations of postadoption contact with birth parents.

To respect autonomy, it can be argued, a society must at a minimum preserve meaningful choices for the men and women who create children they believe they cannot rear. Biological parents must be free to transfer custody of
their children to responsible new adoptive parents; they must be free to select
adoptive parents for their children or to delegate some or all of the powers of
selection to a trusted fiduciary; they must be free to require of adopting parents a means of obtaining information about the continuing well being of their
children. If adoption is family fusion, it would seem to follow that the means
by which birth parents obtain information should be means appropriate to intimates in our culture rather than means open to strangers. Personal letters, personal conversations, and intimate direct contact could be expected.

To act with beneficence, it could be argued, the needs of birth parents who
strongly desire to maintain ties with adopted children and their families ought
to be accommodated, and the needs of children for access to biological kin
and information about them ought to be accommodated. To meet these relational needs it might be supposed that adoptions and adoption records should
be more open than closed. And, again, if adoption is family fusion, modes of
openness appropriate to families should be encouraged to the extent possible.

Finally, to do as justice requires, it is imperative that the adoption process treat birth families fairly and as the moral equals of adoptive families, despite typical disparities in education, income, class, and race. It is imperative, too, that the human rights of birth families be respected. Drucilla Cornell has powerfully argued that birth mothers have rights to "be allowed the space to come to terms with their own life-defining decisions about sexuality and family." These rights could justify ascription of generous rights to surrogate mothers and birth mothers. Cornell conceives of the ongoing interest of birth mothers for inclusion in the lives of adopted children thus:

> What should a birth mother relinquish when she relinquishes primary custody of her child? Only that—primary custody. The equal protection of the birth mother's imaginary domain at least demands that she be allowed access to any information she desires to have about her child, and to have the chance to meet and explore with the child what kind of relationship they can develop.[52]

Arguably, birth fathers have analogous equality interests in knowing their offspring that just societies ought to honor. Grounded in the model of adoption as family fusion, there is an impressive ethical case for a duty of cooperative openness that extends beyond a one-time meeting at the adoption agency or lawyer's office.

In summation, if adoptive parents and birth families are construed as part of a single primary familial unit, whose members are to be treated with respect for their moral autonomy, with benevolent respect for their welfare, and with justice, it makes sense to think that, *prima facie*, adoptive parents have (1) a moral obligation of family-style inclusion to birth parents, and (2) a moral obligation to their children to, for example, meet with the children's birth parents, learn from them, and provide them with information. Adoptive parents have rights, too, in this model. They have a right to birth parents' cooperation in some form of mutually acceptable ongoing contact, so that adopted children have meaningful opportunities to know their full ("true") genealogical identities and their entire ("real") parents and families.

As powerful as the family fusion-based case for open adoption arrangements can appear when viewed through the lenses of commonly held ideals and principles, those same principles ultimately compel a quite different view of things. Below, I elaborate the case for the alternative, family configuration model of adoption, and then urge that we should view postplacement open adoption as an important option rather than a moral mandate.

The Permanent Adoption Imperative

In the United States children of all ages often need homes because their parents are unable to provide for them. Ideally, no child would have to be placed for adoption; ideally policymakers would devote more resources to measures that allow parents to care for the children they bear.[53] It is especially heartbreaking that kind, employed, high school educated birth mothers feel compelled to resort to adoption for primarily economic reasons.

In our less than ideal nation, welfare policies and practices enshrine the permanent adoption imperative: young children whose parents cannot, should not, or do not wish to rear them ought to be placed for adoption with minimal delay in permanent new homes with new parents.[54] The permanent adoption imperative, reflected in, *inter alia*, the Adoption and Safe Families Act (1997) and the Adoption Assistance and Child Welfare Act (1980), requires a pool of competent, loving adults willing to take on the time-consuming, expensive, and emotional process of qualifying for adoption, followed by the burdens of rearing children born to others.[55] We are glad when new families competent to shelter children from harm, want, and uncertainty unconditionally embrace the children who need them. We are saddened when children spend a significant portion of their lives in neglect, abuse, and serial foster homes.

Open record policies, face-to-face pre-adoption meetings, postplacement communication through letters and photos, and postplacement visits are four distinct varieties of open adoption, each of which requires separate analysis. The impact, if any, of each on (1) the size of the pool of prospective adoptive parents and on (2) efficacious adoptive parenting, must be part of the ethical calculus. I want to focus on postplacement contacts because they may be the forms of open adoption that are most likely to turn off and turn away prospective adoptive parents. They are also the form of open adoption most likely to increase the burdens of parenting for adults seeking to rear adopted children. I believe ethical respect for adoptive parents' agency and autonomy, when combined with considerations of beneficent regard for adoptive families and the pool of children needing homes, makes a strong case for a regime in which postadoption contact is strictly optional. We do best by children by attempting to preserve varieties of nondisclosed adoption as meaningful options for the prospective parents who require them as a condition of adoption *and* for the actual adoptive parents who require them as a condition of what they believe to be responsible care.

Preserving the Option

Our domestic adoption practices thwart the permanent adoption policy imperative to the extent that concerns about adoption practices diminish the pool of prospective adoptive parents in the United States. Several practices could diminish the pool. Denying adoptive families the ability to express racial preferences in adoption might reduce the pool, as might requiring genetic testing to prove fitness. It is also possible that open adoption practices could reduce the pool.

Should we be worried about the size of the pool? At present in the United States there are many more people seeking to adopt healthy white newborns than there are healthy white newborns available for adoption. With respect to the pool of potential parents for white American newborns, my concerns about policies adversely affecting the size may be unwarranted. But the pool for nonwhite and at-risk newborns is not so vast as to render my concerns moot. And I see no reason to think that the crowded pool of white parents looking for white newborns could not be significantly emptied by unappealing changes in adoption practices and appealing developments in biomedical technology. The felt needs and desire of whites to adopt will soon be addressed by cloning and other reproductive technologies on the horizon.

Although an attractive, workable option for some, open adoption is not for everyone. Not everyone who would otherwise make a terrific adoptive parent will want to adopt if he or she is expected to participate in open procedures. Some prospective adoptive parents may not be willing to adopt, particularly a child from their own locale, if they cannot do so anonymously or with complete confidence that they will not be compelled to interact with birth parents on an ongoing basis. According to Carol Sanger open adoption "increases the number of children available," presumably by making adoption more attractive to birth parents.[56] It is not clear that open adoption increases the number of families willing to adopt, however.

In the case of international adoptions, adoptive parents may be unable to avoid excluding birth parents from their lives. Even where it is not literally unavoidable, birth parent exclusion can seem natural and justified by great geographic and cultural distances. But adoptive parents in the United States who adopt from their own localities may be expected to participate in a variety of open-adoption practices, precisely because geographic and cultural barriers are perceived as minimal. Private adoption agencies commonly promote a degree of openness in their domestic adoptions. Adoptions Together, an agency that serves families throughout the greater Washington, D.C., and Baltimore, Maryland, region, is just one example of a private adoption agency that encourages birth parents to participate in the selection of adoptive families and encourages adoptive families to meet and maintain contact with birth parents.

Counseling, education, and emotional support can convert some reluctant people into willing participants in open-adoption practices. Private agencies officially committed to ideals of openness have reported success in persuading prospective adoptive parents to meet birth parents face-to-face, at least once. Some adoptive parents have agreed to one or more face-to-face meetings with birth parents partly out of curiosity and mainly out of fear that they would hurt their chances of obtaining a child were they to insist upon complete anonymity. Private agencies report that when initially resisted face-to-face meetings happen, they are generally pleasant and informational. Anecdotally, birth parents and adoptive parents report feeling less anxious about adoption after meeting one another.

I would conjecture that a small number of prospective adoptive parents have been utterly turned off to the process of adoption by the prospect of meeting with birth parents. Those who were turned off may have had concerns about being judged by and potentially rejected by birth parents, coupled with concerns about future emotional entanglement with birth parents who are not complete strangers. Some people who eschew open adoption remain in the pool for domestic adoption, but search for non-open adoption options. Others enter the pool for international adoptions from orphanages, in which contact with birth parents is exceedingly rare.

The greatest threat to domestic adoption is not the one-time pre-adoption meeting. Instead, it is the perceived threat of hardship potentially arising out of ongoing postadoption intimate contact with birth families. When it comes to newborn adoptions, few agencies actively encourage ongoing contact between birth families and unrelated adoptive families, apart from occasional letters and photographs. The story is different when it comes to domestic adoptions involving older children and minority children placed in white homes. Adoption professionals often advise adoptive parents to maintain older children's social ties to prior families, caretakers, and friends, and minority children's ties to appropriate minority communities. Yet, seemingly to maintain a clientele of appealing prospective parents for same-race newborn adoptions, some agency professionals reassure prospective adoptive parents that once an adoption is final, they, the legal parents will call the shots and need not do anything that they find uncomfortable. Prospective parents quickly figure out that in theory they can decline to deliver on promises about postadoption contact they make to agencies and to birth parents.

Adoptive parents should not make promises they do not plan to keep. There is no reason to think many do. Nor should adoption professionals directly or indirectly encourage insincere promises and promise breaking. Adoptive parents who do not make specific promises of ongoing contact do not have ethical obligations of ongoing contact, for reasons I will describe below, but adoptive parents who make specific representations to birth parents are obligated to make a good-faith effort to adhere to them. Sensible people will be reluctant to make promises to perfect strangers that they are not sure they will want to keep, particularly promises about their deepest emotional attachments and gravest responsibilities. Qualified prospective adoptive families may therefore decline to get involved in adoption, fearing that open adoption will produce for them heartache rather than happy families of their own.

Selective Intimacy

It must be admitted that, despite their recognized virtues, open-adoption practices can discourage and complicate adoption. For policymakers, this is a problem of perception and of realities. The perception that postadoption contact is expected but will lead to emotional entanglements and logistical nightmares can discourage adults from choosing domestic adoption. This perception can lead rational adults to conclude that adoption is not a way to have a happy family of one's own. When entanglements and nightmares do occur, the reputation of open adoption as a viable alternative is harmed.

In ways that open records and preplacement meetings need not do, ongoing postadoption contact with birth parents can frustrate the ability of adoptive parents to achieve the genuine and selective intimacy many Americans associate with parent-child families. Many Americans conceive of the family as an intimate union formed around the core values and preferences of the adults who configure them. Parent-child families today are indeed *configured*, that is, intentionally shaped by knowing choices and deeply felt responsibilities. In important respects, marriage is a choice. Partnership is a choice. Divorce and remarriage are choices. Pregnancy can be a choice. Because of birth control, abortion, and prenatal testing, the number, sex, and health of one's children is subject to choice. Whether kin or close friends are part of one's home and family life are matters about which there is considerable choice. (None of this emphasis on the role of choice is intended to deny the major forces that shape motive and desire, and the acts of God that can overtake a family—an unexpected illness, a unanticipated genius, a disability.)

The wish for postadoption birth parent exclusion may sometimes stem from insecurities about losing a child or losing powers of independent decision making. Adoptive parents may fear the continuing moral influence of birth parents, even birth parents who do not intend or expect to monitor or influence adoptive parents' key child-rearing decisions. Adoptive parents may be made uncomfortable by the unequal relationships that often exist between themselves and birth parents. Economic and educational inequalities are typical, with adopting parents being more affluent and better educated than birth families. Informational inequalities are common. Birth parents disclose more information about themselves than adoptive parents do. After years of contact birth parents may know only the first names of adoptive parents and their general line of work. Conversation, friendship, and trust are difficult when personal data disclosures are nonreciprocal. The resultant social discomforts, some of which can be overcome, are only a part of the story behind resistance to open adoption.

The bigger part of the story is an affirmative desire among adoptive parents for self-defined family privacy and intimacy. Open adoption unavoidably introduces an additional level of accountability for parenting and life choices into the home. Open adoption practices strike some people as *dictating* the fusion of families and *mandating* specific intimacies. Adoptive parents may reject intimacy with birth parents because they feel they have little in common with birth families. They may feel that attempts to fuse and blend are strained and stressful. This can easily be the case when birth and adoptive parents are far apart in age, education, or religion, and where they belong to different ethnic, cultural, and linguistic groups.

Effective Adoptive Parenting

How hard can it be to open your life to the people who are, after all, the biological kin of your children? It does not have to be hard, but it can be hard. The uncertain degree of accountability, the mismatch of tastes and temperament, the generational differences. The lopsided, forced intimacy. The time, the emotional work, the money. Reality seldom resembles the family law sagas that end up in textbooks and as television movies. Yet reality can manifest enough emotional confusion and entanglement to turn some prospective parents off to open adoption and to adoption altogether.

Adoptive parents who feel they should spend time with birth parents and incorporate them into their lives may find that they cannot easily do it. Time is a scarce commodity in many families. Suppose you have two adopted children, a sister in Gwen's predicament, aging parents, and a job. Emotional space is a scarce commodity as well. Adoptive parents may have two or more children, two careers, large, established extended families, and many close friends competing for their time and attention. Some birth parents easily blend into adoptive families. Yet young birth parents may have unmet needs for parenting that leave adoptive parents bewildered, feeling like overburdened grandparents of their adopted children.

Adoptive parents may judge that contact with birth parents or a particular birth parent is unwise for a child evidencing special needs unrelated to adoption. Adoptive parents who have two or more adopted children with differently accessible birth parents may conclude that there are emotional risks entailed by postplacement openness. Highly contextual issues of intimate inclusion and exclusion loom especially large in families in which one or more adopted children suffer from attachment, conduct, and or mood disorders.

Clinical studies arguably suggest that adopted children as a class, even including those who may not have suffered grave deprivation or abuse, are at a higher risk than nonadopted children for mental illnesses.[57] A study of adults who had been adopted as children found that they were more likely than other adults to have a history of conduct disorder, antisocial personality, and drug abuse or dependence. Clinical studies have concluded that disruptive behavior, conduct disorders, and attention deficit/hyperactivity disorder are all more common among adopted children than nonadopted children.[58] Fortunately, a number of researchers are skeptical about studies linking adoption to mental illness. There is evidence that mental illness affects a minority of adopted children and that the mental health problems of many adopted children resolve after childhood or adolescence. [59] In the face of ongoing research, however, one ought to respect the decision of an adoptive parent who is reluctant to introduce or sustain open-adoption practices that add stress into their families' lives. Adoptive parents need maximal flexibility to protectively structure the intimate realms of their highly vulnerable children. Although birth parent involvement may be a blessing, when children in the family are troubled or ill, it may also be a stressor and danger.

Mixed-Race

Adults who regard themselves as morally responsible for the upbringing of children commonly view themselves as having an obligation—at a minimum—to feed, clothe, and educate the children. Such adults also view themselves as having an obligation to ensure that their children, or their families', friends', or communities' children, have suitable identities. This is why many African Americans have qualms about both interracial marriage and about transracial adoption. Racial identity groups impose accountability expectations on a person's ascribed group membership relating to child rearing, no less than marriage. In fact, accountability norms are vital to group perpetuation. Exerting moral influence over how children are reared serves to promote the survival of minority groups as distinct groups. African Americans hold one another accountable for rearing children with an appropriate black identity. The community that accepts your interracial marriage as justified may nonetheless exert moral pressure on you to rear your child to form a black identity. Mixed-race children are the future of black culture and are also perceived as a threat to it unless they develop black identities.

Transracial adoption in the United States is one context in which to think about the complex imperative to bring children up to have the appropriate identities, and in which to see its problematic character. In the United States some categories of identification are treated as essential (e.g., gender), but others are treated as not essential (e.g., religion). Officially, under progressive "color blind" civil rights laws, race is supposed to be treated like religion—a weak factor to consider in matching children to families. If black children are adopted by nonblacks, they are adopted by people who are not accountable to other blacks in the same strong way. Thus the moral pressure to rear the child as a black person is substantially lighter. Although the issue is most often put in terms of cultural competence and the need for the child to have culturally competent parents so that the child can develop the appropriate identity, the concern less often articulated is that transracial adoption means some black children will have parents who are not accountable to the racial group.

Open adoption seems to some as the most just and responsive form of domestic transracial adoption.[60] It has been argued that if white people are going to adopt black newborns or older children, for example, they should do so in a way that facilitates African American modes of kinship and black identity. I have heard white parents in nondisclosed transracial adoptions express a sense of obligation to their adopted children and the children's unknown and unknowable birth parents to rear and educate the children in a way that is consistent with the values and mores of an important branch of the child's ancestral family tree.

Indeed, I have on several occasions heard white adoptive parents explain why they are involved in open adoption, in effect by reference to what they felt were their Asian or Black or Mexican American child's social continuity needs. For example, a former colleague who has adopted a Mexican American girl maintains close contact with the girl's biological grandparents to assure social continuity. The child was adopted as a newborn and had no emotional relationship with the grandmother prior to adoption.

The social continuity argument for open-adoption practices is based on the pervasive but mistaken view that children are born with certain thickly constituted social identities that ought to be reinscribed by an upbringing among or in the ways of their social similars.[61] We are said to wrong children, to ignore their basic welfare interests, to mistreat them, when we thwart reinscription. Thus biological parents raising their own children sometimes feel that they wrong their children to the extent that they do not rear them in a way that will assure them an appropriate racial or cultural identity. Orthodox Jews take pains to rear their children as Orthodox Jews. African American parents who live in predominately white communities sometimes take pains to expose their children to foods, rituals, music, and dance that will help their children to not only appreciate black culture in an aesthetic sense but that will enable them to participate in and identify with black culture. Adoptive parents who adopt transracially may feel special incompetence and special pressures to rear their children in a way that will assure them their appropriate identities.

Some adoptive parents and perspective adoptive parents will conclude that neither emotional nor social continuity arguments are sufficiently strong to warrant open adoption. Some will reach such conclusions because they do not believe children are born with certain thickly constituted identities that merit reinscription. They may doubt that social categories of race and national origin, for example, are sufficiently meaningful to design their families' lives around them; they may view their obligations as parents as requiring that they seek to ensure that their adopted children have stable, secure, loving environments likely to give rise to stable personalities and secure individual identities. Other will conclude that seeking social continuity is impractical. Birth families may live in remote places or be deceased or be unknown. A child's biological parents may have come from two or more extremely different and even antagonistic cultural traditions. Which tradition gets reinscribed? What if adoptive parents know that the birth parents were indifferent to their own traditions (e.g., they were nonpracticing Catholics, assimilated Cuban Americans or Jews)? What if the birth parents held offensive beliefs? Plainly there can be no categorical duty to maintain social continuity.

Is there *prima facie* such a duty? Suppose, *arguendo*, that adoptive parents know precisely the social origins of their children and know how to contact birth parents and families. And suppose further that there is no history of abuse and neglect or criminality to warrant keeping children away from birth families. Do a child's interests in social continuity warrant viewing open adoption as a *prima facie* moral mandate? I propose that they do not, at least in the case of newborn adoptions. My proposal rests in part on a tenet, elaborated elsewhere, that no child has a right to a certain identity.[62] The parents of newborns have obligations of beneficence or care to rear their child in reasonably stable and loving environments that prepare the child for its adult roles. Concerns about "appropriate" identity formation often have more to say about adults' feelings of social isolation and insecurities about acceptance than about what an emotionally healthy and happy child actually requires. For children adopted as infants, the interests in social continuity are weak. My proposal also rests on a belief that the desire for a family of one's own is a legitimate one and that it is at odds with expectations of family fusion or cooperative parenting. The intimidating notion that adoptive parents are morally obligated to provide social continuity in the form of family fusion and open adoptions *could* reduce the pool of willing adoptive parents.

It would be a mistake to condemn categorically an adoptive parent's judgment that contact with birth families is—or is not—in his or her particular child's best interest. There are a number of good reasons to pursue open adoption, such as making it possible for one's child by adoption to locate birth parents later in life, and to communicate concerns about health and progress. It would appear that open-adoption arrangements are called for in many circumstances, when adopted children have significant, otherwise beneficial emotional bonds with biological kin—parents, siblings, grandparents.[63] In these cases, however, adoptive parents are likely to conclude without coercion that, to the extent that they can have a happy family of their own, they must provide for the emotional continuity needs of their children through an option-adoption practice of sustained contact.

The permanent adoption imperative instructs the just society to find families for young children who need them. Adoption must be kept attractive to prospective parents. Open-adoption practices—such as unsealed records, face-to-face meetings between birth and adoptive families, and postadoption contact between birth and adoptive families—make adoptive families more accountable and may, as a consequence, make domestic adoption less attractive. Policymakers should avoid measures that make intimate contact between birth and adoptive families a precondition of adoption.

In the ideal world, prospective adoptive parents and birth parents would be able to negotiate and chose freely among various types of open adoption and traditional nondisclosed adoption options. Given a choice, many adoptive parents will choose a degree of openness and accountability because they believe it is something they can manage in the context of their unique lives and something from which they and their adopted minor child will benefit. Birth parents, adoption professionals, and policymakers do best by children if they help to make the adoption process attractive to as diverse and large a pool of qualified people as possible, including people who are not drawn to postadoption contact. As a society we should reserve for ourselves the ability to enable parents to parent effectively and to validate the desire to have a family of one's own, a secure sphere of intimacy and agency.

Accountability and Ethnoracial Community

What, though, about the moral interests of children in identity and continuity? Does child welfare justify an added layer of accountability for adoptive families? Debates about open adoption generally focus on the rights, needs, and interests of children. It could be argued that adopted children are entitled to postadoption access to their birth parents so as to provide social continuity and/or emotional continuity. By "social continuity" I mean continuities of kinship with others with roots in the same biological family, neighborhood, tribe, race, religion, ethnicity, history, or culture. By "emotional continuity," I mean continuities of love, affection, and mutual understanding arising out of shared experiences. Children plainly have a moral interest in social and emotional cotinuities. In the case of newborns adopted shortly after birth, the desirability of emotional continuity provides a weak argument for postadoption contact, if any basis at all. After all, newborns have no emotional ties beyond the biological ties to the mothers who bear them. In the case of older children, adoption disrupts relationships and established patterns of life. Emotional and social continuities are disturbed. It is widely believed that newborns, like older children, have an interest in social continuity after adoption, even where it is conceded that they have no interest or a minimal interest in emotional continuity with families of origin.[64] The ideal of social continuity is part of the thinking behind the federal restrictions on the adoption of Native American children by persons who are not Native American.[65] It is why some African Americans vehemently oppose the adoption of black children by whites.[66]

ACCOUNTABILITY TO RACE

The ideal of social continuity is closely linked to the ideal of group survival, which is ultimately linked to ideals of human diversity. The social continuity ideal surfaces in the open adoption debates, the transracial adoption debates, and in the interracial marriage debates.[67]

Loving v. Virginia settled the question of the constitutionality of laws prohibiting marriages between persons of different races. In *Loving*, the United States Supreme Court determined that state laws banning "miscegenation" violate the Equal Protection Clause of the Fourteenth Amendment.[68] Since *Loving*, a higher percentage of Americans have married across racial lines.[69] The rate of black/white intermarriage has quadrupled. As the number of mixed race families and offspring has grown, the number of theorists who question the very idea of race and racial classification has also grown.

Even so, marriage between blacks and whites remains atypical. African American/white marriages comprise less than 1 percent—about 0.6 percent according to the 2000 census—of all marriages in the United States.[70] The 2000 census showed a mere 363 thousand black/white married couples. The 1990 census showed that 97.6 percent of married black women are married to black men, down only slightly from 99.1 percent in 1960.[71] Homogamy is typical for blacks of both sexes. Out-marriage is morally problematic and emotionally loaded for African Americans. They describe hetergamy as potentially disloyal, inconsiderate, and self-hating. In a remarkable study conducted by University of Michigan psychologist Ruby Beale, black women ranked "seeing an interracial couple" as the second leading cause of stress in their lives, ahead of "racism, housework, economic worries, and more than 100 other potential causes of stress" that she measured.[72] I believe the in-marriage pattern among blacks also can be explained by blacks' sense of moral accountability to one another for their private lives. African Americans feel accountable to one another for the spousal choice. African Americans feel obliged to explain and justify their marriages to whites in particular, but they regard marriages to other blacks as more fully being matters of individual taste and judgment. If your partner is not black, you must explain and justify your choice, in light of the implications of out-marriage for offspring and participation in African American life. You may be subject to social sanctions of exclusion and censure for making the racially wrong choice.

Marrying Black

The ethics of interracial marriage is a frequent topic of discussion and debate among African Americans of all income groups and social classes. Many African Americans are morally troubled by sexually romantic intimacy and marriage between blacks and whites. They see it as a social pathology of fantasy and stereotypes—"jungle fever." Moral qualms surface in books and films about black life, and on the pages of magazines and newspapers marketed to blacks. Discussions of interracial intimacy in the popular press are sometimes prompted by the rise to fame of a mixed-race beauty, performer, or athlete, and sometimes by the coupling of a prominent black with a prominent white. In the nationally circulated African American press, the stance that people should be free to date and marry whomever they like coexists with the stance that blacks have a special obligation to seek black mates. Experts urge black women who are tempted to cross the color line to give older, younger, and lower-income black men a chance before giving up on the possibility of finding a suitable black mate. Black men are criticized for abandoning black women for white partners.[73] The overall message of the black press seems to be that intermarriage can work, but it is best for blacks who marry to "marry black," even if finding a black mate requires extra effort and sacrifice.

Marriage is "private." But it is not incomprehensible to Americans that there should be collective constraints on marriages deemed socially harmful. In the United States today we describe marriage as a private matter, and yet we see the justice of public regulation of marriage. It is only right that public laws should ban certain kinds of marriage—for example, incestuous marriage between children and adults. The Constitution has been interpreted to permit government to regulate marriage in the public interest. More than a hundred years ago in *Reynolds v. United States*, the Supreme Court held that Mormon polygamy could be outlawed consistent with religious liberty and equality.[74] Recent immigrants have urged legal reforms recognizing polygamous unions formed abroad, but the most ripe area for legal reform today is same-sex marriage.[75] The constitutionality of laws prohibiting same-sex marriage has yet to be decided by the Supreme Court. Some gay and lesbian advocates fear the ghost of *Reynolds*, even as they fight for their *Loving v. Virginia*. In the meantime, a national conversation about same-sex marriage is ongoing in state houses and courtrooms.

There was once something of a national conversation about interracial marriage. Like today's conversation about gay and lesbian marriage, it was a conversation full of hate, prejudice, and biological misinformation.[76] The national conversation about interracial marriage abruptly stopped when the Supreme Court handed down the *Loving* decision during the height of the civil rights movement. Although few blacks wanted to marry whites in 1967 and few had the opportunity, *Loving* seemed a fitting complement to the Civil Rights Act of 1964. Blacks had no reason to oppose the new marital freedom law, and whites who opposed the law were silenced by the finality of a Supreme Court decree that echoed the overall direction of national integration policy.

It does not follow from the premise that *Loving* was correctly decided as a matter of legal or moral justice that there are no good reasons for African Americans to question the morality of all or some interracial marriages. Many people believe the law justly permits individuals to choose abortion, even though they believe abortion is nearly always an immoral choice. Many blacks believe the law justly permits interracial marriage, even though (they believe) interracial marriage is nearly always a morally irresponsible choice for which the parties should account. Indeed, interracial marriage raises a number of important moral questions about the requirements of self-respect and group membership. African Americans (and other minority group members, I might add) actively and routinely struggle with questions about the morality of out-marriage premised on group-specific obligations of solidarity and care.

The Genesis of Racial Community

Segregation by race perpetuates cultural differences that impair the formation of personal and intimate relationships among blacks and others who might otherwise live, work, or attend school together.[77] Segregation slows the dissolution of old animosities between the races. Segregation sustains prejudice and stereotyping. Past and present racial segregation helps to explain both the low rate of black out-marriage and the moral qualms blacks feel about out-marriage to whites.

Because public accommodations and workplaces are often racially integrated, it is easy to overlook the fact that blacks and whites live substantially segregated lives. In some areas of the country, residential and school segregation is as extensive as it was prior to the Civil Rights Act of 1964. A 1997 survey of whites with school-age children showed that 41 percent of whites would object to sending their children to a school in which more than half the children were black. Overall, blacks of all social classes (poor, middle class, and affluent) tend to live in segregated, virtually all-black communities. Housing segregation by race is not a wholly voluntary pattern. Economic factors limit choice and mobility—you live where you can afford to live. Fear that prejudice and racism will lead to violence limits choice and mobility—you live where it is safe to live. Well-off blacks seek middle-class and affluent majority black communities, hoping thereby to achieve comfort, acceptance, and community—you live where you expect to flourish. Most American public school children attend schools that are virtually all white or all minority. Schools are segregated because housing is segregated. Compounding the segregation in housing and schools, religious institutions and certain businesses (hair salons, funeral parlors) are often segregated by race.

Segregation is a cloud with a silver lining. Racial segregation based on appearance (skin color, facial features, hair texture, language, etc.) and/or known ancestry (African, etc.) has contributed to the ability of blacks all over the United States to become a culturally vibrant population group. Black society has produced great music, visual art, entertainers, athletes, language styles, and cuisines. Many blacks have common interests, experiences, and viewpoints. Rich and poor blacks, rural and urban blacks, recent immigrant and slave-ancestry blacks feel a subjective affinity for one another despite radically different lifestyles and languages. Blacks use the terms "black community," "black culture," and "black society" to emphasize the matrix of cultural and historical ties binding a population group that is strikingly decentralized and diverse. Being part of the black community, culture, or society does not require any affirmative act of admission. If you have black African ancestry and North American roots or aspirations, you belong. You belong even if one of your parents is not black, and even if you grew up in a white neighborhood or in a white adoptive or foster home. Many African Americans treat black society, which would include their extended families, as where they come from—their community of origin.

A sense of belonging to the African American community is the basis of attributions of obligation, including the imperatives of accountability. The conception of having special obligations to one's community of origin figures prominently in Plato's *Crito*. Socrates was about to be put to death for allegedly corrupting the youth of Athens. When good friends offered him an opportunity to escape from prison and live safely abroad, Socrates refused. He argued that he owed a debt of gratitude to his community of origin for all it had done for him, and that debt meant he could not turn his back on the community when it wrongly adjudicated him to be a criminal. Moreover, Socrates argued, a disobedient escape from prison would set a bad example for the young, rendering him guilty in fact of the crime of which he was accused. Unlike Athens, the black community is not a geographically situated polity with its own systems of laws. Nonetheless, many blacks feel an obligation to the black community analogous to the obligation Socrates felt toward Athens: an obligation to further the group's collective welfare and to yield to its collective judgments, even when that means foregoing personal liberties and sharing resources. I know blacks who deny having any special obligations to the black community, but whose behavior toward other blacks suggests that they are constrained by implicit acceptance of a kind of "second order" obligation to respect the fact that other blacks extend community membership to them.

Interracial Marriage Is a Moral Issue

African Americans' ethical critique of out-marriage strongly relates to the impact of out-marriage on the conditions of social continuity for black families and culture. As I interpret it, the critique is premised on the belief that membership in the black community imposes moral obligations, including obligations about the choice of intimate partners. These obligations are unassumed, nonvoluntary obligations.[78] Three very general moral imperatives appear to lie behind disapproval of out-marriage: (1) respect and care for your community of origin, (2) respect and care for your family and friends, and (3) respect and care for yourself. I believe there is weight to the critique. I comprehend the evolved race-specific accountability practices and ideals. Yet, I believe African Americans should view marriages between blacks and whites as moral challenges rather than moral mistakes. Drug use is a moral mistake; interracial intimacy is a moral challenge.

Respect and Care for Your Community of Origin

As previously observed, many African Americans view themselves as constituting a community. The community in question is not a geographical one, narrowly conceived, because blacks who live hundreds and thousands of miles apart belong to the same community. The community is constituted by cultural and historical affinities that exist whether or not individual blacks attach meaning to them. Loyalty and solidarity, evidenced through involvement with, or participation in, the community is one of the obligations imposed by the black community on blacks.

In general, it is wrong to turn one's back on one's community. We have seen this principle at work among members of the ethnic minority groups "cleansed" from their homelands in Eastern Europe. This ethical notion is strongly held in the United States, sometimes adduced to justify capital punishment for traitors and to justify compulsory military service. Other applications of the notion would justify demands for community service of lesser proportions, such as contributing time and money to charity or holding public office. Opponents of out-marriage construe it as turning one's back on one's community. To in-marry is to validate the community by acknowledging that it can provide one with people of character, beauty, and resources suitable for the intimate relationships most vital to flourishing. To in-marry is to validate the community by signaling an intent to perpetuate the community through childbearing and child-rearing. To in-marry is to be an involved participant in the community through central life activities.

What, then, does it mean to out-marry? Focusing on the obligations of black men to date black women and utilizing metaphors of war, psychology professor Dr. Halford Fairchild summed up the respect-and-care-for-one's-community-based objection to interracial marriage with unusual passion:

> "I feel it is irresponsible for Black men to cross date in today's day and time," says Dr. Fairchild. "It's nice to date whom you want, to say that all is equal, but life is not equal. Black people are defined as inferior and put in second class status. We must recognize our debt to each other. For Black men to date and marry White women in the face of our lingering debt to each other is irresponsible. The brother has sold out. We have a responsibility to each other. We are under siege. We are at war. To sleep with the enemy is treason, racial treason." [79]

To out-marry is to express disappointment with the human products of one's community, to deny the worthiness of perpetuating one's culture, and to reject the significance of community loyalty and solidarity.

Respect and Care for Your Family and Friends

Intimate friends and family ties are of special importance to most people. Moreover, in a society in which government presupposes the existence of family networks to provide child care, care of the sick, and elder care, family members may need us as well as want us. One ought therefore to build a life that includes one's parents, siblings, and other kin. One should avoid designing a life that distances rather than brings together; that hurts rather than pleases; that introduces stresses and tensions into settings that have the potential, otherwise, for uninhibited devotion. It is one thing to go to college and to work with people of all races, but to introduce the political divisions and social division present elsewhere in the society into the home and family is a mistake, particularly if one will thereby lose one's capacity to be an effective member of the family. To in-marry is to signal a willingness to remain involved; to not shift cultural alliances; to not distance oneself.

To out-marry is to invite distance and division. Out-marriage can cause complications that separate a person from his or her black family and black friends:

> Research and personal accounts indicate that interracial couples experience considerable hostility in the workplace, in their social lives and even in their ex-

tended families. And Black/White marriages are more likely to face prejudice than other interracial pairings.[80]

We marry to meld worlds, hoping the whole will be greater than or equal to the sum of its parts. Melded lives can bring a bounty of new kinship, friendships, and holiday celebrations. But if friends and families resist a spouse who is a cultural outsider, or if prejudice and xenophobia abound, interracial couples may find that they are socially diminished rather than enlarged by their marriages. The result can be a melded life together that feels like a net loss.

The loss of society that can come from interracial marriages is not a result of the behavior and attitudes of persons exogenous to the relationship. A white person married to a black person may feel uncomfortable around blacks other than his or her beloved spouse, including his or her beloved's black family and friends; *mutatis mutandis*, a black person married to a white person. Suppose a white professional man joins through marriage an African American family that includes, as they often do, siblings of vastly dissimilar education and employment—a welfare mom, a doctor, and a marine. He marries the sibling who is a doctor. If the white spouse is from a solidly upper middle-class segregated white background, he may be quite unable to relate to the welfare mom and the marine, let alone the father-in-law who never went to college, the cousin just released from prison, and the aunt who "shouts" in church. White men also may have trouble understanding the sense of responsibility their successful black partners may feel with respect to family members in addition to their own children, siblings, and parents. Whites may not understand extended family loyalties that extend far down the kinship chain to nieces and nephews, to great-aunts, and even to "play" cousins of "play" aunts. Even blacks and whites of the same income group and professional class may find that they bring to the marriage inconsistent culturally specific social expectations. The ideal of melded lives may be impossible for some interracial couples to approximate. Thanks to rampant segregation, to out-marry is to invite conflict, stress, and disappointment.

Respect and Care for Yourself

One ought to love oneself. It is wrong to be ashamed of what you are and to devalue your own physical characteristics. These are important ethical ideas. For some blacks, to in-marry is to announce pride in one's racial heritage. It is to announce: "I have no problems with my color, my nose, my lips, my shape, my hair, nor similar traits in others." In-marriage announces: "Should I choose to bear children, I will be glad to pass on my African traits." To in-marry is to demand and get the best for oneself—namely, a partner who can easily comprehend one's value, humor, and needs. To out-marry is to imply a need for white approval and validation; regret about what one is; and aversion to the traits one would pass on to offspring were one to in-marry and bear children. It does not appear that African Americans believe whites and blacks are incapable of loving one another. But I have heard blacks suggest that blacks who marry whites are selling themselves short. (This suggestion often is made about the attractive, affluent blacks who become intimately involved with what are considered less attractive or affluent whites.) To out-marry is to sell oneself short by giving up the opportunity to share one's life with a true peer, someone capable of deep, culturally-based understanding of who one is and what one values.

In Defense of Interracial Marriage

How does one reply to the powerful moral concerns African Americans raise against interracial marriage? "That's private!" would be a poor response, ignoring rather than engaging the claims of community debt and accountability African Americans make with respect to one another. Liberals respond inadequately, therefore, if they reply simply that everyone has a right to marry whomever he or she wants to, racial difference notwithstanding. You love who you love and isn't it great when love defies segregation! Some African Americans who choose white spouses undoubtedly do so feeling morally justified by just the kinds of liberal considerations cited. They feel their autonomous, legal choice of spouse is no one's business. They may even feel that they are doing America a favor.

Liberals do better to acknowledge the practical adversities interracial couples face and cause, but to stress the ideals of romantic love and toleration that interracial marriages often instantiate. Because so many African Americans embrace the seemingly unliberal notions that race is a basis of community and community a source of unassumed obligations of solidarity and care, I want to try and frame a response to the case against out-marriage that reconciles interracial marriages between blacks and whites with black community-centered concerns about respect and care. I believe interracial intimacy and out-marriage can be defended within a framework that takes seriously (without necessarily sharing) African American concerns and values relating to communities of origin.

First, interracial marriage is consistent with the principle of respecting and caring for the black community. Interracial marriage would not be consistent with this important principle if the practice were intended to injure blacks or in fact injured blacks. Black/white out-marriage is a product of integrated association rather than of efforts to harm, demean, or offend blacks. Interracial intimacy is normally the product of living, working, or playing in desegregated environments. If people from different racial communities are thrown together, despite overall segregated housing and social patterns, a few will form attachments to people of other races. Many middle- and upper middle-class blacks live in majority white neighborhoods and work in majority white environments. Many blacks in the military raise families in multicultural and international settings. As young adults, many blacks who have led theretofore segregated lives attend majority white colleges and universities and undertake fields of study that are populated mainly by whites and other nonblacks. Extensive contact with whites in these contexts can result in close friendships, sexual attraction, and a desire to marry.[81]

Second, interracial marriages have not rendered black cultural life less vital. This is partly because out-marriage has not shown signs of ending the pervasive segregation that regenerates black cultural life, and partly because blacks who out-marry make contributions to the black community comparable to those they would have made in any case. Out-marriage is always evidence that segregation has been ineffective. Those who come into contact with happy out-marriages may be moved toward greater racial tolerance. And yet out-marriage—still rare when viewed as an overall percentage of black marriage—has done little to change the fact of pervasive segregation. Indeed, a black woman married to a white man may end up living as the only black in a white community, or a white woman married to a black man may wind up as the only white in a circle of blacks. Blacks who out-marry are not thereby lost to the black community, even if they do come to reside in majority white neighborhoods. Some of the most prominent contributors to African American art, culture, politics, and social life have been married to whites or are products of interracial marriages.[82] Indeed, Marion Wright Edelman, the best-known children's advocate in the United States, is an African American woman married to a white lawyer she met while working as a civil rights lawyer in the South.[83] The offspring of mixed marriages typically identify themselves as blacks and are more likely to be black identified or bicultural than to be black outsiders. Mindful of the moral concerns I am discussing, blacks who out-marry may possess active fears about being lost to the community that lead them to eagerly embrace opportunities for contributing to the black community through their employment, volunteer work, or philanthropy.

Some of the moral opposition to black out-marriage is based on the presumption that out-marriage signals a deficit of black identity that will naturally lead to a diminished willingness to be involved as participants in black life. Blacks who marry whites may live in majority white neighborhoods and come to take on some of the external affects or lifestyles associated with European Americans. But this says nothing about their core identities. They may have strong black identities. Identity issues are real among African Americans who live in isolation from other blacks. I believe it is possible for a black person to wish she were white, "act white," and even forget that she is black,[84] but these possibilities result from integrated lifestyles that can be a product of black wealth, military service, and residential or schooling choices, unrelated to out-marriage.

The fear of genocide through interracial marriage is an important dimension of blacks' moral preferences for in-marriage. The consequences of interracial sex and marriages pressured the federal government to change its still-clumsy racial categorization practices on the decennial census forms,[85] but interracial marriages have done nothing at all to water down African American culture or to erode the existence of a distinct population group. Could it someday? Suppose over time there came to be fewer people in the United States with distinctively visible African features and ancestries because of interracial procreation. This development alone would not signal the end of an African American community or culture.

Segregation and in-marriage have, without a doubt, made African American culture the rich and distinct culture that it is. The continued existence of an African American culture (or a series of African American subcultures) is not dependent upon the perpetuation of a group of people who will forever look substantially different from whites and from other nonwhite minorities. There could be pride enough for a joyous Black History Month celebration even though what it meant to be African American no longer had substantially to do with skin color, facial features, and curl patterns. The existence of an Irish American culture is not mainly dependent upon the ability to tell, based on appearance alone, who is Irish. African American culture and community will die out, not if blacks become tan or beige, but instead, if blacks cease to identify with one another on the basis of common interests and heritage. Whether interracial marriage makes loss of common identity significantly more likely is hard to say. Clearly, all African Americans, not only the small number who out-marry, must take some responsibility for preserving worthwhile cultural products and institutions. For those who out-marry, meeting this responsibility may be more difficult and may, in that respect, represent a special moral challenge. Overcoming obstacles to black community participation erected by blacks hostile toward out-marrying fellow blacks and their families is part of the special challenge.

The obligation of respect and care for family and friends and the obligation of respect and care for self are not addressed by claims that interracial unions do not destroy black identity and erode the basis of vital community life. The ultimately stronger arguments against interracial marriage may be those that focus on the harm to the interracial couple and their families. Interracial marriage is clearly a moral challenge for the individuals who choose it and for their families. African Americans value romantic love and obligations to respect the romantic choices and aspirations of family members and friends. When the love object is of another race, those obligations do not go away. Reciprocal obligations of respect and care suggest that the marrying couple will need to take measures to accommodate the reasonable concerns and emotional needs of family members, and family members will have to take steps to accommodate the reasonable concerns and emotional needs of the marrying couple.

Romantic love is typified by a placement of the object of love at the center of the universe—nothing and no one matter more than the beloved. Inflicting emotional pain and depriving needy people of emotional and financial support in violation of settled expectations are moral injuries, whether resulting from interracial marriage or other intentional acts. The "Guess Who's Coming to Dinner" model of interracial marriage is insensitive and irresponsible. Under this model, which ignores the reality of enmity and the demands of accountability among both races, one springs (or inflicts) a new spouse or fiancé on unsuspecting families and lets the chips fall where they may.[86] This approach may serve only to exacerbate the moral challenges ahead. Every person, family, and relationship is a little different. Interracial marriage will be a morally acceptable choice in some situations and the morally optimal choice in others. Interracial marriage is a morally bad choice for people who have good reason to believe the marriage will not work because they or their spouse would be permanently or substantially isolated from their families and friends as a result of their marriage.

CONCLUSION

We are accountable for personal conduct to members of our families because we choose them, because we are dealt them, and because they need us. We have a right to expect mutual accountability of kin. But who is kin? Who is a member of the family? Our children, yes, but the biological kin of our children? Our siblings, yes, but our racially similar "brothers and sisters"? And why is family the relevant boundary for those "special" and "extra" accountability requirements? Why not race? This chapter has illustrated how accountability for private life in our society extends beyond the nuclear family and includes racial, ethnic, or cultural groups, confounding, on the microlevel of ordinary personal life, the social ideals of strong liberalism. Accountability for private life offers another surprise. Extending with remarkable ease to race, it resists hyperextension beyond the traditional nuclear family after which adoptive families are modeled, confounding feminist innovators seeking to protect birth mothers and minority identities.

NOTES

1. Leon Dash, *Rosa Lee: A Mother and Her Family in Urban America* (New York: HarperCollins Basic Books, 1996).

2. My experience is intended to illustrate and motivate general points in this chapter, not to "prove" them. I have changed the names of the members of my family and have also changed certain other identifying facts. I am deeply grateful to my extraordinary family for their willingness to share our story.

3. I use "war on drugs" in the usual way, to refer to the set of policies and statutes adopted by the United States to regulate the market in illegal nonprescription drugs. But see Roberto Suro, "Drug Control Strategy in Midst of Makeover: Problem Is Recast as a Public Health Issue," *Washington Post,* 2 March 1997, A11. According to Suro, the "war on drugs expression is rarely heard" in the Clinton administration anymore. "Age of Crack" is a term I borrow from the *Boston Review.* See Debate Transcript, "The Responsibility of Intellectuals in the Age of Crack," *Boston Review* 19, no. 1 (February/March 1994): 3–9. The debate was a discussion among prominent African American intellectuals.

4. Jan Narveson, "The Drug Laws: More Nails in the Coffin of American Liberalism," 7. This is an unpublished conference paper. Professor Narveson spoke at "Morality, Legality, and Drugs: An Academic Conference on the Topic of Drugs, Drug Abuse, and Social Policy, Buffalo, New York, September 15–17, 1995. The Baldy Center Program on Human Rights co-sponsored the conference, which was organized by Professor Pablo DeGreiff of the State University of New York at Buffalo's Department of Philosophy. Professor DeGreiff edited and published some of the conference papers, not including Professor Narveson's, as a book entitled *Drugs and the Limits of Liberalism: Moral and Legal Issues,* ed. Pablo DeGreiff (Ithaca, N.Y.: Cornell University Press, 1999). Principal presentations and speakers at the conference included: "Addiction and Gambling," Jon Elster, Columbia University/ University of Oslo; "Constructing Communities: Drugs, Freedom, and the Common Good," J. Donald Moon, Wesleyan University; "Against Liberal Drugs-Talk: Citizenship and Moral Responsibility," John P. Walters, The New Citizenship Project; "Natural Law and Unnatural Disorder: The Problem of Drugs," Michael Moore, University of Pennsylvania Law School; "Constitutionalism, Morality, and Drugs," Samuel Freeman, University of Pennsylvania; "Drugs, the Nation, and Free Lancing," William Connolly, Johns Hopkins University; "The Drug Laws: More Nails in the Coffin of American Liberalism," Jan Narveson, University of Waterloo; and "Drugs and the Overlap between Morality and Law," Pablo DeGreiff, Department of Philosophy, University of Buffalo.

5. Narveson, "The Drug Laws," 6.

6. Douglas N. Husak, *Drugs and Rights* (Cambridge, U.K.: Cambridge University Press, 1992), 2.

7. Husak, *Drugs and Rights,* 2.

8. Husak, *Drugs and Rights,* 2.

9. Samuel Freeman, "Liberalism, Inalienability, and the Rights of Drug Use," in DeGreiff, *Drugs and Limits of Liberalism,* 110–32.

10. Husak, *Drugs and Rights,* 254.

11. Husak, *Drugs and Rights,* 254.

12. Issues relating to the "other" victims of drugs are identified and discussed in Mark A. R. Kleiman, *Against Excess: Drug Policy for Results* (New York: Basic Books, 1992) and in Chester Nelson Mitchell, *The Drug Solution* (Ottawa, Canada: Carleton University Press, 1990).

13. See Michael Moore, "Liberty and Drugs," in DeGreiff, *Drugs and Limits of Liberalism,* 61–109.

14. Narveson, "The Drug Laws," 7.

15. Husak, *Drugs and Rights*, 2.

16. I am relying in the next few paragraphs on widely cited data obtained through the Drug Policy Alliance, Office of National Affairs, 4455 Connecticut Avenue, N.W., Suite B-500, Washington, D.C., 20008; www.drugpolicy.org. The data are from government and private studies conducted between the years 1995–2001.

17. John L. Mitchell, "Did CIA Introduce Crack Cocaine in the Inner City? Undeterred, Waters Crusades for Answers," *Los Angeles Times*, 4 March 1997, A3.

18. *Boston Review*, "Age of Crack."

19. Robert Suro, "Political Rhetoric Overlooks Change in Drug-Use Patterns," *Washington Post*, 24 September 1996, A1, A10.

20. D. R. Neuspiel, "Racism and Perinatal Addiction," *Ethnicity and Disease* 6 (1996): 47–55.

21. See Daniel Klaidman, "The Politics of Drugs: Back to War," *Newsweek*, 26 August 1996, 57–58.

22. Nick Gillespie, "Zero Tolerance for Hypocritical Politicians: Officials Flout Drug Laws They Expect Citizens to Obey," *Baltimore Sun*, 25 August 1996, 7F.

23. Staff and wire reports, "Did Rep. Susan Molinari Smoke Pot? Yes and No," *Washington Post*, 9 August 1996, B3.

24. Philip P. Pan, "Police Relax Standards on Recruits' Past Drug Use," *Washington Post*, 9 August 1996, C1.

25. *United States v. Santiago*, 837 F. 2d 1545 (11th Cir. 1988).

26. See U.S. Department of Justice, "Lifetime Likelihood of Going to State or Federal Prison," 6 March 1997. This report confirmed statistics cited in Jerome G. Miller, *Search and Destroy: African American Males in the Criminal Justice System* (Cambridge, U.K.: Cambridge University Press, 1996). The same basic statistics held true in 2002.

27. See generally Randall Kennedy, *Race, Crime, and Law* (New York: Vintage Books, 1998), xii, 10, 301, 377, 384. Professor Kennedy detailed the relationships in fact and myth between blacks, crack, and law enforcement.

28. The rule has been that a person convicted of possession of five grams of crack cocaine receives a mandatory *minimum* sentence of five years in prison; the same amount of powdered cocaine possession would result in a *maximum* one-year sentence.

29. *Boston Review*, "Age of Crack," 4.

30. *Boston Review*, "Age of Crack," 4.

31. How well do we know ourselves? How possible is it to protect ourselves from actions that lead to moral disaster? See J. David Velleman's discussions of self-understanding, self-awareness, and self-deception urging but problematizing "reflective foresight" in *Practical Reflection* (Princeton, N.J.: Princeton University Press, 1989), 48ff.

32. A good sense of the complexity is evident in books like Husak's *Drugs and Rights*. See also Mitchell, *The Drug Solution*.

33. Narveson, "The Drug Laws," 8.

34. Human Rights Watch Sentencing Project, *Losing the Vote: The Impact of Felony Disenfranchisement Laws in the United States* (New York: Human Rights Watch, 1998). See also www.hrw.org/reports98/vote/usvote980-02.htm.

35. Elizabeth Bartholet, "Where Do Black Children Belong? The Politics of Race Matching in Adoption," *University of Pennsylvania Law Review* 139 (1991): 1163–1256. See also Randall Kennedy, *Interracial Intimacies, Sex, Marriage, Identity, and Adoption* (forthcoming).

36. See Naomi R. Cahn, "Models of Family Privacy," *George Washington Law Review* 67 (1999): 1225–46; and Barbara Bennett Woodhouse, "The Dark Side of Family Privacy," *George Washington Law Review* 67 (1999): 1247–62.

37. *Wisconsin v. Yoder*, 406 U.S. 205 (1972).

38. See for example Cahn, "Models"; Woodhouse, "Dark Side."

39. *Deshaney v. Winnebago Department of Social Services*, 489 U.S. 189 (1989).

40. Annette R. Appell, "Blending Families through Adoption: Implications for Collaborative Adoption Law and Practice," *Boston University Law Review* 75 (1995): 997–1061; Susan L. Brooks, "The Case for Adoption Alternatives," *Family and Conciliation Courts Review* 39 (2001): 43–53; Joan Hollinger et al., *Adoption Law and Practice* (New York: Matthew Bender Co., 1998).

41. E. Wayne Carp, *Family Matters: Secrecy and Disclosure in the History of Adoption* (Cambridge, U.K.: Harvard University Press, 1998), 25–26, 32.

42. See Brooks, "Case for Alternatives," 43–53; and Susan Vivian Mongold, "Extending Non-Exclusive Parenting and the Right to Protection for Older Foster Children: Creating Third Options in Permanency Planning," *Buffalo Law Review* 48 (2000): 835–79.

43. Harold D. Grotevant and Ruth McRoy, *Openness in Adoption: Exploring Family Connections* (Thousand Oaks, Calif.: Sage Publications, 1998).

44. Appell, "Blending Families."

45. See Naomi Cahn and Jana Singer, "Adoption, Identity, and the Constitution: The Case for Opening Closed Records," *University of Pennsylvania Journal of Constitutional Law* 2 (1999): 150–94; Alison H. Young, "Reconceiving the Family: Challenging the Paradigm of the Exclusive Family," *The American University Journal of Gender and Law* 6 (1998): 505–56.

46. Young, "Reconceiving the Family."

47. Young, "Reconceiving the Family."

48. Reuben Pannor and Annette Baran. "Perspectives on Open Adoption," *Future of Children* 3, no. 1 (Spring 1993): 119–124.

49. Cahn and Singer, "Adoption, Identity."

50. Thomas Beauchamp and James Childress, *Principles of Biomedical Ethics,* rev. ed. (New York: Oxford University Press, 2001). I mention these notorious "principles" less to register that the range of consideration at least includes familiar bioethical categories. But see Susan Wolf, ed., *Feminism and Bioethics* (Oxford, U.K.: Oxford University Press, 1996).

51. Nel Nodding, *Caring: A Feminine Approach to Ethics and Moral Education* (Berkeley: University of California Press, 1984).

52. Drucilla Cornell, *At the Heart of Freedom: Feminism, Sex, and Equality* (Princeton, N.J.: Princeton University Press, 1998), 108–9.

53. Brooks, "Case for Alternatives."

54. Brooks, "Case for Alternatives."

55. Three major federal adoption laws are the Indian Child Welfare Act, 25 U.S.C. Sec. 1901 (1988); Adoption and Safe Families Act, Pub. L. No. 105–89, 111 Stat. 2115 (1997); and Adoption Assistance and Child Welfare Act of 1980, Pub. L. No. 99 Stat. 500 (1980).

56. Carol Sanger, "Separating from Children," *Columbia Law Review* 96 (1996): 375–492.

57. Ann E. Brand and Paul M. Brinich, "Behavior Problems and Mental Health Contacts in Adopted, Foster, and Nonadopted Children," *Journal of Child Psychology* 40 (1999): 1221–29.

58. See Janette Moore and Eric Fombonne, "Psychopathology in Adopted and Nonadopted Children: A Clinical Sample," *American Journal of Orthopsychiatry* 69, no. 3 (1999): 403–9; and P. F. Sullivan, J. E. Well, and J. A. Bushnell, "Adoption as a Risk Factor for Mental Disorders," *Acta Psychiatrica Scandinavia* 92 (1995): 119–24.

59. Allen Lipman et al., "Follow-Up of Psychiatric and Educational Morbidity among Adopted Children," *Journal of the American Academy of Child and Adolescent Psychiatry* 32, no. 5 (1993): 1007–12.

60. Steven A. Holmes, "People Can Claim One or More Races on Federal Forms," *New York Times*, 30 October 1997, A1, col. 1.

61. Gilbert A. Holmes, "The Extended Family System in the Black Community: A Child-Centered Model for Adoption Policy," *Temple Law Review* 68 (1995): 1665.

62. Anita L. Allen, "Do Children Have Right to a Certain Identity?" *Rechtsheorie* 15 (1992–1993): 109–19.

63. Jennifer Wiggins, "Parental Rights Termination Jurisprudence: Questioning the Framework," *South Carolina Law Review* 52 (2000): 241–68.

64. Twila L. Perry, "The Transracial Adoption Controversy: An Analysis of Discourse and Subordination," *New York University Review of Law and Social Change* 21 (1993–1994): 33–108.

65. Janet Farrell Smith, "Analyzing Ethical Conflict in the Transracial Adoption Debate: Three Conflicts Involving Community," *Hypatia* 11 (1996): 1–33.

66. James S. Bowen, "Cultural Convergences and Divergences: The Nexus between Putative African American Family Values and the Best Interest of the Child," *Journal of Family Law* 26 (1988): 487–544.

67. An earlier version of this discussion of interracial marriage appeared in my "Interracial Marriage: Folk Ethics in Contemporary Philosophy," in *Women of Color and Philosophy*, ed. Naomi Zack (Malden, Mass.: Blackwell Publishers, 2000), 182–206.

68. The petitioners were a white man and a black woman who returned to their home state of Virginia after getting married in the District of Columbia. Once back in Virginia, the Lovings were convicted of violating a Virginia statute that criminalized marriages between blacks and whites. The Lovings pled guilty and were sentenced to a year in jail. The criminal court suspended the sentence on the condition that the couple agreed to leave Virginia.

69. U.S. Bureau of the Census, *Current Population Reports*, showed 1,260,000 interracial married couples (all races) in 1996, up from 651,000 (all races) in 1980. Interracial marriages "skyrocketed by more than 800 percent" between 1960 and 1990

(Michael Lind, "The Beige and the Black," *New York Times Magazine*, 16 August 1998, 38–39).

70. Robert M. Moore, "Interracial Dating as an Indicator of Integration," *Black Issues in Higher Education* 15, no. 26 (18 February 1999): 120.

71. U.S. Bureau of the Census, *Current Population Reports*, Series P20-537, "America's Families and Living Arrangements: March 2000," Table MS-3: Interracial Couples: 1960 to Present.

72. Richard Morin, "Unconventional Wisdom, New Facts, and Hot Stats from the Social Sciences," *Washington Post*, 29 June 1997, C-5.

73. Cf. George Yancey, "An Analysis of Resistance to Racial Exogamy: The 1998 South Carolina Referendum," *Journal of Black Studies* 31, no. 5 (May 2001): 635–50; Kyle D. Crowder and Stewart E. Tolnay, "A New Marriage Squeeze for Black Women: The Role of Racial Intermarriage by Black Men," *Journal of Marriage and the Family* 62 (August 2000): 792–807; Anita Kathy Foeman and Teresa Nance, "From Miscegenation to Multiculturalism: Perceptions and Stages of Interracial Relationship Development," *Journal of Black Studies* 29, no. 4 (March 1999): 540–57; and Sheryline A. Zebroski, "Black-White Intermarriages: The Racial and Gender Dynamics of Support and Opposition," *Journal of Black Studies* 30, no. 1 (September 1999): 123–32.

74. *Reynolds v. United States*, 98 U.S. 145 (1878).

75. Barbara Crossettes, "Testing the Limits of Tolerance as Cultures Mix: Does Freedom Mean Accepting Rituals that Repel the West?" *New York Times*, 6 March 1999, A1.

76. William Eskridge, *The Case for Same-Sex Marriage* (New York: Free Press, 1996).

77. The University of Michigan compiled a series of studies of American segregation and the impact of diversity in education in *The Compelling Need for Diversity in Higher Education*, a compilation of expert testimony by Thomas Sugrue, Eric Foner, Albert Camarillo, Patricia Gurin, William Bowen, Claude Steele, Derek Bok, Kent Syverud, and Robert Webster in *Gratz et al. v. Bollinger*, 277 F. 3d 803 (6th Cir. 2001), granting en banc, and *Grutter, et al. v. Bollinger et al.*, 288 F. 3d 732 (6th Cir. 2002).

78. See Michael J. Sandel, *Democracy's Discontent: America in Search of a Public Philosophy* (Cambridge, Mass.: Harvard University Press, 1996).

79. See Lynn Norment, "Black Men, White Women, What's Behind the Furor?" *Ebony* 50, no. 1 (November 1994): 44–48.

80. Norment, "Black Men."

81. Surveys suggest that military service greatly enhances the prospects for interracial marriage. About 14 percent of black men and 10 percent of black women who served in the military married nonblacks. For a discussion of the impact of higher education see "News and Views: The Effect of Higher Education on Interracial Marriage," *Journal of Blacks in Higher Education* 30 (June 1997): 55.

82. F. James Davis, *Who Is Black?* (University Park, Pa.: Pennsylvania State University, 1991).

83. African American Marion Wright Edelman, who heads the Children's Defense Fund in Washington, D.C., is not married to an African American. For what it may be worth, she and her husband, noted law professor Peter Edelman, have three high-achieving mixed-race sons. See Mary McCory, "Voting with Conscience, and Feet,"

Washington Post, 17 September 1996, A2; and Barbara Kessler, "Jonah Edelman," *Dallas Morning News*, 23 March 1997, 1J.

84. Anita L. Allen, "Forgetting Yourself," in *Feminists Rethink the Self*, ed. Diana Meyers (Boulder, Colo.: Westview Press, 1996), 104–23.

85. Holmes, "Claim One or More Races." The year 2000 national census forms permitted respondents to identify themselves as belonging to one or more racial population groups, and then to indicate whether they are Hispanic. In the 1990 census, respondents were only permitted to choose a single racial category, even if they were biracial or mixed race.

86. The title of the film reflects the premise of social segregation. The film was released in 1967 and starred Katharine Hepburn, Spencer Tracy, and Sidney Poitier. In the movie, a beautiful young white woman decides to marry a handsome black physician. They spring the news on her shocked upper-class parents; the black doctor similarly surprises his parents.

Chapter Three

Accountability for Health

Ask anyone to list the things he or she regards as most personal. It is likely that health information will appear on the list. Health information is not certain to appear on everyone's list; ours is too diverse a polity for that.[1] But it is likely to appear, and near the top. Health, like sex, family, religion, and finances, is a sensitive domain commonly termed personal.

In the United States, individuals often take pains to protect their illnesses from disclosure. Our moralities approve health privacy. A shared system of etiquette dictates limited disclosure of health-related information. People know that it is impolite to ask certain questions. (They also know that it is impolite to answer certain health-related questions with frank answers.) Legal norms govern health information practices, too. To protect against unwanted disclosures of health information, every state has adopted medical record confidentiality laws. Health insurance innovation, the AIDS epidemic, the Human Genome Project, White House health care reform agendas, and the Internet each spawned proposals for federal legislation regulating health privacy. Federal regulations now mandate more health information privacy than ever before. Congress enacted the federal Health Insurance Portability and Accountability Act of 1996 (HIPAA).[2] The statute mandated both efficiency in health finance administration through electronic standardization of medical records, and medical information privacy through rules requiring patient consent for dissemination of physician medical records to third parties. Privacy rules called for by HIPAA were promulgated by the Department of Health and Human Services a few years after HIPAA's enactment. Of course, good manners and strong statutes can do only so much to accommodate the public's privacy preferences: medical records are still available to hackers, clerical workers, and other strangers. Anyone with a grudge against you and access to your trash can collect DNA and foretell elements of your health future.

Law, morality, and etiquette dictate privacy for health information, but they dictate accountability as well. Health is a domain that is riddled with accountability requirements. Providing others with information about health is a familiar requirement of personal relationships, of receiving health care, of obtaining health insurance coverage, of intimate relationships, of attending school, and of holding down certain jobs and public offices. This chapter will explore the wide terrain of accountability for health in the context of a society that also honors expectations of medical privacy and confidentiality.

As an empirical matter, the recognized grounds for accountability for health appear to be the same as accountability for other personal matters. Accountability obtains by virtue of consent, reliance, dependency, or public need. For example, people are accountable to their insurance companies for health information because they "contract" for accountability by applying for life insurance or enrolling in employee health benefit plans. They are accountable to spouses and friends because of the reliance, hopefully mutual and reciprocal, constitutive of those relationships. They are accountable to their children, because young people have nurturing needs that could be left untended by parents' poor health. They are accountable to political constituencies because of the public need for effective, vital leadership.

Familiar health accountability requirements strike me as reasonable. If I expect the employer-provided health plan that I signed up for to pay for medical expenses, I should be accountable to the plan for information sufficient to prove that my claim is bona fide. The accountability-sensitive federal rules allow nonconsensual access to health information by insurance companies processing health coverage claims, but also to public health researchers and law enforcement. These potential disclosures are more controversial but have defensible bases in conceptions of public need. Unauthorized access by curious neighbors, most marketers, and most employers is, and should be, forbidden by law.

In the legal and administrative realms nearly all the attention goes to accountability for health *information*. It bears emphasis, though, that in the moral and ethical realms, accountability for health is a broader set of imperatives. Accountability for health consists of requirements for more than mere information. It consists also of requirements for explanation and justification. One may be required to not only inform a partner of the fact that one has a sexually transmitted disease, but also explain how one suddenly came to have it when one is supposed to be in a monogamous relationship. A stunned partner might also expect a justification for an infidelity that imposed a significant health risk. Breaching moral accountability norms can lead to a negative moral sanction. Punishment for violating health accountability norms could include censure and loss of a relationship. In some jurisdictions it is considered a criminal offense to knowingly expose otherwise consenting sex partners to AIDS. Legal sanctions could accompany moral sanctions.

TO CLOAK OR TO CELEBRATIZE?

Legal rules limiting access to health information are popular with consumers. People do not always welcome sharing health information with others and may resist accountability imperatives tied to their health. Of course, not everyone is greatly bothered by health disclosures. Sensibilities about the inherent privacy of the human body and privacy of health information are changing. Evidencing new sensibilities, many people in the United States freely disclose health matters that, as recently as twenty years ago, would have been treated as quite personal and intimate. Moreover, the New Accountability demands health disclosures of people in the public eye who would not otherwise freely disclose them.

David Morris explains: "illness has recently emerged from the obscurity of medical treatises and private diaries to acquire something like celebrity status."[3] Specific sick people, specific diseases or disorders, and even specific medications have become famous in recent years. Discretionary openness about health matters is clearly a trend. Openness about health concerns has appreciable public health benefits.[4] Policymakers have to decide whether to continue fashioning policies premised on older, concealment-oriented sensibilities or newer, disclosure-oriented sensibilities. One strategy would be to ignore older sensibilities in an effort to reap public health and efficiency gains. Yet the weight of current governmental and nongovernmental policy assumes the continuing social value of selective concealment of health information. There is little evidence to suggest that the public is prepared to yield complete control over health information to health providers or other third parties.

Why Cloak?

As standard accounts of the value of health information privacy emphasize, people rely upon privacy to help control or limit health disclosures that could result in tangible, material losses.[5] Potential losses can be major. They include loss of employment, loss of insurance, loss of school choice, loss of community standing, and loss of intimacy.[6] Protecting health information through privacy policies serves an important material loss minimization function in a world in which discrimination and rejection can flow from news of health or genetic status. The literature on medical privacy contains good efforts to link medical privacy to material loss minimization and then to link material loss minimization to respect for human dignity (including personhood, personality, reputation, identity, individuality, uniqueness, or spirituality); respect for autonomy (including freedom, independence, self-determination, choice, or control); and respect for justice (including fairness, nondiscrimination, equality, toleration, or limited government).

Even when people do not have to worry much about whether health disclosure will result in the sorts of material losses named above, they will often seek to avoid health disclosures nonetheless. The public cares about health information privacy for reasons other than loss minimization. People commonly rely upon seclusion, secrecy, confidentiality, and other forms of privacy to facilitate what I term (1) "responsive reflection" and (2) "emotional distress minimization," in addition to (3) material loss minimization.

The Value of Health Information Privacy

Health affects mortality and social standing. Self-consciously or instinctively, when a person first discovers a health problem, she may keep the problem a secret in order to allow herself time to react, reflect, and make plans. Some health problems require a good deal of planning about how to meet responsibilities and answer accountability imperatives. Privacy functions as a tool for responsive reflection, that is, reflection in response to new information and belief about personal health. The discovery of health problems may cause anxiety and emotion. Unfortunately, for some, illness leads to shame, embarrassment, and defeat that lower self-esteem and increase feelings of vulnerability. Hoping to manage common forms of psychological distress brought on by health concerns, a person may choose secrecy. Or she may simply fall silent. Secrecy can help avoid the amplification of feelings of low self-esteem and heightened vulnerability. In this respect, privacy functions as a tool of emotional distress minimization.

Ethicists have made the moral case for material loss minimization by reference to the overlapping moral ideals of respect for dignity, autonomy, and justice. The case for responsive reflection and emotional distress minimization can be made by reference to those same ideals but is also supported, more directly, by ideals of respect for social boundaries and needs (including intimacy, friendship, civility, trust, or accountability); and respect for psychological boundaries and needs (including solitude, repose, composure, self-expression, or reduction of social anxiety).

Physician and Patient

Typical discussions of the value of health information privacy start with an account of the confidentiality requirements of the physician–patient relationship. Appropriately, these discussions emphasize the importance of clinical and record-keeping practices that will encourage patients to seek care and speak openly with physicians. The ability of patients to trust their doctors with the truth depends on their expectations of physician competence and confidentiality. Patient openness is especially critical in the delivery of mental health services. In addition to physician-patient confidentiality facilitating health-relevant disclosures, it also promotes individual interests in autonomy. And, because health information can lead to discrimination, confidentiality furthers patients' interests in reputation, employment, housing, access to social services, and companionship.

Current trends fully explain the focus on informational privacy in the context of patient encounters with service providers and third parties who create and share medical records. Emergent uses of medical information and medical information technologies are rapidly challenging traditional conceptions of medical privacy. The day is coming soon when every general practitioner will rely on portable computers to access their patients' medical histories, order tests, consult specialists, transmit referrals, bill insurers, and submit pharmacy prescriptions. Existing computer technology has already increased the ease and attractiveness of transmitting medical information for purposes of referrals, insurance reimbursements, cost containment, research, employment decisions, and better patient care. Many commentators stress the importance of protecting privacy by balancing the compelling need for medical privacy against the compelling societal need for medical information and technology. According to Professor Lawrence Gostin, "[a] national health information policy that encourages the collection of vast amounts of electronic data while creating uniform rules for handling these data may be the best way of reconciling equally compelling public and private claims."[7]

BEFORE AND BEYOND THE MEDICAL GAZE

To illuminate health privacy values and resistance to health accountability observed in society, I consider three distinct contexts of health-related privacy concern: the contexts of (1) encounters with the self, (2) encounters with health care providers, and (3) encounters with third parties. My starting place is the context of self-confrontation, the context wherein an individual is not a medical consumer as much as a family member, friend, co-worker, and fellow citizen grappling with feeling, fate, and the health accountability norms of ordinary life. The privacy yearnings of people who believe they have health-related problems who are not yet, strictly speaking, medical patients helps with understanding the privacy yearnings of those who are and have been. By focusing on what we know about how people feel about wellness and unwellness in their inner lives, we can better understand the overall significance they attach to health information disclosures. Indeed, the effort to grasp the values of health information privacy and accountability in the contexts of encounters with health care providers and third parties is aided by efforts to grasp the felt value of health information privacy and accountability in the extraprofessional context of self-confrontation.

Encounters with the Self

You may not know that you are sick until you see a doctor. Health concerns and health privacy concerns may arise as a consequence of the "medical gaze" of the health care provider who informs you in confidence that you are unwell.[8] However, health information privacy concerns need not first arise as medical privacy concerns. In fact, worries about health information privacy may precede and outlive encounters with health professionals.

The initial context for health privacy concerns is the context of self-confrontation. I mean encounters with one's own body and mind as imperfect, unwell, or declining. An embarrassed, fearful man who discovers blood in his stools may keep this important evidence of disease a secret from his family and physician. A woman who believes she is depressed may tell no one, in order to avoid the stigma of mental illness. Concealment and avoidance of professional care may be in neither person's ultimate best interests and may violate accountability responsibilities to kin and associates who are kept in the dark. But for this man and this woman, informational and physical privacy are important.

Privileged Access

Individuals have exclusive access to many forms of information about their own physical and mental states. They may elect to keep this kind of information to themselves. The following realistic but imaginary scenarios illustrate my point:

> "I discovered a lump in my breast while taking a shower. My first thoughts were about my mother's breast cancer. My next thoughts were about my fear of dying and about how much I am needed by my kids, my husband, and my employer. It took me two days to tell my husband about the lump, and two more to tell my doctor. People at work still don't know."—Cara

> "I noticed blood in my stools, but it wasn't the sort of thing I felt comfortable talking to anybody about. I never did, until a doctor specifically asked me about it during a physical exam I had to have for work."—Lou

"When my sight and memory began to fail, I hoped no one would notice. I couldn't hide the situation forever, and eventually my family forced me to see a doctor."—Kent

As a separate and distinct person, each of us enjoys an intimate relationship with our own body and mind. Many symptoms of disease and injury are invisible to other people. Moral customs and law limit who can touch and observe the body without consent. For these reasons, each person naturally comes to possess some health information about himself or herself in advance of others. Although some unsuspecting individuals initially find out about their medical problems in a doctor's office or in an emergency room, others do not. In the first illustration, Cara discovered a lump in her breast while bathing alone at home, not after consulting with, for example, a radiologist skilled at locating occult tumors. Lou was coping with bloody stools, and Kent with poor eyesight and a failing memory, before they sought professional medical evaluation. Kent, Lou, and Cara's initial health information privacy concerns arose outside of any relationship with a health care provider. They arose extraprofessionally.

Privileged access to health information means that thoughtful individuals have the ability to carefully plan the performance of their accountability obligations. As accountability can be satisfying, we will often perform these obligations without hesitation as they should be performed. We tell the right people at the right time in the right way, offering the necessary explanation, justification, and apology. We can also exploit privileged access to postpone sharing health information. The supportive spouse who really should know about the recurrence of a breast cancer right away could be kept in the dark for months. The price of secrecy is a loss of moral support and care. Ideally persons will reasonably balance their need for time to reflect and feel on their own with their need for comfort and care.

There are important limits to the notion that we have privileged access to information about our own health. Kent's case illustrates that health information can be kept secret but that such secrets may not last. As Kent's condition worsened, it became apparent to his family that he was going blind and losing his memory. We are not always the first among family, friends, and co-workers to know that we are ill or declining. Family members and co-workers might notice deafness and memory lapses before we do. A wife might detect personality changes, weight loss, halitosis, shortness of breath, and other common signs of illness to which her husband is oblivious. Even perfect strangers with whom one does not interact at all can detect health problems that adversely affect outward appearance. The ghastly jaundice of advanced liver disease and alcoholism's unsteady gait are hard to conceal from passersby. Thus, although we have a substantial degree of privileged access to health information, we are social beings who unavoidably share health information. At times, self-deception may interfere with our recognition of illnesses others see quite clearly. Persons invested in their images of essential fitness and vigor may fall prey to self-deception to avoid confronting the truth of illness.

An unwillingness to share health information to which one does have privileged access can be dangerous. It can be deadly, too, if, for example, the undisclosed information concerns AIDS or hepatitis. Nowadays most people in the United States recognize the importance of sharing health information. It is important to share health information with family and friends to reap the rewards of reciprocal love, trust, and interdependency. The capacity of loved ones to function as loved ones is dependent upon their knowing one another's health needs. One of the things people who care about us do is to cajole us to see a physician about our health complaints. It is ultimately important to share health information with nurses and doctors to facilitate appropriate care. It is important to share health information with employers because poor health can interfere with the discharge of our professional responsibilities, and because we may require sick days, disability leaves, and health insurance coverage. It is important to share health information with managed care administrators and insurance companies because they pay the medical bills we expect them to pay. They need to be able to process claims and manage risk efficiently.

Special Contours

To say that individuals ought to share health information is not to say precisely when, precisely how, or with precisely whom. Trust appropriate to marriage or domestic partnership suggests that spouses and partners ought to let one another in on health secrets. Yet, there are good reasons to not always immediately share health concerns with a husband, wife, or partner. When many of us experience hidden problems with our bodies or minds, we commence a series of judgments about whether, when, how, and with whom to share invisible symptoms and our feelings about them. The nature of the judgments we make will reflect our character, but also our knowledge of medical matters, such as how to tell serious from less serious symptoms; our beliefs about the requirement of civility and accountability, such as when it is appropriate to burden others with our health problems; and our capacity to be reasonable and responsible in difficult situations.

Clearly, too much health-related secrecy is risky because early treatment is critical for success in treating many illnesses, and because talking about health concerns can relieve unhealthy stress. From a moral point of view, initial secrecy about health concerns can nonetheless be beneficial. Out of regard for others, it is best to avoid indiscriminately sharing information about ambiguous symptoms. A certain percentage of symptoms of illness resolve spontaneously. We all know that sharing health information imposes a social burden on the people with whom we share. The convention of responding "I'm fine" to the question "How are you?" reflects the expectation that persons will keep to themselves both major health concerns that raise issues too personal or complex for casual conversation, and minor health concerns of the sort that are likely to resolve on their own or with simple treatment. People who are too free with information about their aches and pains are less welcome company than people who exercise reserve. At the same time, we can feel betrayed by reserved family members and friends who conceal nagging health worries from us for too long. Being mum about health symptoms, though, affords individuals the opportunity to analyze subjective evidence of unwellness before imposing on others for care and concern. Certain symptoms mandate medical care without delay, but rushing to a physician before figuring out whether the intermittent minor headaches are on the left side or the right, or whether the best way to characterize sporadic dizziness is "light-headedness" or "vertigo," can result in frustration for both patient and physician.

Responsive reflection is only part of the story of why people will try to keep health information a secret. Another part of the story is less felicitous. Efforts to avoid blows to self-esteem and vulnerability can prompt the secreting of health information. Experiencing our bodies as imperfect, unwell, or declining can be a source of shame, embarrassment, fear, and defeat. These responses lead us to elect forms of solitude and secrecy that avoid the amplification of feelings of low self-esteem and powerlessness. The problem, though, is that these responses isolate us from willing sources of care and concern among family, friends, and professionals.

The visceral sources of shame and embarrassment attendant to illness are unpleasant to acknowledge privately, much less to speak and write about. Sick people seldom resemble the ideal products of diet, exercise, cosmetic surgery, airbrushing, and electronic enhancement dished out by the media. The sight, sound, and smell of unhealthy bodies can be unpleasant. Sadly, we may be repulsed by our unwell or declining bodies and may correctly believe that others are too. Pain, one of the key indications of unwellness, can itself be a source of embarrassment. Pain can trigger emotions and behaviors we are embarrassed to let others observe. Pain, like other symptoms of illness, can turn sufferers into objects of unwanted pity and attention. Self-esteem premised on attractiveness, vigor, or independence sometimes goes out the window with illness and aging, to be replaced with feelings of low self-esteem and heightened vulnerability.

Fear motivates us to keep information about our health secret. We fear that shortness of breath may signal a weak heart, and who wants to see a physician who may advise bypass surgery? So we are silent. The lump in the breast may mean cancer. Who wants to hear that diagnosis? Again, we are silent. We have been unable to get pregnant and want help, but dread hearing the words "infertile" applied to us by intimates, peers, or professionals. We silently suffer. Because we fear losing our mates, our livelihoods, our community standing, and our lives, we are drawn to secrecy. Illness can make attractive people unattractive, strong people weak, powerful people helpless. Failing bodies can make us feel that we, as persons, are failures too. If health problems repeatedly interrupt plans and projects, frustration and a sense of defeat may set in. In the worlds of commerce or ideas, lack of productivity caused by prolonged illness means actual material failure. We may feel doubly defeated by poor health that is caused by bad habits—habits like drinking, smoking, drug use, and refusing to exercise.

Health Chat: The New Openness

One could easily exaggerate the importance people attach to keeping health information to themselves. Some people barely hesitate to share health information with family, friends, health providers, employers, and insurers. Moreover, although polling data suggests that a majority of Americans believe the privacy of health information is important, voluntarily sharing health information with the general public is far from rare. There appears to be a national trend toward greater openness about medical matters. Former senator Robert Dole publicly announced that he suffered from erectile dysfunction and had participated in the Viagra trials.[9] His aim, he said, was to call attention to a widespread problem and its treatment. Entertainment and sports celebrities know the practical limits of confidentiality for people in the public eye. But some have bested the tabloids by coming forward on their own to reveal that they suffer from Parkinson's disease (actor Michael J. Fox), prostate cancer, Alzheimer's disease (President Ronald Reagan), or HIV/AIDS (professional basketball player "Magic" Johnson, Olympic swimmer Greg Louganis, and professional tennis player Arthur Ashe).[10] An artist who underwent what she felt was an unnecessary, mutilating mastectomy permitted the *New York Times Magazine* to run a photograph of her postsurgical chest on its cover in connection with a story about breast cancer surgery.[11] A Pennsylvania woman permitted her mastectomy to be broadcast live on the World Wide Web.[12] Another woman gave birth live on the Internet.[13]

Recent changes in social mores permit and reward openness about medical matters once deemed too personal for public discussion. Many television programs feature graphic video coverage of actual emergency room care and surgery. The family of a bipolar teenager allowed MTV to film the teen's fits of irrational anger for an arresting program on the mental illness that first aired in July 2002. People seem to be comfortable participating in medical programs and seem to enjoy watching them. On television, in newspapers, and in magazines we see families like our own coping with organ transplants, conjoined twin separation, hand transplants, genetic diseases, and disfiguring accidents. For some people loss minimization and distress minimization concerns are absent or insufficient to compel privacy.

Consensualism, though, is very much a part of the new openness. Most people still want to feel that they have a degree of control over the disclosure of health information. Controlling access to health information may be impossible for persons whose health privacy needs clash with their desire to exploit the benefits of openness:

> "My girlfriend knew I was HIV positive. She didn't want her family to know though, because she knew they wouldn't want me around. So we didn't tell them and they were cool with me. One night I was on the 6 o'clock news describing the AIDS Clinic I work for. I said I was HIV positive. A friend of my girlfriend's sister saw me on TV and spilled the beans. Now the whole family knows and guess who's not been invited back to dinner?"—Chin

How do we make public policy for a diverse population whose privacy interests are this complex? Chin's case turns upside down the assumption that family and friends are more likely to share our secrets than strangers and co-workers. Families are not always confidants. Chin was comfortable talking about his health problem with an anonymous television audience and with the people at work, but not with his (partner's) family. Sometimes it is within what are supposed to be the most intimate relationships that loss minimization and distress minimization (and hence privacy) are most needed.

The seeming trend toward highly "public" openness about health matters could mean Americans are prepared to accept health information policies that stress the societal benefits of information accessibility over the societal and individual benefits of stringent privacy protection. On the other hand, there is scant basis for believing most Americans are prepared to surrender choice and control outright. In our liberal society the most popular legal policies for the present would be the ones we have: policies that presumptively vest alienable rights to choose and control health disclosures in the individual. In this way people with consistently traditional privacy sensibilities would be protected, and persons with the newer sensibility or idiosyncratic admixtures of old and new could elect the privacy they want. They would ideally make those selections in caring and self-caring ways.

Encounters with Health Care Providers

The second context in which concerns about health privacy arise is the context of encounters with health care providers. These providers are the paramedics, nurses, medical students, doctors, hospitals, and researchers discharged on a confidential basis to make imperfect, declining, and unwell minds and bodies better. A man experiencing erectile dysfunction speaks openly about his condition with his urologist but expects strict confidentiality. He expects informational privacy. A hospital patient balks at the idea of a television news crew filming her trip to the emergency room. She expects physical, informational, and proprietary privacy. A dying cancer patient demands pain medication of her physician in a dose sufficient for terminating her life. She wants a level of decisional privacy to which the law for the most part says she is not entitled.

The physician-patient contract entitles physicians to payment for services and the patient to nonnegligent care. We do not ordinarily regard the physician as someone who, like a family member or lover, is morally entitled to health information because of promises, reliance relationships, and dependencies. People seeking medical care do well to disclose health information to the physicians with whom they consult. It is self-defeating not to do it. For prudential reasons it should be done. Another way to think about it would be this: an agreement to do one's utmost to help the doctor do his or her utmost is a moral requirement and an implied term of the physician-patient contract.

Confidentiality and Exposure

Encounters with professional health providers could be viewed as privacy-preserving because confidentiality norms limit outsiders' access to patient information. But encounters with health providers require privacy sacrifices. Specifically, informational and physical privacy must be sacrificed. The frank talk, undressing, and submission to the eyes and hands of strangers are standard requirements of medical care. Ordinary rules of social interaction are suspended. To interpret vaginal warts or rectal tears, physicians may ask patients about their sex lives, resulting in perceived accountability. Patients who are young or modest or gay may balk at questioning about sex and sexuality. Doctors are not robots, but human beings with religious perspectives and social agendas that can openly clash with those of their patients. (I was once offended by a pediatrician who chewed out my eight-year-old for sporting "something only bad men in jail have": an "ugly, disgusting" tattoo. My son had a temporary tattoo on his forearm, acquired at a birthday party. Out of earshot of my son, I let the physician know that I was offended. He explained that he was trying to discourage young men from developing a taste for real tattoos, which he viewed as health hazards. I explained in return that several of my son's closest African American role models bear tattoos, including my brother, his favorite uncle, who is a lawyer and has never spent time behind bars.

Patients cannot expect complete physical privacy, although health providers usually try to respect patients' needs for modesty and seclusion:

> Complete physical privacy is inconsistent with the demands of modern health care. The modern delivery of health services presupposes that patients . . . accept nudity, touching, and observation as unavoidable aspects of examination, treatment, surgery, and hospitalization. . . . [Patients] have sometimes characterized unauthorized medical treatments as invasions of privacy, along with the presence of inessential medical attendants, spectators, or cameras. The desire for physical privacy may lead patients who have a choice to choose single over shared hospital rooms . . . and physicians of their own sex. Norms of quietude surrounding hospitals reflect the sentiment that patients have heightened physical and psychological needs for solitude and peace of mind.[14]

To the sacrifice of physical privacy, as to the sacrifice of informational privacy, patients quietly bring the feelings of shame, embarrassment, fear, and defeat that arise extraprofessionally.

The confidentiality promise and professional manner of health care providers make the sacrifice tolerable, but without eliminating all of the vulnerability and low self-esteem many patients feel. Fragile self-esteem and vulnerability follow individuals to their doctors' offices. Although it is vital to good practice, a physician's creation of health record data potentially transmitted among third parties may adversely affect the patient's sense of worth and social power. When we disclose our health secrets to health care providers, we hope that their professional attitudes and the tradition of patient confidentiality will mean a minimum of third party disclosures of a type that could heighten feelings of shame, embarrassment, fear, or defeat. A patient is willing to call attention to unsightly lesions on his skin because he believes the nurse and doctor will be clinical rather than emotive about what they see and because he believes that information about the causes of the lesions— allergy, cancer, or AIDS, for example—will be kept confidential. Mandatory reporting requirements for sexually transmitted diseases make sense to the extent that patients' perceived privacy needs will not lead them to shun care.

The privacy sacrifices people make in exchange for professional care are resented, of course, when professionals perform poorly, breach confidences, or violate trust. In the well-known case *Moore v. Regents of the University of California*, a leukemia patient sued California research physicians over what he felt was fraudulent care and the appropriation of cells for commercial exploitation.[15] A man who agreed to premarital blood testing sued for privacy invasion when his physician also performed an AIDS test.[16]

If health providers are discreet and records are truly confidential, informational privacy is protected. Informational privacy is lost, though, when physicians violate patient trust:

> "Years ago I placed a newborn daughter for adoption with the help of my obstetrician. Recently I picked up the phone and the voice on the other end said 'Hi, I'm your daughter.' I asked how she'd found me. She said she'd gotten my name from my doctor, by fibbing about having a medical reason to know about her birth mother's medical history. There must be laws that say this isn't supposed to happen."—Kim

The tradition of physician–patient confidentiality addresses informational privacy concerns but does not begin to address all of the other categories of privacy concern (viz., concerns about physical, decisional, and proprietary privacy) that arise in the context of encounters with health care providers.

When medical record informational privacy is assiduously guarded through confidentiality practices, patients' interests in physical privacy may be neglected:

> "Seeing my wife deliver our son was amazing. I never felt closer to her than I did at that moment. We took classes together, so that I would be able to help out. I kept my cool, coached her, comforted her. It was great. But then I found out some guy I don't even know watched the whole thing! This guy was the husband of one of the maternity ward nurses. Our doctor let him watch! It was bad enough that so many doctors and nurses—and my mother-in-law—had to be there, but at least they had our permission."—Akil

Akil's doctor violated his trust by authorizing a direct physical intrusion. Patients rarely appreciate having to give up more physical and decisional privacy than they think is required by care:

> "The day I turned 60, I was diagnosed with lung cancer. I went in for surgery to remove part of my right lung. After the operation I woke up in the intensive care ward and prayed to God for letting me pull through. But then I discovered that they had put me in the same room with a man! He was a white man too. I was so shamed. They wouldn't have put no rich white lady in a room with a man."—Rita

> "After the abortion I was led into a large room with six reclining chairs. I sat in one chair. The other chairs were filled with women who had also just had abortions. I kept thinking the woman with red hair looked like someone I knew, maybe a neighbor in my apartment complex. Everybody's always talking about the right to privacy, but getting an abortion is not really very private. Anyone on the street can see you go in the front door. Then you sit in a waiting room where everyone can see you and people get bored so they try to talk to you. And

then they put you through counseling to make you talk about your personal feelings and second-guess your decision. Then you end up on display in the room
with the recliners hiding your emotions."—Soo Yi

Patients like Rita and Soo Yi suffer in silence these felt privacy indignities
called for by efficient delivery of health services. However, violated expectations about the privacy of medical encounters have been the basis of numerous
lawsuits brought throughout the United States against physicians, hospitals, and
other health care providers.

Feminist perspectives on physician–patient encounters have emphasized decisional privacy implications of communication between physicians and patients. Drawing on the insights of Jurgen Habermas and Seyla Benhabib, Janet
Farrell Smith has argued that communication within the physician-patient dyad
is not simply about "information delivery," but also about marshaling power and
authority to direct treatment. Patient voice, judgment, and choice become sec-
ondary to that of the more powerful white jacket.[17] Resisting accountability is a
potentially deadly way patients can resist the superior authority of the physician.

The Litigation Paradox

Lawsuits are public acts that ordinarily result in records open to the public.
Suits claiming breach of confidentiality open confidential matters up to public scrutiny. In a number of instances patients have sued because of breaches
of confidentiality. Kim's case, above, is based on an actual adoption disclosure case.[18] Patients have also sued when their interests in physical privacy
are invaded. A hospital, physician, and nurse were sued for privacy invasion
by a married couple who discovered that the physician had permitted the husband of a staff nurse to observe the birth of the couple's daughter.[19] Akil's
case, above, is based on this litigation. The unwanted observer was on hand
solely to kill time as he waited for his wife's shift to end so that he could drive
her home. An otolaryngologist was sued for privacy intrusion by the estate of
a deceased patient whose cancer surgery wounds the physician photographed
without consent as the man lay dying in his hospital bed.[20] The patient's wife
informed the doctor that her husband had expressed a desire to be let alone,
but the doctor persisted in his picture-taking, propping and adjusting the patient's unwilling head to get the best shots. In other lawsuits, interests in propriety privacy have been centrally at issue. A hospital and a newspaper were
sued by an elderly heart patient after the hospital's public relations office gave
the newspaper a photograph of the patient for use in an article about charity
care; the patient, who was depicted with her walker, was a paying patient.[21]
The plaintiff felt bad that her identity was appropriated for a journalistic use
that further offended her by portraying her in a false light.

In the Supreme Court's "right to die" cases, patients (or families on behalf of patients) sought to be free of unwanted treatment, nutrition, or pain. These cases show that encounters with health care providers can turn into struggles over decisional privacy as families, patients, and providers battle over who has the right to decide the fate of comatose and hopeless patients. Physical privacy concerns are part of the struggle as well, because when providers treat and feed hopeless patients, opponents liken their conduct to assaults on bodily integrity, tortious intrusion, and battery.[22] The Supreme Court's reproductive rights cases[23] assign privacy rights to pregnant women that mean a degree of decisional privacy, confidential record keeping, anonymous reporting, and freedom from spousal notification,[24] but as Soo Yi's case was designed to illustrate, the process of exercising the abortion right can in practice also raise physical and informational privacy concerns for patients.

Hide the Scars

Notice that medical care can create new bases for resisting accountability when patients return home. "Tell me what the doctor said," is an oft-heard request in families and among close friends. Patients, however, may resist accountability within their intimate circle concerning what the doctor said. "The doctor said the pain is due to vaginal warts, a sexually transmitted disease, Mommy," is not what the sixteen-year-old is eager to report to her fundamentalist parents. Her vaginal warts may prevaricate into a yeast infection for purposes of answering the parents, the prescribed medication hidden under the mattress.

Surgery and chemotherapy are notorious for creating body image problems that outlive encounters with health providers. Even minor surgery can lead to privacy seeking:

> "A hand surgeon removed an entire fingernail in order to extract a thorn that had become embedded in the nail bed. I thought the surgical wound looked grotesque, so every time I changed the bandage, I locked the door of the bathroom to make sure my roommates didn't walk in on me. I didn't mind if my roommates saw me totally naked, as long as I had a Band-Aid on that finger!"—Pat

After a surgical procedure, especially major craniofacial surgery and amputations, the patient takes home concerns about body image and social acceptance that may lead to new selective concealment strategies. Pat's decision to lock the bathroom door and wear a bandage while awaiting nail regrowth was a simple way to avoid shame and vulnerability following minor surgery. Hiding what one thinks of as disfigurement beneath a bandage, a beard, clothing, or a tattoo are ways to reduce social anxieties, bolster self-esteem, and avoid unwanted attention.

Encounters with Third Parties

The third and final context in which concerns about medical information arise is the context of encounters with third-party users of health data. Medical privacy concerns arise, finally, in the context of encounters with third parties who use (or seek to use) health data. Third parties conceivably include family members, schools, employers, insurance companies, pharmacists, research scientists, and retailers who assert a right to know or a need to know details of others' health and health requirements. A person seeking to buy life insurance discovers that she is required to undergo HIV testing and give written permission for the insurer to examine medical records dating back ten years. A man purchasing incontinence protection and over-the-counter medication from a supermarket is unhappy to learn that the retailer not only records his discount card purchases, but also sells what amounts to information about his health needs to other businesses. An army recruit is troubled that she is required to submit tissue samples for storage in a military DNA bank. The insurance purchaser faces physical and informational privacy losses with testing and record-disclosure requirements. The "adult diaper" purchaser faces informational privacy losses and resents the junk mail that appears in his mailbox. The military recruit has informational and proprietary privacy worries about agents of the government coming to own her genetic identity through an appropriation of her tissue.

The demand by third parties for personal health information is great. Most people in the United States are only vaguely aware of the range of third parties who obtain (and would like to obtain) health information contained in medical records. Few stop to read or think about the authorization forms we routinely sign as a condition of care, granting permission to third parties to examine our health records. Limited awareness translates into limited discontent.

Sometimes people do become aware of illicit third-party uses of health information. The plaintiff in a negligence action against a hospital sued an insurance company for securing information from his physician under a false pretext.[25] A plaintiff in a malpractice suit brought a breach of confidentiality suit against a hospital that obtained medical information about him from a surgeon at another hospital.[26] In *Whalen v. Roe*, a group of prescription drug users sued unsuccessfully to block implementation of a state law requiring that the names, ages, and addresses of persons purchasing certain prescription drugs be reported to the state.[27] The Supreme Court held that although the Fourteenth Amendment protects the privacy of personal information, the New York mandatory reporting law included confidentiality strictures that would adequately protect informational privacy.

Most salient for typical Americans are the health information demands that third parties make directly on individuals. Employers, life insurance brokers, even the media make demands. A media production firm was sued for invasion of privacy by an accident victim videotaped while receiving care in a rescue helicopter that the court analogized to a hospital room.[28] The media defendant urged that the accident victim's rescue was newsworthy.

The insurance industry and self-insured employers are major users of health information. In the managed care setting, patients understand that their physicians may simply be unable to keep diagnostic and treatment information strictly confidential. Doctors are required to share what they know with network administrators, who will review and approve (or disapprove) certain procedures and treatment plans in advance. Prior to managed care, physicians shared information with third-party insurers too. Through the Medical Bureau and other mechanisms, the insurance industry as a whole shares personal health information to help manage risk and detect fraud.

Policymakers for the insurance industry should carefully weigh the effects of health information dissemination on the willingness of patients to conceal information from doctors and to assume unfair financial burdens. Patients are already driven to avoid care for mental health problems or to pay cash, minimizing the risk of creating a widely disseminated health record that could be used for destructive purposes. Consider Donna's case:

"I plan to run for public office someday. I am now a successful lawyer. I have been in psychotherapy for depression for a year. I have been paying for therapy in cash. I'd hate to have my mental health history in an electronic record on some insurance company or government computer. When I see my primary care doctor (she's part of the managed care network utilized by my firm's health plan), I never mention my depression or the prescription antidepressants I take. I pay cash for my antidepressants and hope the pharmacist and the state agency they report to can be trusted."—Donna

Insurance is not the only reason employees are asked to yield health information to employers. Employees in the public and the private sector find that they are required to give health data to their employers for a variety of reasons, including determining their compliance with drug and alcohol prohibitions and eligibility for workers' compensation or sick leave. As these illustrations show, health and genetic data can be demanded by employers:

"My supervisor wanted to know why I was absent from work so often. I kept saying 'medical problems.' Eventually, I became afraid of losing my job, so I revealed to the owner of the company that I had MS, multiple sclerosis. The owner told my supervisor 'in confidence,' my supervisor told his best friend in the office 'in confidence,' and now everyone knows. I feel so self-conscious. Everyone at work pities me and treats me with kid gloves. I did not lose my job. I didn't lose pay. But I feel less equal and discriminated against anyway."—Mary

"I wouldn't want to give the government my DNA. I was lucky to be getting out of the army just when they started requiring active duty military personnel to provide samples for the big data bank outside of Washington, D.C. The official idea was that if you got killed overseas and it was impossible to identify you from a visual inspection of your remains, they could do a DNA test. But who trusts the government to only do what they say they are going to do with valuable information? Who knows what else they might find out about you or your family from a DNA test before you die? You might find yourself not getting a promotion or a good assignment and think its for one reason, only to discover its because your genes say you're going to die young, or get senile. Then they'll start discharging guys who have what somebody decides is the 'gay gene'."—Juan

HIPAA limits the ability of employers who provide health benefits to access patient medical records for purposes of making employment-related decisions. In an actual case, *Miller v. Motorola*, a woman sued her employer for revealing to co-workers that she had undergone a mastectomy.[29] Marines unsuccessfully sued hoping to avoid providing blood and tissue samples collected for purposes of DNA identification in the event of death in battle. They feared possible DNA analysis by the Department of Defense or other government agencies for purposes other than the identification of remains.[30] The court eventually declared the lawsuit moot following the discharge of the service members and changes in the law. Surreptitious employee DNA testing by a railroad company aimed at determining which employees might be genetically predisposed to carpal tunnel syndrome led to a two-million dollar settlement with the Equal Employment Opportunity Commission.[31]

Employees have enjoyed mixed success suing to avoid drug and alcohol testing that they say reveals health information to third parties. A woman sued her employer for firing her after she declined to consent to a urinalysis for drug and alcohol testing.[32] Railroad employees and U.S. Customs Service workers brought major lawsuits complaining of privacy losses connected with drug and alcohol testing.[33] Employees working closely with mentally retarded clients in a state facility successfully sued to avoid mandatory AIDS testing.[34] Courts try to balance individuals' legitimate expectations of physical and informational privacy against employers' and government's interest in efficiency, health, or safety. Like employees, athletes are asked to submit to mandatory substance testing. Student athletes unsuccessfully alleged that a National Collegiate Athletic Association's random drug testing program invaded their privacy.[35] Other students engaged in extracurricular activities and subjected to drug testing lost in the Supreme Court.[36]

Increasingly salient to the American public are the quasi-voluntary health disclosures we make in the course of drug store purchases and retail transactions using credit cards or stores' discount cards. Retailers who document customer spending patterns in effect collect health information and threaten informational privacy interests:

"I have a problem with incontinence and poor nutrition. I bought some 'adult diapers' and Ensure with a credit card, using my supermarket's discount card. Two weeks later I began getting catalogues in the mail from companies that want to sell me geriatric home health aids. Clearly, my supermarket recorded my transaction then compiled and sold a mailing list. This really bothers me, and more than it would if I wound up on a list of people who bought garden seed or potato chips."—Phil

Why does Phil want information about health-related purchases to be treated differently than information about garden seed or potato chips?

I suggest it is because health information commonly arouses deep feelings of shame, embarrassment, fear, and defeat that other classes of information seldom evoke. Fear of losing insurance or jobs can be great, and so loss minimization is an obvious reason for wanting privacy. Distress minimization deserves emphasis too. The feelings of low self-esteem and heightened vulnerability that lead people to conceal health information from family and physicians also travels to encounters with third parties.

If I buy flower seeds and begin receiving unsolicited gardening catalogues, I will not feel significantly diminished or vulnerable. I might even relish contact with companies I would not otherwise know about who sell products I would not otherwise know about. I might like to think that many people have access to information about my passion for gardening. By contrast, I may be burdened and embarrassed by my incontinence. I may be dispirited by unsolicited reminders of my health problems in my mailbox. I may resent being on a mailing list for drab home health aid catalogues. I may not want to be classified as unwell, diseased, or declining. I may dislike third-party uses of health information for these reasons, even if I do not expect losses, such as loss of insurance, employment, or intimacy. I may want my privacy simply to minimize health-related distress.

Knowledge that personal health data are collected by or circulated among third parties can be disturbing for another related reason. It widens the domain of felt accountability. The problem is more than the idea that others possess facts they can use to materially harm, humiliate, and misconstrue, as the privacy experts stress. It is also that others knowing something that is likely to make one feel obliged to engage in an especially difficult set of performances—to explain and justify something profoundly affecting, to face sanction for something that is deeply personal and affecting. Feeling bound to account to intimates is hard enough. Feeling impelled to account to an uncertain host of strangers is deadly.

Focusing on loss minimization and emotional distress minimization helps to illuminate why there was so little public opposition among the people of Iceland to the decision of the Parliament of Iceland to allow the commercialization and scientific use of the "Icelandic Genome."[37] A Gallup poll found that only 19 percent opposed the Parliament's action to transfer records to the biotechnology firm Decode.[38] A premise of the successful proposal was that the people of Iceland are genetically homogeneous. Descended from a small group of ninth-century Viking settlers, the people of Iceland, into recent times, have lived in relative isolation and have shunned out-marriage. In addition to perceived genetic homogeneity, they have a tradition of excellent family and medical record keeping. A government-supported national health plan eliminates the problem of private insurance and access to care. The decision of Parliament has made it possible for medical and genealogical records to be combined in a search for clues to the genetic bases of illness, health, and longevity. Researchers agree that computerized data culled from the Icelandic people "could be of unequal power in understanding cancer, heart disease, mental illnesses, and other major diseases."[39]

In Iceland, genetic informational privacy probably seems relatively unimportant when compared to the benefits of making a contribution to world science. Material loss minimization through privacy is not a large issue because material losses are not reasonably anticipated. Everyone is believed to have similar genes, and because everyone has similar genes, few need to worry about genetic discrimination. In the United States, racial and ethnic differences, along with a national history of racism and anti-Semitism, make genetic discrimination a concern. Emotional distress minimization through privacy is similarly not at issue in Iceland in connection with wholesale national genomic disclosure. The people from whom genetic information is collected are on the whole genetically healthy and similarly endowed when compared to fellow citizens. Access to genetic health information taken from typical Icelanders creates no basis for shame, embarrassment, fear, or defeat of the sort that arouses feelings of low self-worth and heightened vulnerability. Although the privacy of genetic data may be a mild concern in Iceland for the reasons mentioned, it does not follow that medical privacy in other contexts would not be valued by the Icelandic people for the same reasons tied to reflective responses, emotional distress, and material (especially, reputational) loss for which Americans value health privacy. An individual with a sexually transmitted disease, cancer, or mental illness may be selectively secretive and desire assurances of confidentiality from health professionals and the government in Iceland no less than in the United States.

CONCLUSION

Human beings have plenty of morally sound reasons for concealing health information, some of which relate to the proper discharge of accountability imperatives. Concealment of health information is, at least sometimes, a good thing. But it is not always a good or prudent thing. It is not a good thing when one is accountable to reliant or dependent others for health information that they need right away to take practical steps to cope with the material and emotional consequences of illness. I believe the shame, embarrassment, fear, and defeat people feel when they are ill or getting old impairs their ability to meet accountability demands, to speak frankly to health care professionals, and to be objective about health privacy policies.

Metaphorically speaking, the desire for health privacy is itself linked to health—to the health of the constitutive relationship each person has with his or her own body and mind as seats of personal identity, and equally to the health of the divergent relationships each person has with families, friends, and others. The social and psychological needs of persons facing health concerns, combined with their practical needs for insurance, employment, and community standing, call for a political order that understands accountability and that protects medical information privacy. Americans, some of whom no longer treat their health concerns as deeply private, appear to want the ability to choose whether to conceal or disclose health information. Although a degree of choice is currently vested in the individual, once a person becomes a patient a complex of commercial and governmental forces effectively render control over medical information a chimera. To make medical information privacy for patients a reality, the public and private sectors in the United States ought to embrace public policies that aggressively countermand unnecessary, unreasonable, and nonconsensual disclosures and aggregations of health information. Concretely, nonconsensual disclosures and aggregations of health data for purposes not directly related to care, insurance payment, or paramount public health research should not be permitted. Firms, whether or not covered by HIPAA, should adopt a bias against commercially motivated information disclosures, for example, by requiring consumers of health-related products to specifically "opt in" to participation on mailing lists. Health care identification and security devices that would raise privacy concerns should be redesigned or avoided. These are but a few policy parameters to consider.[40]

If people feel shame-faced, unworthy, and vulnerable when they confront health concerns, should legislators validate those feelings by making their palliation a goal? Policies that allow for necessary accountability but protect settled expectations of privacy and privacy needs are justifiable.[41] At the same time, to reap the joint moral and public health benefits of disclosure, one must support public health education aimed at encouraging the public to become more accepting of the consequences of illness and aging.

NOTES

An earlier version of this chapter was printed as part of the 1999 Robert H. Levi Lecture Series, "Privacy and Medical Information," by the Bioethics Institute of Johns Hopkins University, and appears with permission.

1. Geri-Ann Galanti, *Caring for Patients from Different Cultures: Case Studies from American Hospitals* (Philadelphia: University of Pennsylvania Press, 1997). Galanti describes significant variations in patient privacy preferences among American immigrant and ethnic groups.

2. *Health Insurance Portability and Accountability Act of 1996*, Pub. L. No. 104–191, 110 Stat. 1936 (1996) (HIPAA). Concerning HIPAA:

> "The privacy provisions of the federal law, the Health Insurance Portability and Accountability Act of 1996 (HIPAA), apply to health information created or maintained by health care providers who engage in certain electronic transactions, health plans, and health care clearinghouses. The Department of Health and Human Services (HHS) has issued the regulation, 'Standards for Privacy of Individually Identifiable Health Information,' applicable to entities covered by HIPAA. The Office for Civil Rights (OCR) is the Departmental component responsible for implementing and enforcing the privacy regulation."

Department of Health and Human Services, http://www.hhs.gov/ocr/hipaa/ bkgrnd.html (official website of the United States Department of Health and Human Services, last accessed 17 July 2002).

3. David B. Morris, *Illness and Culture in the Post Modern Age* (Berkeley: University of California Press, 1998), 62.

4. Morris, *Illness and Culture*, 62.

5. Lawrence O. Gostin and James G. Hodge Jr., "Piercing the Veil of Secrecy in HIV/AIDS and Other Sexually Transmitted Diseases: Theories of Privacy and Disclosure in Partner Notification," *Duke Journal of Gender Law and Policy* 5 (1998): 66, 70; and Lawrence Gostin, Joan Turek-Brezina, Madison Powers, and Rene Kozloff, "Privacy and the Security of Health Information in the Emerging Health Care System," *Health Matrix: Journal of Medicine* 5 (1995): 2, 21–24 (stressing autonomy values and justice concerns). See generally Charles Culver, James Moor, William Duerfeldt, Marshall Kapp, and Mark Sullivan, "Privacy," *Professional Ethics* 3, nos. 3–4 (1994): 3–25.

6. See, for example, Neil Holtzman and David Shapiro, "The New Genetics: Genetic Testing and Public Policy," *British Medical Journal* 316 (1998): 852–56, who describe denial of health and life insurance, along with employment constraints, as risks

of genetics-related health disclosures. See also Gostin and Hodge, "Piercing the Veil" (1998), 61 ("Disclosure of their status can result in social stigma among family and friends. They are also vulnerable to discrimination in employment, housing, and insurance."). Gostin and Hodge mention embarrassment, litigation, and domestic violence as potentially adverse consequences of health disclosures.

7. Lawrence O. Gostin, "Health Information Privacy," *Cornell Law Review* 80 (1995): 453, 527.

8. Michel Foucault, *The Birth of the Clinic: An Archaeology of Medical Perception,* trans. A. M. Sheridan Smith (New York: Pantheon Books/Random House, 1975), 3–20, 107–122.

9. Donna Britt, "Would We Really Value Open Leaders?" *Washington Post,* 20 August 1999, B01.

10. See Lloyd Grove with Beth Berselli, "The Reliable Source," *Washington Post,* 28 September 1999, C03, describing an interview with Michael J. Fox; Staff, "Reagan's Condition Has Deteriorated; Sensible Talk Impossible, Wife Says," *Washington Post,* 19 December 1999, A36; Lloyd Grove with Beth Berselli, "The Reliable Source," *Washington Post,* 2 December 1999, C03, describing Magic Johnson's work as an AIDS foundation supporter; and Annie Groer with Ann Gerhart, "The Reliable Source," *Washington Post,* 25 July 1996, C03, describing Louganis' participation in an AIDS March.

11. Susan Sachs, "Artist Sees Hope in Mastectomy Ruling," *New York Times,* 28 March 1999, sec. 1, col. 4, p. 43. The forty-five-year-old artist goes by the name of "Matuschka."

12. On October 20, 1999, the Health Network (TheHealthNetwork.com) webcast live the mastectomy and breast reconstruction surgery of a forty-seven-year-old nurse by Dr. Beth Du Pree, a surgeon at the St. Mary Medical Center in Langhorne, Pennsylvania, as part of Breast Cancer Awareness Month.

13. In June 1998, a woman who revealed her name only as "Elizabeth" gave birth live over the Internet to "Baby Sean" in the Arnold Palmer Hospital in Orlando, Florida. The mother declared her motive to be public education. See Ellen Goodman, "Internet Birth a Blow to Privacy," *Buffalo News,* 20 June 1998, 3C.

14. Anita L. Allen, "Privacy in Health Care," in *Encyclopedia of Bioethics,* rev. ed., ed. Warren T. Reich (New York: Macmillan 1995), 2064–73.

15. *Moore v. Regents of the University of California,* 793 P. 2d 479 (1990).

16. *Doe v. Dyer-Goode,* 566 A. 2d 889 (Pa. Super. Ct., 1989).

17. Janet Farrell Smith, "Communicative Ethics in Medicine: The Physician-Patient Relationship," in *Feminism and Bioethics,* ed. Susan M. Wolf (Oxford, U.K.: Oxford University Press, 1996), 184–215.

18. *Humphers v. First Interstate Bank of Oregon,* 696 P. 2d 527 (Or. 1985).

19. *Knight v. Penobscot Bay Medical Center,* 420 A. 2d 915 (Me., 1980).

20. *Estate of Berthiaume v. Pratt,* 365 A. 2d 792 (Me. 1976).

21. *Weller v. Home News Publishing Company,* 271 A. 2d 738 (N.J. Super. Ct., 1970).

22. *Cruzan v. Director, Missouri Department of Health,* 497 U.S. 261 (1990); *Vacco v. Quill,* 521 U.S. 793 (1997); *Washington v. Glucksberg,* 521 U.S. 702 (1997).

23. *Griswold v. Connecticut*, 381 U.S. 479 (1965); *Roe v. Wade*, 410 U.S. 113 (1973); *Planned Parenthood v. Casey*, 505 U.S. 833 (1992).

24. *Planned Parenthood of Central Missouri v. Danforth*, 428 U.S. 52 (1976); *Thornburgh v. American College of Obstetricians and Gynecologists*, 476 U.S. 747 (1986).

25. *Hammonds v. Aetna Casualty & Surety Company*, 243 F. Supp. 793 (N.D. Ohio 1965).

26. *Moses v. McWilliams*, 549 A. 2d. 950 (Pa. Super. Ct. 1988).

27. *Whalen v. Roe*, 429 U.S. 589 (1977).

28. *Shulman v. Group W Productions*, 59 Cal. Rptr. 2d 434 (Cal. Ct. App. 1996).

29. *Miller v. Motorola*, 560 N.E. 2d 900, 903 (Ill. App. Ct. 1990).

30. *Mayfield v. Dalton*, 109 F. 3d 1423 (9th Cir. 1997).

31. *Equal Employment Opportunity Commission v. Burlington Northern Santa Fe Railroad*, No. C01-4013 MWB, settlement reached (N.D. Iowa, 6 May 2001).

32. *Borse v. Piece Goods Shop Inc.*, 963 F. 2d 611 (3rd Cir. 1992).

33. *National Treasury Employees v. Von Raab*, 489 U.S. 656 (1988) and *Skinner v. Railway Labor Executives Association*, 489 U.S. 602 (1989).

34. *Glover v. Eastern Nebraska Community Office of Retardation*, 867 F. 2d 461 (8th Cir. 1989).

35. *Hill v. NCAA*, 865 P. 2d 633 (1994). See *Vernonia School District 47J v. Wayne Acton*, 515 U.S. 646 (1995).

36. *Board of Education v. Earls*, 122 Sup. Ct. 2559 (2002).

37. Nicolas Wade, "Scientists at Work/Kari Stefansson, Hunting for Disease Genes in Iceland's Genealogies," *New York Times*, 18 June 2002, sec. F, col. 2, p. 4.

38. The Parliament passed the bill by a vote of 37–20 giving the medical records and DNA of the entire nation to a biotechnology company founded in 1996, Decode, along with exclusive rights to create a centralized data bank. See Jackie Crosby, "Iceland: The Selling of a Nation's Genetic Code," Minneapolis (Minn.) *Star Tribune*, 10 February 1999. See also Abi Berger, "Private Company Wins Rights to Icelandic Gene Database," *British Medical Journal* 318 (2 January 1999): 11; and Ragnheidr Haraldsdottir, "Icelandic Gene Database Will Uphold Patient's Rights," *British Medical Journal* 318 (20 March 1999): 806. Opponents of the bill included the Icelandic Medical Association and Mannvernd, and the Association of Icelanders for Ethical Science.

39. Crosby, "Iceland."

40. Crosby, "Iceland."

41. In a different context, one relating to legal protection of interests in contract and property, Laurence Tribe describes "settled expectations" that "should be secure against governmental disruption" as those that are "focused and crystallized." See Laurence Tribe, *American Constitutional Law* (Mineola, N.Y.: Foundation Press, 1988), 587.

Chapter Four

Accountability for Sex

Sex is private, but we are clearly accountable for sex. First, we are accountable to our intimate partners for our sex lives. Most married people hold one another accountable both for sexuality within the marriage and for sexuality outside the marriage. Sexual dysfunction, as well as sexual infidelity, demands a reckoning. Accountability for sex is not just about who or who else a person may have slept with. It is also about the frequency, sincerity, variety, competence, and safety of sex. In addition to intimate partners, we are also, secondarily, accountable to our families and friends for sex. This is obviously true for children and teenagers whom parents want to shelter from premature and unhealthy sex. But it can also be true of adults whose parents, extended families, or wider kinship groups assert a "say" over the choices they make about their sex lives. Thirdly, groups, including religious and ethnic groups, commonly assert a "say" over the sex lives of members. Members may regard their group's having a "say" as highly appropriate. Or, they may not.

Accountability to an affiliative group for sex can take on cruel and discriminatory faces. *Boy Scouts of America v. Dale* reflects the discriminatory visage of civic groups. Under an interpretation of the First Amendment's guarantee of religious freedom and private association, on 28 June 2000 the United States Supreme Court upheld the right of the "morally straight" Boy Scouts of America to expel a loyal adult homosexual scout who spoke out in favor of gay rights. Acting *in loco parentis*, an Atlanta church known as the House of Prayer ran afoul of the child cruelty standards for organizing disciplinary child beatings. Reverend Arthur Allen went to prison for thirty days in 1992 after beating a sixteen-year-old girl for nearly half an hour as church members held her down and looked on in approval. The girl was being held accountable for sex—she was accused of having become sexually active against the wishes of her parents and church.

Our society justifies all of this accountability for sex within private life by reference to familiar commitments, expectations, and dependencies characteristic of intimate and affilial spheres discussed in chapter 2. As the number and intensity of close interpersonal relationships varies from person to person, so too does accountability for sex vary from person to person. Social norms regard the religion, education, ethnicity, age, and ties of an individual as among the factors that may go toward determining his or her sex accountability quotient. Some people will therefore have personal lives marked by considerably more or considerably less accountability for sex than others. We can limit accountability somewhat by isolating ourselves from others. Those of us who are glad for the special accountability that is constitutive of close, intimate relationships still find that accountability for sex is rarely an easy, frictionless matter. We sometimes would rather maintain silence and secrecy than face the constraint, shame, and sheer emotionality that accompanies answerability for sex. The New Accountability has meant that Americans are more deeply answerable to wider communities than in the past.

Accountability for sex in private life is a commonplace rule. Lovers, kin, and membership groups have a say about our sex lives. But what about accountability for sex in our more public lives? Accountability for sex outside of what is typically defined as "private" life is also a commonplace rule. As gay men and lesbians know firsthand, laws criminalizing homosexual acts and penalizing homosexual status amount to accountability to employers and the general public. Wide-ranging accountability for sex also extends to heterosexuals. This chapter traces the significance of accountability for sex when accountability extends beyond otherwise intimate contemporary realms. In this chapter I will focus on the accountability for sex of, first, ordinary employees and, second, that special class of employees we call public officials. I will argue that accountability for sexual conduct at work and intermixed with work is justified, notwithstanding privacy concerns.

ACCOUNTABLE TO THE BOSS

Employees are accountable to their employers. They have to be, notwithstanding the desirability of privacy at work. Employees are paid to perform certain tasks, and from a business profitability perspective, it is imperative that employers have a way of knowing whether and how efficiently those tasks are being performed. Employers need and are entitled to information. To ensure that employees are informationally accountable, employers may rely on honest employees' self-reports and the evidence of tangible work products, such as the quantity of manufactured goods. But employers may also rely on information provided by supervisors and "spies" hired to observe workers, and on evidence obtained from cameras and recordings. Because employers are legally liable for the safety and security of workplaces, they will typically monitor workers to ascertain that federal, state, and local government health and safety standards are met. Increasingly, employers will also seek to ensure that workers conform to modes of conduct that make liability for sexual harassment unlikely. Workers who violate workplace conduct codes may be accountable in more than the informational sense. They may be required to truthfully report intimate interpersonal contact with coworkers and face termination if they violate rules against, for example, dating. Employees subject to random drug and alcohol testing face stiff sanctions if found to have violated drug policies, and their subjection to sanction means they are accountable in the strong sense of accountability as punitive answerability.

Some types of workers are more accountable than others. Pilots and railroad engineers have responsibilities for passenger safety that make them highly accountable to their employers. Domestic workers, especially maids and nannies, are often exceedingly accountable. They may live in their employers' homes and have long hours. It is not unheard of for child care workers to labor under the eye of video cameras that allow absent parents to monitor their conduct all day long. Plant, factory, or shopbound wage laborers are similarly accountable to employers. Seasonal agricultural workers who live in accommodations provided and controlled by their employers are intensely accountable, even after hours. Highly compensated professionals are accountable to their employers, too. Young attorneys in a big law firm may have private offices, telephones, and computers, but they will be required to account for how they spend their time, dividing each day into ten-minute increments for the purpose of properly billing clients.

Sexual Harassment

Accountability for sex is a tool of workplace discrimination. One of the purposes of sexual harassment law is to ensure that working men and women will not be treated as accountable to employers and co-workers for sex. A worker should not be called into her boss's office and grilled about her sex life. She should not have to explain why she does or does not find her boss attractive. A woman who refuses to allow herself to become an object of pornography for co-workers should not lose her job. No one should have to put up with images and conversations at work that demean his or her sex and sexual orientation. Catharine MacKinnon has described sexual harassment law as a "public weapon" and "one of the more successful legal and political changes women have accomplished."[1] However, a number of commentators have condemned sexual harassment laws on the grounds that they have made the problem of accountability for sex in the workplace worse.

In the *Unwanted Gaze* and in a subsequent article in the *New Republic*, Professor Jeffrey Rosen condemned the law of sexual harassment in the workplace as an example of the unwanted gaze of government and business undermining the dignity of workers.[2] Rosen's widely publicized views merit close examination. Title VII of the Civil Rights Act of 1964 prohibits employers from discriminating on the basis of sex and certain other traits.[3] (Title IX of the Education Amendments of 1972 bars sexual harassment in schools receiving federal monies.) Current Equal Employment Opportunity Commission regulations and Title VII jurisprudence endorsed by the Supreme Court treat sexual harassment as employment discrimination. Victims of sexual harassment have a remedy under Title VII for employment discrimination when employers are responsible for either "hostile environment" harassment or "quid pro quo" harassment.[4] Title VII has been under intense scrutiny by legal scholars, some of whom say Title VII sexual harassment law clashes with rights of free speech and worker privacy.[5] In like vein, Rosen believes Title VII appropriately provides a remedy for quid pro quo harassment. Rosen argues, however, that the "hostile environment" doctrine invites unduly extensive scrutiny of the personal lives of workers. Rosen suggests, in effect, that a policy of employee accountability for interpersonal misconduct at work is most defensible when the consequence of misconduct is loss of employment opportunity rather than when the consequence is the creation of an inhospitable workplace.

Feminists who believe it imperative to be able to speak openly and freely about the injuries suffered "in private" and concerning "the private" will be reluctant to embrace Rosen's analysis of Title VII jurisprudence. Symbolized by the slogan "the personal is political," feminists advocate inviting the public to gaze into traditional spheres of personal, sexual, and domestic life in order to discern and address subordination, discrimination, and inequality.[6] Title VII plaintiffs alleging sexual harassment believe the goal of accountability for interpersonal conduct can trump the goal of protecting perpetrators from the unwanted gaze. Plaintiffs want the very gaze that, for alleged perpetrators, is unwanted.

Privacy at Work?

Can there be both privacy at work and accountability for wrongful interpersonal conduct at work? Both would seem to be important. We need privacy at work. Many employees are spending well over forty hours per week in offices and other workplaces. Rosen argues that privacy at work should include what Erving Goffman termed "backstage areas where people can joke, let down their hair, and form intimate relationships free from official scrutiny." It is hard for anyone who values privacy to altogether oppose Rosen's borrowed idea of a "backstage."[7] We cannot be "on stage" all the time. Rosen firmly believes that what happens backstage should remain in that context.

Rosen brings a contextualist accent to his libertarian case for privacy. Individuals are entitled to privacy to avoid having their words and deeds taken out of context. Invasions of privacy cause harm by taking information about personal matters out of the intimate contexts where they belong and thrusting them before the public eye for what inevitably turns into prurient, curious distortions and misunderstandings that limit our freedom and cause us shame, humiliation, and embarrassment.[8] Indeed, some gay people may have preferred the closet if they had known that information about their sexuality would turn their meaningful same-sex relationships into tawdry items for gossip and misplaced moralism. I believe the desire to avoid having his conduct interpreted out of context led the British playwright Oscar Wilde to the deception and lawsuits that ultimately led to his incarceration and premature death. For Rosen, employers and their workers should not be generally accountable for the words and behaviors that fall short of crimes or torts and that deny no one employment opportunity.

The general point Rosen makes—through Goffman's metaphor of the "backstage"—about the importance of privacy at work is appealing. However, sexual harassment law arose because women were being routinely, and as a matter of course, *forced* onto men's "backstage" for unwanted jokes, informality, and intimacy when they wanted to remain out front in their professional roles. Men and women who complain of sexual harassment have done so in part because a boss, supervisor, or co-worker forced them to endure words or behavior more suitable for a date, kitchen table, or sleazy motel room.

One of the primary purposes of the U.S. law of sexual harassment is to improve economic opportunities for previously excluded women by making employers and employees more accountable for sex-related interpersonal misconduct in the workplace.[9] Workers are made more accountable by holding their employers liable. As a practical matter, the law of sexual harassment requires that victims of harassment be willing to make public otherwise private facts about themselves and the perpetrators of the harassment. From the point of view of a person victimized by harassment who brings a formal sexual harassment charge, the resultant privacy losses are more or less voluntary. The gaze is wanted, if only reluctantly, as a cost of legal vindication. From the point of view of persons accused of sexual harassment, sexual harassment law constitutes an "unwanted gaze"—an invasion of their privacy—as their "backstage" words and actions, some pertaining to their intimate lives, are turned into objects of legal scrutiny.

Numerous theorists have argued that the privacy of men and the spheres of life they control are overvalued, thus shortchanging women. Feminists have argued that only by shining a bright light into traditionally private sanctuaries can justice be done. "Unwanted gazes" must become "wanted gazes." Professor Anita Hill became a heroine to some feminists because—at considerable cost to her own privacy and that of Justice Clarence Thomas, their families, and their friends—she opened the door to governmental, media, and public scrutiny of the sex-related tastes and habits of a prominent judge.[10] Although Paula Jones failed to become a heroine of the feminist movement, she also jettisoned sexual privacy, inviting the gaze of the public in order to pursue lucrative legal claims against President Bill Clinton.[11] Both women believed the powerful men they sought to expose had behaved badly toward them and that the men should be made publicly accountable in spite of, and because of, the sexual nature of the alleged interpersonal misconduct.

Anita Bernstein has argued that the hostile environment type of sexual harassment is a brand of incivility or disrespect that merits a Title VII remedy. Rosen argues that the law of sexual harassment is "excessive." It is a heavy-handed way to attack a problem that is better seen as a privacy-norm breach than gender discrimination, he says.[12] Rosen offers a concrete proposal for minimizing the unwanted gazes brought on by sexual harassment law. He suggests jettisoning the hostile environment doctrine and encouraging women whose work environments are filled with demeaning sexual innuendo, offensive language, leering, and overtures to bring tort actions for invasion of privacy against individual responsible offenders. In this way, "highly offensive" privacy-invading sexual harassment will have a remedy, but the more merely offensive, tasteless, and privacy-invading sexual harassment will not.[13] Nor should it, Rosen believes. Minor breaches of social norms and etiquette should not be elevated to the level of legal wrongs, and they cannot be without inviting unwanted gazes.

Rosen's argument presupposes that employers and supervisors will face so few plausible suits for hostile environment under the privacy-invasion rubrics of tort law that they will be able to relax surveillance of e-mail, intimate relationships among co-workers, and other workplace conduct. Employers anticipating what are really breaches of taste and etiquette will not feel compelled to aggressively monitor workplace speech and conduct, Rosen concludes. The "wanted gaze" of accountability for interpersonal conduct will be narrowed by blinders of limited liability. But what if employers remain worried about norms? And what if the number of tort actions match the number of Title VII actions for hostile environment?

Rosen suggests that an otherwise respected, upwardly mobile professional worker like Professor Anita Hill, faced with a boss who likes to describe dirty movies and make sexual innuendos, will have no Title VII claim and perhaps no good privacy tort claim either. A victim of a single act of sexual impropriety, an otherwise respected worker like Paula Jones, would have no Title VII claim either, though her tort claim might pass muster under the tort liability standard. According to Rosen, "If and when Bill Clinton exposed himself to Paula Jones in a Little Rock hotel room, the injury she suffered may be better described as an invasion of privacy than as a form of gender discrimination."[14] Clinton's alleged invasion of Jones's privacy objectified, belittled, and insulted Paula Jones, according to Rosen, and such leering and exposure is wrong for those reasons, not most problematically on account of sex inequality. If Clinton had been a woman and Jones a man, we would more naturally think of such behavior as a breach of etiquette than as sex discrimination, Rosen suggests. As a privacy invasion complained about in a tort action, both exposing one's penis to a stranger simply because one finds her attractive and prattling about pubic hairs and pornography could be deemed "highly offensive" and actionable—or not.

Of course, one might object to the "wanted gaze" of accountability to victims of sexual harassment on the basis of concern for the victims' privacy. Paula Jones and Anita Hill may have deserved privacy, even if President Clinton and Justice Thomas did not. Indeed, feminists have often expressed concern that, ironically, victims of sexual harassment, like victims of rape, can remedy privacy-invading wrongs only by giving up more privacy.[15] However, Rosen's attack against Title VII reflects his voluntarist libertarian impulses rather than feminist or nonvoluntarist impulses. Legal liability for sexual harassment must be restricted, he argues, because it leads to unwanted scrutiny of private life that distorts through decontextualization. Rosen objects to the "wanted gaze" of victims of sexual harassment on the basis of concern about the perpetrators. His perpetrator focus is redeemed somewhat by the fact that every victim is, in theory, also a perpetrator, so vulnerable are we all to breaches of social norms. We are all human.

Still, Rosen's criticism of hostile environment discrimination is troubling. We are all human, but some of us are female humans. Rosen's polite attacks on feminism and the law of sexual harassment in the workplace are no doubt the most controversial aspects of his book. As feminists have emphasized, it is important to give up some privacy—as liberalism has defined it—to get protection and access. We ought not to want too much privacy for ourselves and others, because privacy can shield neglect and violence. Rosen believes that, in response to feminism, our society now calls attention to sexual intimacies in ways that are hurtful and harmful to legitimate privacy interests.

Many forms of what is called sexual harassment are invasions of privacy. As I argued more than a dozen years ago, the invasion of privacy torts should be employed against sexual harassment in the workplace.[16] I disagree, though, with Rosen's *non sequitur* that the hostile environment doctrine should be dropped from Title VII jurisprudence in the interest of workplace privacy. Rosen's argument against the hostile environment doctrine depends critically on an ability to clearly distinguish *quid pro quo* harassment from hostile environment harassment. A semantic distinction can be made between the two, but, at root, liability for both is premised on a policy decision to combat unjust female exclusion from the workplace. The hostile environment doctrine reflects the judgment of the courts and fair-employment lawyers that the ability of women to be at work rather than at home depends both upon employers' willingness to hire and promote women who want to work outside the home and upon women's willingness to endure working outside the home.

Once upon a time, men and women both understood that a woman's decision to enter the workforce was a decision to subject herself both to the frustration that comes from having one's potential and accomplishments undervalued and to the indignities of sexual harassment. A working woman had two choices: be a realistic tough cookie and take the crap male co-workers and bosses dished out, or to be a crybaby and go home. For the women who "had to work," the option of going home did not exist. Women in food service and clerical positions had it bad. Women who tried "male" occupations had it really bad. Three decades ago, husbands took a certain pride in the fact that their wives did not have to earn money in order for the family to survive. But they also slept easier knowing that their wives would not have to leave home only to become objects of leering, uninvited sexual overtures and other forms of sexual harassment.

Professor Rosen believes the position of women in the workplace is elevated and secure today, partly due to Title VII's ban on overt discriminatory exclusion based on gender and its ban on quid pro quo harassment. He seems to assume that incivility does not typically function to deny women the economic opportunity that is a promised civil right. Yet, when women who have a choice about whether and where they work outside the home are making their choices, those choices are being wrongfully constrained by beliefs about, among other things, the amount of unchecked sexual harassment they are likely to face in various settings.[17] To jettison the hostile environment doctrine would be to fail to understand that quid pro quo harassment and hostile environment harassment still work in tandem to deny women the equal employment opportunity promised by Title VII's vision of civil rights.

It *is* discrimination on the basis of sex for employers, managers, and co-workers who hold sway over economic fates to repeatedly demean, humiliate, or embarrass employees because of their gender through sexual overtures and innuendos. Rosen argues that law is often less effective than social norms and technological solutions, which can achieve the same policy result without threatening the privacy of innocent people in the process. In short, the legally buttressed "wanted gaze" sometimes should be rebuffed in favor of nonlegal "norms" to protect people from "unwanted gazes." This may be true, but Rosen has failed to provide evidence or persuasive arguments indicating that women would not more frequently self-exclude in favor of domesticity or stereotypical "women's work" under the truncated Title VII regime he advocates than under the current regime.

Just how should people behave at work? Although Rosen sees privacy-invading sexual harassment as a kind of incivility that breaches norms of etiquette, he is too conventionally liberal in the end to proffer idealized conceptions of good conduct and relations between men and women as such. Wendy Shalit, whose take on privacy is less voluntarist than Rosen's, is a fellow critic of contemporary sexual harassment laws, but one who dwells unashamedly on the virtues: modesty for women and honor for men. In her book, *A Return to Modesty: Discovering the Lost Virtue*, Wendy Shalit invokes Jewish law prohibiting exposure of the intimate to develop a criticism of contemporary American culture.[18] Shalit reports becoming interested in traditions of sexual modesty after seeing an old photograph in which a young Jewish couple stood side by side, but without touching or looking at one another. The Jewish law of *tzniut* required that the body of an unmarried woman remain unseen and untouched, even by her fiancé. Respect for a woman requires that she not be subjected to (or treated to!) physical intimacy, even if she herself desires a lover's touch. Privacy cannot be waived.

Wendy Shalit's book is provocative and curious. It goes against the mainstream of privacy voluntarism. Shalit argues for the resurrection of sexual modesty, defined as premarital virginity and chastity, as a respected virtue for women. Shalit, a twenty-something, upper middle-class, college-educated, self-described feminist when she published her book, wants young women to want modesty (for moral and prudential reasons). And she wants parents and others to impose rules and expectations consistent with sexual modesty. Shalit believes, in effect, that norms mandating unwanted privacy are a good thing. At least in the moral domain, privacy should not be deemed wholly optional and voluntary. Shalit objects to sexual harassment laws on the ground that they address the outer man of action rather than the inner man of conscience and virtue. She wants men to feel an obligation of male honor to treat women in accordance with "the ideal relation between them and women."[19] Ideally, men would treat all women as ladies—with respect and without debasement, she insists.

The choice that must be made is between a legal regime that provides more meaningful employment opportunity or a legal regime that provides more privacy and uncoerced virtue. Shalit's "retro"-chic book is evidence of a writer seeking (in vain, I believe) in sexual modesty and manly honor a weapon against rampant sexual harassment. Rosen's advice to a young woman concerned about hostile environment sexual harassment would be that she try to be a tough cookie, advocate social norms, and wait until things get bad enough to bring a tort suit. My advice: Forget the false veil of sexual chastity; do not hold your breath for the resurgence of manly honor; and cooperate with efforts that may include responsible, privacy-sensitive employer monitoring and enforceable conduct codes designed to minimize sexual harassment and other forms of gender-related misconduct not related to sexuality as such.[20]

Rosen has decried the "fall of the private man," represented by the direction of current sexual harassment law. He has thereby placed himself in a camp occupied by other scholarly libertarians and some important legal feminists, including Professor Vicki Schultz.[21] However, let us not forget that there are two dimensions to the "fall of the private man" and the destruction of privacy. The fall that occurs because other people do not respect a man's privacy—the "unwanted gaze"—is one dimension. The fall that occurs because a man does not respect his own privacy—the "wanted gaze"—is the second. The "unwanted gaze" and the "wanted gaze" equally lead to the destruction of privacy. When a man seeking sex in a professional setting exposes his penis and sexual fantasies to an arbitrarily selected strange woman, we discern a lack of respect for his own privacy as well as his lack of respect for hers. The private man at work who cannot keep his zipper up or who indulges in uncivil conversation about his sexual life, his medical problems, or his personal financial woes is hardly a private man at all. Off-the-job privacy rights to socialize with co-workers and to engage in high-risk and unhealthy activities have something to commend themselves. Yet, we need to find a way to address the "fall of the private man" without precipitating the fall of the working woman.[22] Jettisoning hostile environment law is clearly not the way to go about it.

ACCOUNTABILITY TO THE GENERAL PUBLIC

Like the rest of us, public officials are accountable for private life. Unlike the rest of us, public officials' intimate secrets will on occasion be of legitimate, nationwide interest. The public and the press do not need to know everything about the President of the United States and other public officials. However, in a range of circumstances, they properly claim a right to information about aspects of officials' lives—medical, financial, and sexual aspects—that would ordinarily be considered personal and private. Medical information, for example, is ordinarily considered personal and private. Indeed, recent federal statutes reinforce that understanding of medical information by mandating privacy and data security with respect to the collection, transfer, and storage of health records. Candidates for public office may have a constitutional right against mandatory drug tests.[23] Yet, it is beyond serious debate that if a vice president prone to heart attack has been hospitalized for cardiac problems, he must, in a timely fashion, share with the general public and the press the details of his illness, care, and prognosis. Like medical information, financial information is ordinarily deemed personal. Yet the public and press reasonably expect candidates for office and office holders to disclose details of their investments and tax payments. In addition to medical and financial information, information about a person's sexuality or sexual relationships is commonly characterized as personal and private.

In dramatic contexts, the public and press have made credible claims to know the details of the sex lives of public officials accused of sexual harassment and other sex-related misconduct. The claim that the public has a right to know about the sex lives of public officials can be understood as a claim about accountability for private life. We learn that the president or a member of Congress may have had an affair with an intern and we want accountability. That is, we want complete information, honest explanations, and, if appropriate, fair punishment and apology.

This section is an examination of the accountability of public officials for sex.[24] I will do three things here. First, I will describe past and current accountability norms with respect to public officials' sex lives. Second, I will argue that despite abuses, current demands for sexual accountability by officials have substantial merit. Third, I will urge recognition of limits on the degree and manner of accountability for sex to the general public. Attention to character and conduct is a requirement of good democratic self-government, but there are practical limits to how much we, as a polity, can and should demand disclosures about sex in the name of these virtues. Ironically, at the same time that "protect privacy" has become a battle cry of ethicists and consumer advocates, there has been an explosion in the market for information about private life. The appetite for personal information is so great that most media organs—shielded by the First Amendment's freedom of the press—would be at a distinct economic disadvantage were they to refuse to profit from the public's co-dependent exhibitionism and voyeurism. Very often it seems as though it is not so much a question of whether the media will serve up privacies, but how. As Americans have witnessed in sex scandals over the years, where the bounds of just accountability are egregiously breached or threatened, officials can be expected to take suboptimal measures to protect their sexual privacy, even lying. Holding an official to account for sexual conduct serves legitimate purposes when intimacies deliberately or inadvertently become commingled with official responsibilities or the affairs of government to such an extent that the public cannot adequately tend its business without incursions into private life.

Caring about Sex

We care about other people's sex lives. We discuss, debate, and gossip about sex, observing complex, evolving norms of propriety and civility. Why do we care about people's sex lives? We care because we fear sex (it can be dangerous) and we like sex (it is stimulating). A person's sexual conduct can become a matter of general interest and conversation if it is (1) criminal; (2) illegal, though not a crime; (3) improper, though not illegal; (4) entertaining; or (5) an interesting combination of all of the above.

First, private sexual activity can become a matter of public conversation if the sexual conduct in question is criminal. Sexual conduct can be tantamount to criminal battery, rape, or malicious disease transmission; it can be fornication, adultery, homosexuality, sodomy, prostitution, lewdness, or obscenity; it can be incest or bestiality. Criminal prosecutions are matters of public offense and prosecution, and criminal sexual offenses are discussed.

Second, private sexual behavior can become publicly discussed sex because it violates laws other than criminal laws. Alienation of affection, breach of promise, civil battery, and sexual harassment are examples of (past and present) sex-related noncriminal law offenses.

Third, sex can become a matter of public conversation because it is deemed improper, that is, because it violates social norms or expectations that are not criminal or civil wrongs. A very old person taking a much younger lover, a professor dating an undergraduate student, and a man seducing his lover's daughter are all troubling relationships that may offend our sensibilities. Society has come a long way since the marriage of the black entertainer Sammy Davis, Jr. and the Scandinavian beauty May Britt was a scandal, but for those who disapprove, interracial sex is still improper.

Fourth, sex can become the focus of public conversation because it is entertaining, that is, because it is amusing, interesting, or even arousing. Reports of sex between celebrities, for instance, can be interesting. Certain kinds of sex acts are interesting because they are bizarre. Moreover, discussing sex can feel good and can titillate; it can be erotic or arousing. This is one reason why talking about sex in professional and employment settings is problematic, even in the context of presidential impeachment. We are not supposed to get aroused at work.

Fifth, sexual conduct can become a matter of general discussion if it is some combination of criminal, civilly wrong, improper, and entertaining. At the peak of his career when, as they say, "he could have had any woman he wanted," police caught the handsome white film star Hugh Grant having oral sex with a black prostitute. The public talked about the Hugh Grant incident because it involved a crime, a glamorous celebrity, and a social impropriety. When NBC sportscaster Marv Albert pled guilty to assaulting a former lover whom he repeatedly bit, the public talked about the court case because he was a seemingly normal media personality accused of what some people would say is bizarre sexual conduct.

Opening up about Sex

In certain settings and to a certain degree, people like to talk about sex, and it is important for them to be free to do so. Any notion that the discussion of sex must be confined to a sacred private domain and can never be the subject of public discussion cannot endure. Moreover, although some sex talk and publicity about other people is gratuitously invasive, revealing serious crimes and hypocrisy seem to be good justifications for publicizing secret private lives. Illegal sex between teenage pages and members of Congress merits public disclosure and action, however embarrassing to the offending congressmen. If President Thomas Jefferson took the public position that blacks were morally inferior and unfit for the society of whites and if he was having an intimate relationship with his black slave Sally Hemings, his hypocrisy would have merited disclosure. A gay politician who condemns homosexuality as immoral and advocates restrictions on gays should be "outed." Likewise, aggressively antiphilandering philanderers should be outed. This view led a former Newt Gingrich campaign worker to reveal that she had had an adulterous affair with the future speaker of the house during his first marriage.[25] Anne Manning said she came forward "because when Gingrich talks about family values and acts righteous . . . it just gets my back up." When confronted about Anne Manning's claim that she had sex with him while he was married to his first wife, Gingrich had no comment.

Although many public officials guard their private lives from the prying eyes of the public, some individuals intentionally call attention to their formerly secret sex lives. Individuals may have varied motives for self-disclosure. An official can be motivated solely by the belief that he or she will soon be found out by others. Such strategic considerations help to explain why Democratic Representative Barney Frank of Massachusetts, who courageously revealed in 1987 that he is a homosexual, announced that he had paid a male prostitute for sex and then hired the man to become his $20,000-per-year personal aide. Representative Frank's admission came after a Washington newspaper published a story in which former Frank aide Steven L. Gobie claimed that he had run a prostitution service from Frank's Capitol Hill townhouse. In 1990, the House voted to reprimand Frank for ethics violations tied to Gobie. The House found that Frank improperly used the power of his office not only to fix thirty-three of Gobie's parking tickets, but also to attempt to shorten Gobie's probation for sex and drug convictions.

Self-disclosure is not always a matter of damage or spin control, as it was in the Frank-Gobie case. Former Republican senator from Kansas and presidential candidate Robert Dole called attention to his erection disorder to promote public awareness about the medical condition. Dole revealed on CNN's *Larry King Live* that he had participated in the medical trials of the then-new impotence drug Viagra and wholeheartedly endorsed the product. On the one hand, the public did not need to know that Senator Dole suffers from penile erectile dysfunction. On the other hand, his disclosure called attention to an unduly embarrassing, widespread condition and the availability of a new treatment. President Dwight D. Eisenhower's impotence was a secret that was revealed only when his alleged romantic partner, Kay Summersby, wrote a book describing their several failed attempts at sexual intercourse.

The End of Discretion and Reserve

How did we get from Eisenhower's shame to Dole's cheer? At one time, family, friends, employees, and journalists adhered to an unwritten code of privacy. Under this code, the sexual intimacies of public officials were concealed from the general public as secrets and confidences. The code kept truth from the public, but it was a reflection of respect for sexual privacy. Not everyone's sexual privacy was accorded the same protection. But the typical, mainstream white male politician of the 1940s and 1960s could count on a large degree of discretion. The extent of privacy protection in previous generations is remarkable. President Franklin D. Roosevelt's long-time affair with Lucy Mercer was known to many but not publicized or publicly acknowledged in the press. First Lady Eleanor Roosevelt's suspected infidelities, both heterosexual and homosexual, were safeguarded secrets as well. Presidents John F. Kennedy and Lyndon B. Johnson allegedly exploited the code of privacy and enjoyed robust extramarital sex lives as presidents.

When I first saw Marilyn Monroe's infamous performance of "Happy Birthday, Mr. President," I did not suspect that Monroe and President Kennedy had been lovers. Nor did I suspect that Monroe and Robert Kennedy were lovers; that the first lady had refused to attend her husband's birthday party because she knew Monroe would be there; or that Monroe's performance in a deliberately-selected, see-through dress into which she literally had been sewn may have fueled the fears of John and Robert Kennedy that the mentally unstable film star would reveal her alleged secret affairs with the president and his sibling attorney general.

Some private sexual conduct is clearly immoral. As a general matter, however, sexual privacy has moral, political, and psychological value. What is that value? A body of philosophical, jurisprudential, and psychological literature argues that privacy, including sexual privacy, is important. Philosophers ascribe to privacy varieties of utilitarian and deontic value tied to autonomy, independence, self-expression, love, friendship, bodily integrity, judgment, and democracy. Jurisprudential scholars stress privacy's value as it relates to limiting government and individual rights in liberal democracies. Psychologists say privacy is a key to our well being, especially to the reduction of social anxieties.

Sexual privacy is among the most important forms of privacy. The old code cloaking the sex lives of officials was thus well motivated. You might be forced to testify before Congress about your political beliefs, but you were unlikely to have to talk publicly about your sex practices. The code protecting privacy—and male prerogative—was a distinct feature of public life from World War II until the 1970s—the era of civil rights, feminism, the sexual revolution, the war in Vietnam, and general skepticism about the uses and abuses of government power.

The significant increase in the public accountability of officials for sexuality and sexual conduct was a product of the 1970s. As suggested to me by Washington lawyer Tom Birch, the turning point seems to have been 1974, when the police came across the battered and intoxicated duo of Representative Wilbur Mills, a Democrat from Arkansas, and ex-stripper Mrs. Eduardo Battistella (a.k.a. Fanne Foxe, the Argentine Firecracker) brawling near the Tidal Basin in Washington, D.C. Until that unlucky night, facts about the sex lives of presidents and other prominent men and women in government generally were not considered news fit to print in the mainstream press. Three days after the police fished his suicidal companion out of the Tidal Basin sporting two black eyes, Mills issued a statement. It was clearly that of a man accustomed to getting away with dodging questions about his "improper" personal life. He did not expect to have to answer the many questions raised by his absurd, insincere explanation of what happened that night. Numerous witnesses linked Mills to a lavish social life centered around strip clubs, but Mills' public statement described the ex-stripper Battistella as a friend of the family. Amazingly, he blamed his wife's inability to accompany him that evening because of a broken foot as the main reason for the regrettable appearance of impropriety. Wilbur Mills' egregious misconduct (and the fact that he was caught) helped to put an end to the era in which public officials could expect discretion concerning the intimate details of their sex lives, even when those lives included fornication, adultery, promiscuity, substance abuse, and children born out of wedlock.

The Wilbur Mills incident, however, was only the beginning of this new era of disclosure. In 1976, the post-Vietnam, post-Watergate press published the claim of Elizabeth Ray that she was on the payroll of Democratic Representative Wayne Hays of Ohio for the purpose of serving as his mistress. The press also published stories revealing that two congressmen had sexual relationships with seventeen-year-old House of Representatives pages in 1973 and 1980. Because minors were involved, it was right for the House to censure formally the two congressmen in question, Representatives Daniel B. Crane, a Republican from Illinois, and Gerry Studds, a Democrat from Massachusetts, in 1983. Sexual misconduct was not new to the news when the media caught married presidential candidate Gary Hart with Donna Rice on his lap. Against this background, Democratic Representative Mel Reynolds of Illinois could not reasonably expect sex with a teenage campaign volunteer to remain a secret; he eventually was convicted of sexual assault and attempts to thwart the investigation.

The society-wide ban on open discussion of sex in the United States eventually yielded to a standard of permissible public discussion of sex. If youth culture's sexual revolution made disclosures about officials' sex lives appealing, post-Vietnam, post-Watergate ethical resolve made them seem necessary. Discussion started as euphemistic, eventually became explicit, and now is often graphic. To take an example from popular culture, couples on the television game show "The Newlywed Game" in the 1960s were coyly asked about "making whoopee." The contestants on the show in the 1990s, however, were asked outright about having sex. The new openness could be explained partly by the "sexual revolution" of which radical feminism was but an element. The sexual revolution was a sweeping rejection of traditional sexual morality and gender roles, embracing birth control, abortions, premarital sex, and nonmarital cohabitation. Sex came out of the closet and into the street. Women left the kitchen and went to the office. Consensual adult sex outside of marriage gained acceptance, but because of the women's rights movement and feminism, sexual exploitation and sexual harassment declined in acceptance and eventually became illegal.

In the early 1980s, politicians began to call for a return to "family values" that some felt were lost in the 1960s and 1970s. Although the rhetoric of "family values" took hold during the Reagan and Bush presidencies, it was impossible to stop all of the cultural momentum of the sexual revolution that was redefining the family and the overall moral tone of society. Since the 1980s, an American culture obsessed with sex and sexy products has coexisted with an American culture obsessed with ideals of sexual propriety. This bipolarity in the American psyche helped to explain why the investigation and impeachment of President Clinton was both pornographic and moralistic. Now that conversing about sex has became permissible, it appears that probing into the sexuality and sex lives of officials knows no inherent limits. We investigate. We talk and we judge. We hold accountable.

Too Embarrassing, Too Contentious

If a member of Congress has maintained a politically damaging secret liaison with a woman who winds up missing and possibly dead, the public and press cannot ignore the fact. His sex life has to be scrutinized. It has become the business of the public. As citizens of a democracy we are asked to concern ourselves with at least some of the intimate sexual conduct of our public officials. We are asked to evaluate propriety and impropriety, legality and illegality, and then to deliberate with fellow citizens about the significance and implications of our evaluations.

Some of the things we are asked to do we cannot do easily or well. There are two reasons we cannot easily engage each other on the topic of sexuality: we are embarrassed, and we are in radical disagreement. First, we are embarrassed by talk about sex. We do care about other people's sex lives and we do talk about it. But there are felt limits that, I believe, impair the most responsible and serious forms of conversation about sex.

In the aftermath of the sexual revolution, Americans are fairly comfortable discussing sex with some close friends. The unspoken rules of civility governing the mainstream permit conversations about sex with peers of the same sex. When civility rules bar explicit language, it is still possible to discuss or allude to the sex lives of public personalities For instance, it was easy to debate the moral significance of President Jimmy Carter's adulterous thoughts, Democratic Senator from Virginia Chuck Robb's assignation with Miss U.S.A. Tai Collins in a Manhattan hotel room, and former Washington, D.C., Mayor Marion Barry's videotaped drug-laced affair. In each case, however, the precise sexual activities at issue remained unclear.

The Clinton-Lewinsky affair escalated into an impeachment trial of the president, making it an affair that ought to have been discussed. Because we knew more about the affair than many of us would have liked to know, however, it was not fully discussible. It is one thing to talk and joke about Hugh Grant and Marv Albert among friends; it is something else to discuss the removal of a president from office for perjury, obstruction of justice, and sex with a subordinate when doing so requires close attention to the details of sexual expression. A male law student in his twenties told me he deliberately avoided reading the Starr Report because he thought it was none of his business. A public document issued by a public official about the president of the United States was none of his business? The details about the president and Ms. Lewinsky made public by Kenneth Starr are the kinds of subjects parents probably would not want to discuss with their children. They are also the kinds of matters one might be reluctant to discuss in law school, at work with colleagues of the opposite sex, at church, or at polite social gatherings. We do not want to be accused of sexual harassment or bad manners, and we certainly do not want to risk becoming sexually aroused in inappropriate settings.

Second, we disagree about sex. We disagree for many reasons, including our age and our regional, religious, and ethnic diversity. We disagree about what kinds of sexual conduct should be criminal; we disagree about what kinds of conduct should be a basis of civil liability; we disagree about reasonable social expectations; we disagree about what is interesting; we disagree about when sex should be discussed in public; and we disagree about how explicitly certain sexual conduct should be discussed. These are disagreements about law, morality, and etiquette. These disagreements incorporate, but transcend, the so-called cultural wars. These disagreements are so deep that we may be unable to work through them in the interest of civil public discourse and collective governance.

The problem of discussing sex predated the independent counsel's investigation into President Clinton and the ill-fated impeachment trial. But the public response to the notorious Starr Report, the House impeachment proceedings, and the Senate trial well illustrates dimensions of the problem. It illustrates both conversation-stopping disagreement and embarrassment. Whether the impeachment and trial of a president seemed to be only or mainly about a sex scandal depended upon one's attitudes about the regulation of sexual conduct and the "discussibility" of graphic sex. If one believes that lying about sex to protect the privacy of one's consensual sexual activities is justified, one probably disapproved of the discretion exercised by the attorney general, the independent counsel, and members of Congress. If one believes that the oath of office taken by the president and the integrity of the grand jury system require blunt truth about sexual privacy under any and all circumstances, one probably approved of the efforts to oust Clinton.

Collectively scrutinizing the sex lives of public officials with frankness and civility is prohibitively difficult and, some would argue, counterproductive. In an article recounting adultery committed by Martin Luther King Jr., Franklin D. Roosevelt, and John F. Kennedy, veteran journalist Anthony Lewis concluded: "straying from the straight and narrow does not disable one as a statesman, a general, or a civil rights leader." He argued that we surely are not better off now that "prurient interest in the sex lives of politicians" is out of Pandora's box. Some of the more "intelligent, sensitive Americans" will no longer aspire to office, and the natural tendency to lie to protect one's sexual privacy will be exploited easily by enemies.

Feminists concerned with the lack of public scrutiny of domestic abuse and sexual exploitation in the workplace have joined the call for higher standards of accountability for what was once defined as private life. Proponents of communitarian and republican conceptions of a democratic community call for the rejection of a sharp divide between private lives and public virtues. Forming and remaining a community may require that the sexual lifestyles of our public officials be appropriate topics for public scrutiny. Civic republicans argue that if we are to avoid becoming disenchanted with and alienated from our democracy, we must be permitted to demand leaders who exemplify our substantive constitutive values.

Feminists taking issue with Anthony Lewis rightly argue that we must take the bad with the good. Unleashing prurient interest in the sex lives of politicians was a necessary evil as we pursued the laudable goal of combating sexual harassment and other forms of gender oppression. Now that the national understanding of sexually offensive conduct has improved, many feminists are seeking a new public-private balance that vests the government with the power to deter and punish sex-related offenses while otherwise leaving consenting adults alone. Feminists who refused to support Republicans seeking to oust President Clinton believed the Republicans "got" the importance of prosecuting sexual harassment but "forgot" the importance of limiting government intrusion into the sex lives of consenting adults.

Communitarians and civic republicans would also take issue with Lewis. For them, conformity to collectively recognized standards of sexual virtue is among the legitimate expectations of public office; it is of no consequence that a nation might end up with a merely competent leader (a Dan Quayle) rather than a gifted leader (a Franklin Roosevelt). In the view of communitarians, the merely competent person may be the leader who best reflects our publicly announced, shared values and who therefore best inspires and leads us.

Lewis' concern about the quality of leadership is not entirely off target. The specific concern I have is that self-righteous individuals may believe they have a political vocation solely because they satisfy superficial criteria of moral virtue and look good on television, rather than because they have real vision and commitment. To these concerns, I would add that unrelenting attention to and investigation of ordinary sexual immorality distracts officials from their core policymaking responsibilities. The intelligent, sensitive minds we do manage to attract into public service are wasted on speeches and reports about their colleagues' sex lives.

This concern cuts two ways, revealing a point of disagreement with Lewis. Although I agree with Lewis that great and popular leadership by sexual rogues has been commonplace in American history, I believe that leaders such as presidents Clinton and Kennedy would have been even greater were they not so busy managing complicated, covert sex lives. Sexual affairs may represent lost opportunities for great leaders to become truly superb. Although there are costs to the new sexual accountability standard, a benefit of the standard is that it may deter the kinds of sexual conduct that waste our leaders' talents and that others can exploit politically. With fewer sex scandals, government might become more efficient, open, and participatory. I say "could" because we just do not know what government by sexual saints in all three branches might look like. We have not yet experienced it. Perhaps scandals of other sorts would erupt to fill the vacuum. Indeed, if sex were no longer a political issue because the men and women in public life were leading "proper" sex lives, I fear that politicians would seize upon other personal matters—such as problem children or the use of prescription mental health drugs by family members—to cast the shadow of unfitness on their political foes. But then, some journalists and political opponents turn public attention to such personal matters already. For instance, former Democratic presidential candidate Michael Dukakis of Massachusetts was embarrassed by efforts to probe his wife Kitty's mental health history. Substance abuse by the daughters of President George W. Bush and his brother, Florida governor Jeb Bush, is widely reported. We need to tackle the sexual privacy problem for people in the public eye, but sexual privacy is not the only kind of privacy about which we must worry.

Elected officials really should be the kind of people whose vices—sexual or otherwise—do not amount to abuse of power, corruption, and injustice. In these respects, their conduct must not jeopardize public trust in government. Leaders should be, and should appear to be, of good moral character. But can strong political leaders be moral? Citing the example of Nobel Peace Prize–winner President Jimmy Carter, Richard L. Berke argues that too much virtue can be a flaw in a leader. Berke suggests that to reach the highest offices of government, "a person, no matter how upright in public, has to be a master at the inherently devious game of politics." Sex need not have a role in that "devious" game, yet during John F. Kennedy's Camelot years in the White House, access to the president was often limited to those who could also be trusted to remain silent about his licentiousness.

There is no elegant solution to the current dilemma of needing to talk about sex but being challenged in our ability to do it well by embarrassment and disagreement. It appeared that, bruised by the escalation of the Clinton-Lewinsky affair into a doomed Senate impeachment trial, our country will begin a process of voluntary self-correction, shifting the balance toward greater respect for the privacy of public officials and aspiring officials. We are unlikely to return to the extremes of yesteryear when President Kennedy's habitual romps with prostitutes went unreported. But we may advance to the point when our presidents and politics are not unduly pornographic and good leaders are not forced to resign from office over ancient marital infidelities. The media frenzy surrounding Congressman Condit's problems in the Chandra Levy case suggest, though, that the public and press are not prepared to leave public officials alone, at least in cases in which they may be guilty of criminal misconduct in addition to breaches of professional ethics and their marriage vows. Condit's secret affair came to light only during a police investigation of the young woman's mysterious disappearance.

The Case for Accountability

Talking about and judging other people's sex lives is not all bad. In fact, it is sometimes good and sometimes even obligatory. There are better and worse justifications for doing so, however. I would like to consider three often-heard justifications for holding public officials accountable for sexuality and sexual conduct. The first is that holding or pursuing public office entails a voluntary waiver of privacy expectations. On this view, being an office holder or candidate renders one fair game. The second is that officials ought to be held to special ("high") standards of moral and sexual virtue. On this view, although officials and candidates may not consent to opening their sex lives to all, the public has legitimate expectations of sexual virtue that justify scrutiny and accountability. The third is that the public has a right to know how the affairs of state are conducted and that officials and candidates are accountable for their sex lives to the extent that they relate directly to official responsibility or competence for office. I believe the third justification is sound. I also believe the general case for officials' accountability framed in the discourse of the public's right to know and the official's competence for office is strong, whereas the case framed in the discourses of voluntarism and moral character is weak.

Justification 1: Voluntary Waiver, Reciprocity

Opinion is divided, but some commentators have argued that public officials (and also public figures) knowingly sacrifice their privacy when they pursue public office or step into the limelight. A related argument is that in exchange for public scrutiny, officials receive prestige and financial compensation not enjoyed by typical citizens. A further, related argument is that the extroverted people who seek public office do not have the same need or desire for privacy that ordinary people have. The problem with these lines of argument is that many people who seek public office do not, in fact, intend to sacrifice or bargain away their sexual privacy. They continue to need and want privacy. Moreover, the responsibilities of office rarely require complete abrogation of sexual privacy, and the rewards of office holding are not obviously fair compensation for this complete abrogation of sexual privacy.

Let us begin with the claim that politicians do not need or want the privacy wanted and needed by others. Even assuming that there were a political "type," it would not follow that everyone who seeks or enters public office shares a privacy preference profile. Some office holders will want more privacy than others. The public may be unaware of just how much a given public official craves privacy.

Ordinary citizens who want privacy can take steps to avoid attention. Certain forms of self-help, however, are not available to public officials who want privacy. The practical realities of public life render attempts by high-ranking public officials to retreat from view all but impossible. Trying to retreat may come across as suspicious or unseemly. Even voicing disapproval of intrusion and publicity can be politically dangerous. A couple of years ago, I participated in a panel discussion about privacy and public life. The panel included a newer member of Congress from a prominent political family. During the discussion he made the familiar statement that as a public official, he has a responsibility to open his financial and family life to public scrutiny. After the panel, away from the microphones, the young congressman was less glib. He revealed that he actually deeply resented the loss of privacy that accompanied his role as a celebrity public servant but that his congressional staff warned him of the potential political consequences of saying so in public.

Public servants need the sexual privacy that we know they are unlikely to get, particularly once they are suspected of improper intimacy or a glamorous liaison. Officials' need for privacy stems from universal feelings of passion, desire, and a need for un-self-conscious expression. Although it would be hard to prove to a mathematical certainty that officials need privacy, the burden of proof should not rest on those who ascribe to public servants a need freely ascribed to other people. To the contrary, the burden should fall on those who assert that officials are different and do not need privacy.

Admittedly, public officials' own reckless behavior can give credence to the suggestion that they are a breed apart, people without the usual need for genuine privacy and intimacy. Former New York mayor Rudolph Giuliani made poor choices about the time, place, and manner of his separation from his wife that invited tabloid publicity. President Clinton is an obvious case of reckless self-tabloidization: if one really needs and yearns for sexual privacy, would one conduct an affair with a young intern under the watchful eye of White House staff while attempting to defend oneself in a sexual harassment suit and while being investigated by an independent counsel? President Clinton, like the rest of us, needed to have a private sex life. Regrettably, however, Clinton exhibited a taste for risky extramarital sexual conduct that is hard to satisfy while serving in the highly visible roles of governor and president. His flawed conduct might not have come to light thirty years ago, however poor his judgment. Public servants' lack of judgment is often fatal to sexual privacy today. Also fatal are other people's disclosures of secrets—sometimes prompted by profit, sometimes by concerns about public trust and the discernment of character.

The assertion that people who enter public life have diminished spiritual, psychological, or moral needs for privacy compared with ordinary people seems only that—an assertion. It is an assertion that does not clearly follow from valid concerns about accountability. The public's genuine need for accountability from its officials may simply clash with the officials' personal needs for privacy. It is for that reason that the public must be circumspect in its demands for accountability about private life. Many people disapproved of Independent Counsel Kenneth W. Starr's investigation of President Clinton's relationship with Monica S. Lewinsky, not because he demanded sexual accountability from the president and a young woman, but because he probed more deeply into their sex lives than the public's concern about trust and accountability obviously required. The privacy implications of the investigation discredited both the independent counsel's report and the impeachment proceedings in Congress. We owe one another our best efforts to understand better the kinds and extent of privacy that are consistent with public responsibilities and to consider how, if at all, in the present context of moral pluralism, those privacy interests can be protected.

The claim that officials reciprocally exchange privacy for prestige and money is interesting but ultimately unpersuasive. Although there are respects in which office holding is a privilege of citizenship for which officials should expect to have to "pay" with additional sacrifices, there are equally important respects in which it is a duty of citizenship one must bear, for which one ought to expect to earn special rewards. If office holding is viewed as a duty, the public should make it as attractive as possible to a diverse range of qualified members of the community. No one will want to assume a duty that pays below-market wages, that takes one away from one's family, and that involves a complete loss of financial, medical, and sexual privacy.

Justification 2: "High" Moral Virtue

Sex scandals—complete with raw, lurid tales of sex and lies about sex—have affected both major political parties and every branch of the federal government during the past twenty years. The lives of judges, members of Congress, and presidents have been tainted by sex-related scandal. According to the usual justification for playing the sexual morality card, a history of improper sex is allegedly a good indication of bad character and bad judgment. Political leadership requires good character and judgment, we are told, and public trust in government depends on them. So appealing are these arguments that some of us who would rather not hear another word about anyone's bad marriage and noncriminal sexual practices believe that it is our duty to hang tough and listen anyway, as a matter of civic responsibility.

The politics of sexual virtue is complex. Sexual virtue requirements for public office have always existed. For instance, being openly gay or divorced would once have ruined a person's chances for national office. To some extent, the mere appearance of sexual virtue once sufficed for participation in national politics, allowing a sexually promiscuous man such as John F. Kennedy to occupy the White House. Although knowledge of President Kennedy's egregious habit of adultery would have influenced the American people's view of him, the people were not told. Instead, the journalists and government employees who knew about Kennedy's lifestyle kept quiet. The norms of investigation and disclosure changed between the Kennedy presidency and the Clinton presidency, however, making White House swims with naked beauties or oral sex in the Oval Office harder to keep secret.

The problem with expectations of high moral virtue from our officials is that such expectations in practice have rather arbitrary and unfair boundaries, if any boundaries at all. For example, it seems of late that a certain standard of sexual virtue is fast becoming a de facto requirement of high public office. The new standard for national office holders prescribes sexual "propriety" and proscribes "impropriety," defined as conduct which, if disclosed, would result in a loss of favor with a significant element of the general public. Propriety neither mandates celibacy of men and women in public life nor requires postponing sex or cohabitation until marriage, as it required years ago. The new standard does, of course, despise illegal sexual conduct, including sexual harassment in the workplace, sex with minors, and solicitation of prostitution. Moreover, the new standard favors heterosexuals because many people believe homosexual conduct is inherently improper.

Although no longer a crime, adultery clearly violates the sexual virtue rule because it is improper. The privatization of responsibility that has characterized public policy since the earliest days of the Reagan presidency has turned the idealized nuclear family into the powerfully symbolic fulcrum of national prosperity and well being. (It is "symbolic" because the nation's recent prosperity coincides with a remarkably high rate of nonmarriage, delayed marriage, divorce, single parenting, and gay cohabitation.) Adultery violates the sexual virtue standard because marital infidelity is thought to be a moral crime against the cornerstone of the family—the marital vow. Deception, lies, and cover-ups concerning adultery are compound violations of the sexual virtue rule. In fact, some people seem to think that lying about putative sexual misconduct to protect privacy is as evil as engaging in sexual misconduct in the first place. They say that if one "makes a mistake," one should be man or woman enough to admit it. Thus in August 2001, twelve female members of Congress appeared together on "The Larry King Show" to decry Representative Condit's affair with intern Chandra Levy.

Experience in the nation's capital suggests that officials accused of adultery, sexual harassment, solicitation of prostitution, or sex with teenagers eventually will have to face their opponents. This is not an entirely bad situation, because conduct with real victims merits real punishment. The consolation for the accused is that if the putative misconduct is limited to past, consensual, adult heterosexual adultery, one's political party may mount a defense. Loyal supporters of the accused offender might argue, for example, that his or her recent conduct has improved or that the ability to admit his or her private error to the public and to suffer the consequences is evidence of exemplary character and judgment. Nevertheless, it goes almost without saying that politicians cannot afford to defend colleagues who have sex with minors or who sexually harass co-workers, thanks to the President Bill Clinton/Paula Jones, Justice Clarence Thomas/Anita Hill, and Senator Bob Packwood/Jane Does debacles. Anyone who wants to survive as a ranking government official today had better be either sexually chaste or lucky enough to have discreet intimates, a tolerant constituency, and nerves of steel.

High-ranking public officials are among the most likely victims of egregious intrusion and unwanted publicity. For example, when the Senate considered Judge Robert Bork's nomination to the Supreme Court, someone obtained copies of Bork's video store records detailing the films he had rented. Congress swiftly passed a federal law prohibiting unauthorized disclosure of video rental records. Ironically, our privacy-deficient officials are in the best position to design, promote, and implement public policies sensitive to the many assaults against privacy. Our elected officials and top bureaucrats should focus on getting us and our government to take valuable forms of privacy more seriously. A robust democratic community is little helped by preference-falsifying leaders who are afraid to undertake aggressive campaigns to promote sexual privacy. Our leaders, however, fear the consequences of taking up the torch for sexual privacy. Specifically, they fear that the public will suspect that they have something shameful to hide or that they will tumble down from their shaky perches on the political Olympus like so many Gary Harts.

Leaders who came of age before 1970, when marital infidelity and secrecy about marital infidelity were tolerated as prerogatives of successful men, often do have something to hide. By today's new standard, these men have wayward, improper pasts that political opponents, mainstream journalists, scorned lovers, and others can legitimately, if controversially, bring to light to assist the public in evaluating the individual's competence, character, and credibility. Laches and statutes of limitations apply to neither former murderers nor former adulterers. The sexual virtue bar is so high that it scarcely helps men with tarnished pasts to point out that a radical change in mores has occurred since their decades-old trysts or that they have reconciled with their wronged spouses. As the House faced the possibility of impeachment hearings in September 1998, Republican Representative Dan Burton of Indiana—the conservative chairman of the House Government Reform and Oversight Committee, which investigated President Clinton's campaign finances—was forced to admit that he had conducted an extramarital affair and had fathered an out-of-wedlock child. Republican Representative Helen Chenoweth of Idaho admitted a six-year affair with a married man, but only after her public denouncement of President Bill Clinton's morals angered her ex-lover's wife into outing her. Illinois Republican Representative Henry Hyde's past affair with a married woman came to light as he prepared to chair the House Judiciary Committee's impeachment hearings. Hyde, who was in his forties at the time of the affair, now dismisses it as a "youthful indiscretion." Gingrich's designated replacement as House Speaker, Louisiana Republican Representative Robert Livingston, resigned during the pendency of the House impeachment debate after admitting that he also had engaged in marital infidelity.

Republican Senator Robert Packwood of Oregon tumbled down after years of fighting off charges of making uninvited sexual advances to women. In 1995 he resigned from Congress, brought down by a ten-volume report documenting "sordid, grossly embarrassing sexual and official misconduct." The nation was "treated" to evidence from Packwood's own diary, which detailed his financial and sexual misdeeds and described his "sense of 'Christian duty' to propose sex" to seemingly lonely women. Although we do not need elected representatives like Packwood any longer, public life nevertheless is enriched by leaders representing a diverse range of sexual values and experiences that express personality, build character, and make us wiser. For all the scandal that enveloped their lives, Barney Frank and Newt Gingrich contributed something of value to our national Congress.

This is the problem of unclean hands. Controversial sexual conduct and misconduct are so commonplace that the fingers of shame inevitably are pointed by men and women who themselves, by their own standards of judgment, have cause for shame.

Justification 3: The Right to Know

The call for sexual disclosures by public officials has been most plausible when grounded in a defensible set of assumptions, reviewed here, about the political morality of the right to know. The right to know is a right asserted both by members of the general public and by the press. The idea of the "public's right to know" is in essence the idea that people in a free society are entitled to be well informed. The right to know is the claim that society is obligated to adopt laws and promote practices that channel useful and important information to the general public.

Notwithstanding the language of "rights," the public's right to know is not reducible to one specific legal entitlement satisfied by one specific law, or to one specific moral entitlement satisfied by one specific act. In fact, it might be helpful to think of the public's right to know as a collection of several distinguishable *rights* to know, each with its own set of correlative obligations. The public's rights to know include the right to know how government conducts itself; the right to know how government officials and candidates for government office conduct themselves; the right of access to information contained in government files and records; the right to important information, both about current events and issues and about the history and achievements of the past, insofar as they bear on current events and issues; the right to know the opinions and ideas of fellows citizens; the right to know how public figures conduct themselves; the right to know how businesses and other nongovernmental entities receiving government aid or affecting the public welfare conduct themselves.

The idea that the public has a right to know encompassing some or all of these seven rights plays an important role in democratic political systems. In the ideal democracy, citizens are free and self-governing. Access to information enables each person to make the sound, independent judgments about matters of personal and collective concern that are required by responsible citizenship. Access to information also enables citizens to effectively evaluate and criticize government and the other institutions that affect public well being.

A free press, freedom of information statutes, public schools, public libraries, and consumer advocacy groups are some of the many institutions and practices that can fulfill societal obligations implied by the public's right to know. The role of the free press is especially noteworthy. Major media have taken on the professional responsibility of channeling news and information to the public. The American people, like people in countries the world over, are vitally dependent upon their newspapers, radios, televisions, and computers to keep them informed. The media have invested heavily in court battles to vindicate publications and investigative tactics that they believe are warranted by the public's right to know.

By tradition, the principle of freedom of the press, enshrined in the United States in the First Amendment of the federal Constitution, is closely associated with the idea of the public's right to know. The American media have staked out turf as the constitutionally empowered defenders of the public's right to know. The law books are filled with cases of newspapers, magazines, and television networks seeking judicial approval for the acquisition, publication, or investigation of family, medical, sexual, employment, or financial information others deem appropriately private. The impossibility of drawing a fine line between entertainment and news on the one hand, and the personal and the commercial on the other, complicates deciding whether the public's right to know justifies private invasions of the sorts just described.

The idea of the right to know includes the right of access to officials and candidates for public office. It is widely agreed that government officials are accountable to the general public for their official acts and misconduct while in office. Like officials, candidates for high office may be required to disclose financial and medical information to the public so that their fitness and suitability for office can be judged. The price of accountability for public officials and candidates for office is very high and can include justifiable, but humiliating, sexual privacy losses. As previously noted, former United States Senator Robert Packwood was forced to open his personal diaries to public scrutiny in proceedings to oust him for sexual and financial improprieties. Other members of Congress accused of inappropriate sex with teenagers, sexual harassment, and sexually motivated nepotism have faced humiliating public exposure of what they considered their personal lives. Yet exposure is called for by the ideal of the well-informed polity when sexual intimacies are inextricably commingled with public responsibilities.

"Commingling" Invites Accountability

One school of thought maintains that, when it comes to high public officials, virtually every aspect of their lives is a matter of legitimate public concern, simply because they are officials. The ideal of the transparent public official is defended by appeal to the values of accountability and trust. The assumption made is that the public can better trust officials who are utterly accountable—who have no significant secrets and who are willing to account for all aspects of their personal and professional lives.

Trust, "a fragile good" according to Sissela Bok, is an issue for American democracy. The men and women elected to public office are supposed to represent the interests of their constituencies. The public needs to be able to trust elected and appointed officials to do what they are elected to do. The Vietnam War, the Watergate affair, the Iran-Contra affair, and the Clinton-Lewinsky affair all illustrate that the president and his closest advisors cannot be trusted absolutely. They are capable of crimes, cover-ups, omissions, and outright lies. Outside of Washington, politicians and officials disappoint as well. They lie, distort, steal, cheat on their spouses, sexually harass women, demean minorities, abuse drugs and alcohol, evade taxes, accept bribes, hire undocumented workers, and they even assault, plot to kill and—occasionally—actually kill their adversaries.

It is hard to quantify trust or to say just how much trust the U.S. political order requires to remain effective and legitimate. Ascertaining the amount of trust Americans actually place in officials is not easy. Polls only reach a small segment of the population, and the answers people give to pollsters may overstate or understate their actual feelings. On the one hand, several trends could suggest a perilously low level of trust in government: the tone of political discourse is often cynical; the number of people interested in engaging in serious political discussion is small; voter turnout is low, compared to that in other democracies; and antigovernment activism is flourishing. On the other hand, I suspect the vast majority of people living in the United States would say that government is legitimate and effective and that they can rely on it. It does reliably offer them security and services worth having. Although it is commonplace to interpret low voter turnout as a sign of disenchantment and disengagement with politics, one might also read it as evidence that those entitled to vote actually do trust that the candidates will adequately serve their needs. Indeed, I believe that most people in the United States, despite their sometimes vociferous complaints, feel very secure with their government. They do not necessarily believe that all public officials are always ethical and fair, but they do believe that they are, on the whole, mostly ethical and fair enough.

Another school of thought—the one with which I identify—argues for accountability as a response to the need for trust but defends a reserve of privacy for public officials, on the grounds that opportunities for privacy are the moral and social needs of everyone. The difficulty facing the perspective that officials should be opaque rather than transparent is the need to decide what information should be off-limits. Matters of health are usually considered private, but these may affect the public assessment of fitness for office. Matters of marriage and child rearing are considered private, but these may affect public assessment of character and judgment, properties valued in public employees and especially in high public officials.

Rather than defining any category of information as off-limits, I believe we should look to whether the official has commingled what are often considered private realms with realms of public responsibility. If there is inextricable commingling of realms, as there was in the Packwood case and in Paula Jones' lawsuit against President Clinton, a detailed scrutiny of sexuality and sex may be called for, notwithstanding privacy concerns.

I believe the quality of our democratic government is diminished if public officials are not accountable for their sex lives and if our leaders expend their time and energy pursuing and concealing countless sexual affairs. I also believe that some potentially good leaders refuse to serve because they fear destruction of their private lives; leaders dedicate public institutions and financial resources to investigating and prosecuting sexual "improprieties" that are not—or should not be—crimes; and the general public is asked to evaluate, but cannot talk about, the sex lives of public officials because of fundamental disagreements about the content of law, morality, and etiquette.

It seems clear, therefore, that from now on public officials must work hard to create subjectively meaningful private lives and to protect their own privacy while at the same time acting on William Galston's assumption that "every aspect of their lives may become widely known." Some officials will do just that. Many public officials will create and protect privacy by studied conformity, that is, leading lives that do not require extraordinary concealment. They will marry, be faithful, have children by their spouses, and so on. A few in public life will opt to protect privacy by open nonconformity. They will live their lives as they please, but they will do so openly, so that outsiders cannot sensationalize what would otherwise be secrets and lies. A few public officials will opt for intelligent forms of secret nonconformity. They will experience sexual freedom, but only among well-chosen close friends and lovers on whose loyalty and confidence they can count, even when relationships sour. And then there will be the few who will be reckless with their sexual privacy, repeating the mistakes President Clinton was accused of making with Paula Jones and Monica Lewinsky. When the reckless are exposed, they can try the "no-comment denial" or admit impropriety and try to move on. Congressman Gary Condit took this latter route, but not before initially denying an affair with Chandra Levy. Like President Clinton, he tried the lie first.

Should Officials Lie?

My claim has been that officials can be highly accountable for their personal or private lives, including sexual intimacies, notwithstanding the value of privacy. But this is not to say that officials are not sometimes justified in thwarting others' efforts to make them accountable for information, explanations, or sanctions. Isn't deception the antithesis of accountability? In the realm of sexual privacy, we are quite often justified in thwarting others' efforts to obtain information, elicit explanation, and punish. Indeed, we are justified in lying to protect sexual privacy. But are public officials ever justified in using deception? I think they might be, in instances in which the press or general public probes sexuality that has not been commingled with professional responsibilities, or not inextricably so.

Lying to protect privacy is not always a morally acceptable departure from the general principle of truthfulness.[26] For example, when the supposed "sexual privacy" at issue concerns rape, incest, child molestation, sexual harassment, or exploitation, privacy is no excuse or justification for lying. Any plausible defense of lying to protect privacy will have to be qualified.

A qualified defense of lying to protect sexual privacy is consistent with the widespread moral belief and religious doctrine that lying sometimes is a morally justifiable response to others' seeking of information to which they have no right. Lying to a would-be murderer about the whereabouts of the would-be victim hoping thereby to thwart a crime is the right thing to do. Lying to the unjust, however, is not always the morally best alternative. Lying to a would-be "busybody" to thwart an ordinary invasion of privacy in everyday life may not be the right thing to do either. A passenger on a train has no right to ask a stranger traveling with a child whether the child was adopted. And yet, because of the importance for children of knowing the truth about their origins and feeling good about who they are, the stranger may be obligated to answer truthfully and cheerfully. In instances in which lying in response to prying is the morally best response, it is due to the fundamental importance of certain forms of privacy.

A defense of lying to protect sexual privacy is based on the premise that privacy is a human need and moral entitlement akin to freedom and equality. Three decades of reflection and observation by philosophers and psychologists inform this premise. In the North American context, privacy is not a mere luxury or an optional good. Lying about sex has evolved as one way well-meaning people from all walks of life cope with the interplay of conflicting physical, emotional, and social imperatives. Therefore, lying about sex is something Americans should not condemn too quickly or categorically.

Lying Is Ordinary

Broadly defined, lying includes intentional falsification and deceitful concealment.[27] To lie is to make false statements or to conceal the truth knowingly, voluntarily, and with an intent to deceive. So defined, lying is a perfectly ordinary event.[28] People lie all the time. Liars lie, but they are not alone. Ordinary people who value and practice a high degree of honesty also lie. Some highly regarded professionals lie as a seeming requirement of their work.[29] Physicians and nurses lie to patients to ease their distress. Social psychologists lie to research subjects in studies of human behavior. Law enforcement officials lie to criminal suspects to encourage cooperation and collect evidence. Diplomats and government bureaucrats lie to gain advantage over foreign governments in international affairs. Lawyers lawfully conceal truths unfavorable to their clients, for indeed, in the adversary system, "the very institutional framework of a legal system may be used to hide the truth. . . ."

The frequency and significance of deception is not the same in every segment of the population or for all personality types, but men, women, and children of all cultural and economic backgrounds lie. Women, who typically engage in a greater number of social interactions than men, may lie more often than men.[30] Small children may lie more often than typical adults. Lying and related forms of deception "appear to be normal rather than abnormal, a workaday attribute of practical intelligence."[31] People who lie too much or too little strike us as unkind. Studies suggest that average Americans will admit to telling at least a couple of lies a day, and actually tell more. Lying is frequent and pervasive because it works. Lying works because even experienced lie detectors can distinguish lies from truth only about half the time.[32] Not all lies work, though. There are many reasons why lies fail. Our lies fail because they are discovered or we give ourselves away through facial expression, demeanor, or outright confession.[33]

The Truth-Telling Bias in Western Ethics

Despite the prevalence of lying, western moral traditions generally advocate truth telling over lying. Secular moralists and theologians have written extensively about the ideal and actual ethics of lying.[34] The Catholic theological tradition consistently regards lying as a grave sin. The Catholic doctrine does, however, appear to allow some untruthful assertions on certain occasions. The Jesuits are often associated with the doctrine of "mental reservation." This permits one to speak falsely or misleadingly, so long as one makes a mental note of the truth. The standard example of when this doctrine may apply is the situation in which a murderer comes to your door looking for someone you know to be at home. When asked if the intended victim is at home, it is permissible to say that the intended victim is not, as long as you make a mental note that what you really mean is that the intended victim is at home, but not for the purposes of the murderer. The Catholic teaching is that you may lie or equivocate in this situation because the truth is sought by someone whose unjust intentions deny him or her the right to it.

Immanuel Kant advocated an absolute, categorical duty to speak the truth without regard to the consequences.[35] He rejected the notion that it is just to lie to the unjust, pointing out that an outcome worse than the one the liar hoped to avert could come about as a consequence of the lie. For example, suppose you tell the murderer that the intended victim is not at home, hoping to mislead the murderer and send the murderer on his or her way. Unknown to you, the victim is climbing out of a side window, hoping to escape while you distract the murderer. Relying on your lie, the murderer leaves the house, encounters the victim attempting to escape, and kills the victim. Had you told the truth, the murderer might have come inside to search the house, giving the victim time to complete an escape.

Most contemporary philosophers who have taken up the subject of lying—
F. G. Bailey, Sissela Bok, Christine Korsgaard, David Nyberg, Alasdair Mac-
Intyre, and Mary Mothersill, to name a very few—have argued that the
wrongness of lying is to some extent contingent upon the circumstances.[36]
They typically conclude that, although lying is sometimes justifiable, the better moral principle is that we should strive toward the highest possible
degrees of honesty in our public and private lives. We should be honest in
dealings with our friends, families, coworkers, fellow citizens, and government. We should also be honest with ourselves. In everyday life, judgments
about the morality of particular instances of lying seem to depend upon who
is doing the lying (e.g., a friend, a child, a thief), what the lying concerns
(e.g., sex, health, business), and who is being lied to (e.g., a dying patient, a
judge, a racketeer).

Why is truth telling better as a rule than lying? Philosophers have argued that
individuals should avoid lies to promote knowledge of the truth about ourselves
and others in important relationships, to show respect for moral persons' dignity as rational human beings, and to achieve integrity and self-respect. Experts
also contend that "society is better if truth-telling prevails as the rule in public
and private affairs,"[37] for truth telling encourages the trust that is a basis for mutual reliance in commerce, government, social life, and families.

Motives for Lying

If truth telling is so valuable, why do people lie? And why is all lying not
clearly wrong? There appear to be a number of distinct reasons or motives for
lying. Accounting for why people lie has been a recurrent concern of philosophers. Motives matter to philosophers' moral assessment of lying because
"we react very differently to identical actions if we believe that they arise
from very different motives."[38] It is one thing to lie to prevent a murder, but
it is something else to lie simply to pad a bank account. Accounting for why
people lie has also been a subject of particular interest to social psychologists.[39] After extensive empirical studies of adults' and children's motives for
lying, researcher Paul Ekman compiled a list of nine different reasons people
lie. According to Ekman, the most common reasons people lie are to avoid
punishment and to obtain rewards. People also lie to protect others from punishment, to protect themselves and others from the threat of physical harm, to
win admiration, to get out of an awkward social situation, to avoid embarrassment, to maintain privacy, and to exercise power over others. Of special
interest to this chapter is the eighth reason on Ekman's list: people lie to maintain their privacy. Philosopher David Nyberg has also expressly recognized
the privacy motive, noting: "we have learned to use deception . . . to gain and
protect privacy."[40]

Lying to maintain privacy is a complex motive, for there are several distinguishable dimensions of privacy a person might seek to secure through deception. Dimensions of physical, informational, decisional, and proprietary privacy all can be furthered by lying. An adulterer like President Clinton might lie, first, to conceal his affair; second, to conceal the trysts themselves; third, to maintain a sense of independence—a sense of being free, autonomous, and able to make one's own decisions about sex, love, and intimacy without unwanted interference; and fourth, to preserve dignitarian interests and any economic interests in his good name and reputation. Three of the four dimensions of privacy protected by the lying adulterer merit further comment.

First, a person might lie, for better or for worse, to maintain informational privacy. The person might lie seeking to keep private some confidential or secret information about a sexual relationship, as in the case of President Clinton; information about a medical ailment, as in the case of tennis great Arthur Ashe, who managed to conceal his AIDS from the public for some time; or information about financial affairs, as in the case of the former Secretary of Housing and Urban Development, Henry Cisneros, who lied to the FBI in a background check about tens of thousands of dollars he paid to an ex-mistress. People also lie to protect the privacy of information about their families, as in the bizarre case of Judge James Ware of San Jose, who hid information about his uninteresting family background. Judge Ware repeatedly lied in professional settings, claiming that as a child living in Alabama he had suffered through a vicious hate crime perpetrated against his brother. At first, Judge Ware lied to gain sympathy and attention rather than informational privacy, but then, as time passed, he needed to continue his lies to keep the truth of his dull background from being exposed. Former Labor Secretary Robert Reich tactfully lied about the miserably low esteem in which he held others while he served in the Clinton administration. Only after the publication of his notoriously inaccurate tell-all book, *Locked in the Cabinet*, did the bulk of his former Washington associates learn Reich's true impressions.[41]

Second, lies can protect opportunities for physical privacy, like solitude and trysts. When President Clinton told White House staff members that he was receiving Ms. Lewinsky into the Oval Office to examine the papers or accept the pizza she pretended to deliver, lying was a way of getting time alone for intimacy.

Third and finally, lying can be motivated by a desire to conceal and facilitate independent choices relating to aspects of life that we usually tag "private." People commonly lie to protect their independence. In constitutional law, privacy often signifies independence or autonomy. Philosophers and psychologists who talk about lying to protect independence often have in mind the very same things that we in the legal community have in mind when we talk about the decisional privacy of the abortion choice or the decisional privacy of a terminally ill patient electing to terminate life support. President Clinton's lies to friends and aides about the nature of his relationship with Ms. Lewinsky were designed to allow him the freedom to continue a relationship of which he knew most others would disapprove on moral or prudential grounds.

I am primarily interested in the most self-focused kind of lying for privacy—lying to protect one's own privacy. It is worth noting, however, that people also lie to protect the privacy of others. They lie attempting to conceal facts about others' affairs. President Clinton's secretary, Betty Currie, may have done this. We lie sometimes to protect our friends, members of our families, or our lovers. We may also lie because we believe that we have a professional duty to guard zealously the confidentiality of personal, business, legal, and medical information about other people.

Public Figures and Public Officials: A Comparison

People lie about sex. Indeed, as the television comedians say, people lie during sex. That people lie to avoid disclosure of facts about their sex lives and to enjoy sexual independence is a reality observed in everyday life that psychologists have studied and confirmed. In light of the current diverse mix of sexual mores, public officials may decide that carefully concealing their sex lives is essential to the freedom and intimacy they understandably crave. Immediately after President Clinton confirmed his improper relationship with Monica Lewinsky, Americans were eager to understand two rather remarkable phenomena: that intelligent people who know they will be scrutinized undertake the kinds of sex lives about which they will probably have to lie, and that these same intelligent people sometimes lie in such sloppy and public ways that their lies can be uncovered easily and with disastrous consequences.

A famous lecturer, wit, and playwright, Oscar Wilde had a complex and troubling sex life.[42] He was married and fathered children by his wife, Constance. While married, he undertook a series of three homosexual relationships with other artists. He also engaged in sex and sex play (voyeurism) with numerous other men. Wilde lied to his wife and many of his associates about his sexual practices. Wilde was remarkably reckless about the lies he told, lies that might otherwise have vouchsafed his identity and freedom. On the one hand, he often made efforts to keep his illicit romantic and sexual affairs secret, particularly from his wife and children. On the other hand, he freely and openly associated with well-known homosexuals, with advocates of homosexual tolerance at Oxford, and with notorious and flamboyant homosexuals and indiscreet young male prostitutes in London and abroad.

Wilde's lies can be looked upon with great empathy, given the severe legal penalties for open homosexuality in Wilde's time. Why, however, was Wilde willing to risk criminal prosecution? Why was he not deterred by the harshness of the law? It was fairly safe, if one was discreet, to be an educated, upper-class homosexual. Wilde knew that most homosexuals were not exposed and prosecuted in London. More importantly, Wilde may have felt that sexual risks were worth taking if they allowed him to live more authentically. His identity and freedom were diminished by a life restricted to conventional heterosexual marriage.

While still officially denying homosexuality, Wilde virtually abandoned his wife and children in favor of living with the handsome, petulant, and self-centered poet, Lord Alfred Douglas. Douglas's father, the Marquess of Queensberry, disapproved of his son's relationship with Wilde and demanded in vain that Wilde break things off. Prodded by Lord Douglas, Wilde took lying about sex to extraordinary heights when he brought a defamation action against Queensberry.

Wilde's great folly was to sue a powerful opponent and to bring libel charges that he could only defend by easily disproved lies. The libel allegations focused on a hateful note Douglas's father scrawled on the back of a card left for Wilde at Wilde's club. Queensberry and his lawyers maintained that the Marquess's note described Wilde as a man "posing as a Somdomite [sic]."[43] So far as Wilde and Lord Douglas were concerned, the note condemned Wilde as a sodomite. In defamation actions, truth is obviously a defense. The Marquess's lawyers had no trouble rounding up male prostitutes willing to testify against Wilde. They secured hotel staff willing to testify to finding men in Wilde's bed and fecal stains on Wilde's bed sheets. Thus, Wilde's futile attempt at a face-saving lawsuit against Queensberry led to his conviction for sodomy and a sentencing to two grueling years of hard labor, a sentence that broke his health and ruined and shortened his life.

With lies we desperately try to preserve our freedom and our identities—our actual identities rather than the masks we must wear as a price of admission to conventional mainstream society. Wilde went too far in trying to protect his life as an eccentric gay artist, much as President Clinton went too far in trying to protect his life as a daring ladies' man. Clinton recklessly engaged in a clandestine extramarital sexual affair with Lewinsky and then boldly lied about that fact on national television and in private meetings with his closest friends and confidants. Like Wilde, Clinton allowed himself to become smitten with a self-centered young lover and then entrusted his remarkable and historic career to an immature lover's judgment. Like Wilde, Clinton wound up hurting and embarrassing his family by an affair with a beautiful, younger, and less gifted person. Like Wilde, Clinton sought to turn the truth tellers, whom he regarded as having inappropriately pried and distorted the truth, into moral monsters. Wilde literally put Queensberry on trial, and Clinton tried, with some success, to put Kenneth Starr and the Republican Congress on trial in the minds of the American people. Like Wilde, Clinton temporarily sought refuge in technical definitions of sexual conduct in an effort to escape the law. Clinton denied a "sexual relationship" with "that woman" on national television because he could honestly say he never had experienced full penetration penile-vaginal intercourse with Lewinsky. Wilde denied that he was a sodomite because he could honestly say that he did not practice penile-anal intercourse with Lord Douglas.

To lie about sex in such a fashion, a person must possess character traits and status not shared by everyone. Perhaps one has to feel and be very powerful and enjoy taking risks. But, perhaps, as I believe, one need only have a very strong urge to be the genuine person behind the masks donned for public roles and private responsibilities. Wilde emerges as more sympathetic than Clinton because conventional morality increasingly regards legally enforced homophobia as unjust but continues to regard monogamy as a legitimate requirement of marriage. A recent film version of Wilde's life paints Wilde sympathetically as a tragic hero, a gifted genius in love with someone who did not deserve his love. Similarly, *Primary Colors*, a veiled film version of Clinton's presidential campaign, paints Clinton as a tragic hero, a brilliant communicator with a pathetic weakness for illicit sex and greasy food.

Privacy and the Fixation of Meaning

We must grapple with the following question: if you take privacy seriously, don't you have to make a virtue out of telling lies to protect privacy?[44] Shall we ascribe a right to lie in response to prying, snooping, and prejudiced questions; a right to lie to protect information about, and distortions of, the details of our sexual practices? Shall we extend that right to public officials and public figures to the same extent as ordinary citizens and resist the temptation to dismiss the problem quickly with the fiction that public officials and public figures "waive" their rights to privacy by thrusting themselves into the limelight?

Sometimes we lie because we do not expect other people to appreciate what we regard as our true identities and the private lives in which our true identities emerge. Sometimes we lie because telling the truth can lead to rejection, ridicule, censure, or punishment. Lying can keep the world out and allow us to escape the offensive meanings others assign to our conduct. It may be easier to say, "I'm allergic to shellfish," a lie, than to reveal that one belongs to a religious minority reviled as a radical vegetarian cult. It may be easier to say, "I'm not a lesbian" when one is indeed a lesbian than to invite disapproval, rejection, or even beatings.

Keeping conduct private is a way to escape having to see oneself in the shameful, hateful, and ridiculous terms in which others may see us. Although nearly every adult engages in some type of sexual activity, we all have unique combinations of acts, habits, emotions, language, styles, props, and tastes that are our own. Disclosure of our sexual selves could undercut our ability to be our sexual selves. Disclosure may make the sexual conduct or partnerships we once enjoyed impractical. Disclosure may subject us to shame and ridicule or decrease our ability to experience joy and intimacy our way. After the Starr Report and the impeachment, it is unlikely that Clinton will ever again enjoy the role of Monica Lewinsky's cigar-toting lover, "Handsome," without feeling ridiculous.

These considerations about the importance of privacy and sexual expression help explain what is going on when powerful men seek refuge in technical definitions of sex in lieu of truth telling. They are trying to fight off the imposition of others' interpretations of their identities and conduct. Oscar Wilde denied that he was a sodomite because he wanted to disassociate himself from the negative connotations of homosexuality in the minds of those who disapproved of it and were disgusted by it. He disliked the derogatory meanings others in his society brought to their understandings of homosexuality: depravity, filth, frivolity, and godlessness. In his own mind, he was participating in the "New Aestheticism," a realm of intellectual and spiritual beauty higher than ethics itself. For him, intimacy with young men was not reducible to particular sexual acts or to fecal stains on a sheet. These "Greek" relationships, as he understood them, were part intellectual, part aesthetic, part pedagogical, part paternal, and part erotic. The parts formed an inseparable whole. Wilde felt as though Queensberry, who sought him out at a theater and club, was intentionally destroying his private life. Wilde wrote to a friend that his "whole life seems ruined by this man. The tower of ivory is assailed by the foul thing. On the sand is my life spilt."[45] Wilde lied because he was unable through force of character and art to persuade an entire society of what he thought was the true nature and significance of his relationships with men, and because he was unable to get his wife, the world, or Queensberry to see these relationships' true meaning and his true identity. Wilde lied to keep his private world and his self-esteem intact. He did not enjoy the lies that he repeated to his own lawyer, but they seemed necessary.

President Clinton lied because he believed there was no postfeminist interpretation of his extramarital affair with a young intern that the public would accept uncritically. His relationship could be construed as the sexual exploitation of a young female subordinate, or worse, as sexual harassment, Paula Jones-style. For Clinton, I conjecture, the meaning of his affair was harmless and represented consensual titillation, sexual gratification, fun, diversion, and friendship. Lying was an effort to preserve a private domain in which those meanings of the affair could flourish. I have known nonmonogamous married couples who lied to most acquaintances about their arrangements because they did not expect other people to understand the real meaning of their conduct—whether loyal, liberating, fun, expressive, intimacy-expanding, or experimental. Indeed, despite all the talk of Bill lying to Hillary and betraying her, for all we know, the President and his wife shared a private "meaning community" in which affairs were allowed and not considered a breach of their mutual commitments.

Given the importance of privacy and sexual privacy just described, is it always morally permissible to lie to someone making inquiries about one's sex life? The answer is surely no. Parents, spouses, and partners may, by virtue of their responsibilities and our commitments to them, have a right to know the details of our sex lives. A more plausible principle than "one has a right to lie in response to all inquiries into one's sex life" is the principle that "one has a right to lie in response to all unjustified inquiries into one's sex life." Nonetheless, even this principle seems too strong and too simplistic. What inquiries will be unjustified? Consider an example involving sexual harassment. In the context of sexual harassment in the workplace, for example, rebuffing rude, invasive questions with falsifications seems morally acceptable. Are you busy tonight? Is your husband out of town? Do you like dirty movies? You know how to show a guy a good time, right? In the above situation, falsification would seem appropriate and certainly not unethical.

Suppose, however, you are a gay man on an airplane and you strike up a conversation with the stranger next to you who asks if you are gay. Further, suppose you are a straight black woman and the person beside you asks if you date white men, not as a come-on, but because he wants to know more about your social perspectives solely for purposes of the conversation. Perhaps the right thing to do in these cases is to answer honestly, but then explain that you believe posing such questions is akin to prying. From the perspective of progressive liberals, proudly affirming homosexuality and racial tolerance when one can do so safely better serves the truth teller and his or her society.

What if you are a candidate for a seat on the Supreme Court and you are asked by the Senate Judiciary Committee whether you enjoy viewing sexual pornography? Should you answer truthfully? This highly personal question seems improper when put exclusively to the second black man in history with a chance at a seat on the Supreme Court. Refusal to answer could be read as an admission, equaling "sudden death" for the candidate. Denial may be the ambitious candidate's only practical option. A judicial candidate ought not to have to reveal his or her sexual tastes, particularly lawful ones, to others as a condition of holding a public office. No one has a right to such information. It is not self-evident, however, that one therefore has a right to lie, that one ought to lie, or that lying is more ethical under the circumstances than refusing to answer or telling the truth. Willingness to speak the truth, even when it is embarrassing, damaging, and sought without good cause, may be a self-destructive virtue we expect of public officials.

The morality of the situation is not self-evident; the psychology, however, is. In the past, we were reared to expect that we could properly do certain things in private without public accountability. When the privacy ethics under which we are reared clash with a novel tell-all ethic of hardball politics and mass media journalism, we are unsettled. We may find ourselves unable to humiliate and shame ourselves with truth telling. We may lie as a result, and who really can blame us? I believe Justice Clarence Thomas did all of the things Anita Hill alleged; however, I do not entirely blame him for not acknowledging it to the Senate.[46]

It is easy to understand, and, therefore hard to fault, some lying. Lying is an ordinary strategy. We all know it. This is why the public did not turn en masse against President Clinton. He should not have had the affair, but his efforts to cover it up with lies to friends, family, and strangers are what you would expect from someone who stands to lose so much self-esteem and prestige. Regrettably for the president, his transparent lies caused Mr. Starr to seek very intimate details of his sexual habits to disprove his story and, once those details were collected, Starr made the case that they should be revealed to the public. But who among us could easily bear, with grace, having the raw details of his or her sex life exposed for all to read about?

An important issue raised by the Clinton impeachment was whether the president lied under oath. In a secular legal system, oath taking is symbolic. Few Americans today believe, as their common-law predecessors may have, that they place their mortal souls on the line by making false statements under oath. It should not be surprising then, given the functions of privacy, that people will lie, mislead others, and omit facts to maintain privacy, even under oath. Ironically, a person threatened with having her intimate life scrutinized in an official government forum has the greatest incentive of all to attempt the good lie. We should expect lies, omissions, equivocations, dissembling, and so on of persons rightly or wrongly put in such a situation.

Many legal doctrines recognize that requiring people to be truthful about matters they deem very private compromises privacy interests and invites dissimulation. One of the goals of the Fifth Amendment right against self-incrimination is the protection of privacy. The attorney–client, physician–patient, clergy–penitent, psychotherapist–patient, and spousal privileges all have goals of protecting the privacy of individuals. In 1998, the Supreme Court narrowed the "exculpatory no" doctrine, which immunized from criminal liability persons who make certain false statements.[47] The surviving doctrine presupposes the temptation to lie when the truth will almost surely lead to prosecution and conviction.

I am reluctant to describe the Clinton-Lewinsky affair as substantially exploitative of Ms. Lewinsky. First, exploitation is a matter of degree. To a degree, Clinton exploited Lewinsky. To a degree, Lewinsky also exploited Clinton and the members of his staff whom she pressured to grant her special privileges and access, even to the detriment of their own careers and morals. Lewinsky was aggressive and persistent in her raunchy and romantic relationship with Clinton. Yet, the "casting couch" is no longer a young woman's only route to a rewarding career. Lewinsky knew that she was not required to have sex with the president to obtain or retain employment in government service or in the corporate sector. The second reason is that the public does not know, cannot know, and should not know enough about the president's sexual relationship with Ms. Lewinsky to declare its content as exploitative. The kinky encounters described in the Starr Report sound like encounters lots of people in peer relationships enjoy.

When philosophers assert that lies by public officials erode trust, they are resting on a time-honored axiom that workable cooperative enterprises require participants to be truthful, trustworthy, and reliable. The axiom is doubtless true, but it does not entail that workable cooperative enterprises will fall apart if leaders are sometimes not truthful about matters of direct relevance to their official duties. In addition, it certainly does not entail that workable cooperative enterprises must fall apart if leaders are sometimes not truthful about matters that the public may deem tangential to their official duties, such as sex, and that are well understood as matters in which moral failure and lapses in judgment are ordinary and predictable. I am suggesting that the conclusion that lying about sex erodes trust in public officials overlooks how much the U.S. public of today and yesterday understands and discounts sex and privacy-related deception.[50]

Secrecy and deception about national programs and policies are components of presidential power. Many presidents, including some of the greatest presidents, falsified and concealed important personal facts from the American people during their terms in office.[51] Some believe Thomas Jefferson's secret was Sally Hemings, a black slave by whom he allegedly sired a child; Grover Cleveland's secret was an out-of-wedlock son he took responsibility for named Oscar, whose mother Cleveland had committed to an insane asylum; Warren Harding's secret was a mistress smuggled into White House closets for sex, and their daughter, Elizabeth Ann, whom Harding declined ever to see or to support; Woodrow Wilson's secrets were dyslexia, a series of strokes, and an extramarital affair with Mary Peck; Franklin Roosevelt's secrets were a mistress and a bout with polio that left him completely unable to walk; John F. Kennedy's secrets were addictions to prescription drugs and sex; and Ronald Reagan's secret, sadly visible before he left office, was Alzheimer's disease.

Sissela Bok raises the following series of key questions.[52] She asks: "Why . . . should lying to the public not be . . . legitimate, in cases of persistent and intrusive probing? What is it that turns an official's lie to the public into a matter of public concern, no matter how rightfully private the subject of the lie itself?" Her answer is that "the credibility of public officials is crucial in a democracy." Bok further states that "[a]ppeals to privacy can be exploited to cover up wrongdoing just as much as national security can . . . ." Moreover, she makes the slippery-slope argument that lies lead to further lies, lies by the liar and lies by those who emulate the liar. Bok states finally: "when distrust becomes too overpowering within a family, a community or a nation, it becomes impossible to meet joint needs." Addressing the duties of public officials in this area, Bok finds that in exchange for the privileges that they have been granted, "public servants, doctors, clergy, lawyers, bankers, journalists and other professionals have a special responsibility" to "consider to what extent their actions erode or help restore this social good of trust."

Bok's most powerful argument is that, for the sake of trust, public officials have a special obligation to avoid deception regarding their private lives, even when their private lives have been perhaps unjustly probed. Notice that Bok rejects the justice-of-lying-to-the-unjust principle as applied to public officials. She also avoids the fiction that public figures waive privacy and expectations of privacy by thrusting themselves into the limelight. My response to Bok is to agree that trust is vital, but to disagree that trust in government hinges crucially on officials never lying to protect privacy. In some contexts, "deliberate deception need not in general pose a significant threat to trust."[53] This is not to say that we should take pride in lies and liars, particularly those whose reckless behavior greatly affects the efficiency of two branches of the national government and subjects our nation to ridicule. We should, however, take pride in our capacity for empathetic understanding of the realm of sexuality as a realm of propriety and impropriety, of a mixture of communal and self-defined modes of intimacy and expression that may or may not conform to social expectations. A significant segment of the public appears to accept the notion that a president is justified in lying to protect the privacy of his or her family.

I defend the right of presidents and other public officials to have private lives sometimes defended by deception. This is not to advocate lying on national television and under oath without conscience and concern for consequences. Privacy is a context for correcting, as well as making, sexually related mistakes. Suppose an official has an extramarital affair, confesses it to his or her spouse in private, and begins to rebuild their marriage in earnest. To deny the affair to the public in an effort to avoid further damage to a marriage is not plainly immoral, and not plainly the kind of deception that, if found out, would significantly erode public trust in government or invite more lies.

In a best-selling practical guide to truth telling in personal relationships, Dr. Harriet Lerner asserts that people seek privacy primarily to protect their dignity and ultimate separateness as human beings, rather than to fool others or engage in acts of deception.[54] For this reason, she argues, we can proudly speak of and exercise our rights to privacy. When it comes to lying to protect privacy, however, Lerner's neat dichotomy breaks apart, for in these contexts, we seek both to fool and to protect our dignity and separateness.

Adrienne Rich suggests that even lying justified by an appeal to privacy can be a product of cowardice and an attempt to "short-cut through another's personality."[55] Because of his manipulative behavior and his cowardice, I do not defend President Clinton's handling of his private life. In my estimation, Clinton was wrong to involve himself with Lewinsky in the shadow of the Paula Jones case, in the corridors of the White House, and in the context of a very public marriage. Having walked on the "Wilde" side, he was wrong to go further down that road by desperately and pathetically using the public airwaves and government employees to further his deception. It was almost as if the president thought he was a private citizen lying to a gullible spouse behind closed doors, circa 1958, rather than the most watched and investigated man on the planet lying to the planet in 1998.

CONCLUSION

Accountability for sex requires openness and honesty. It is difficult to speak openly about sex, although doing so has recently gotten easier and become more acceptable. Tune into television and be amazed by what the stand-up comics will say. Consider the success of *The Vagina Monologues*. But it is one thing to speak openly about sex for purposes of art, entertainment, and amusement, and something else to speak openly about sex when called upon by a disappointed partner or probing journalist to reveal one's own sexual conduct. Accountability for sex implies judgment by others whose morality and tastes may cause them to judge us about dimensions of the irrational self that it is most painful to have judged. But in a society that offers ample opportunities for sexual inaccessibility it is not intolerable that people in foreseeable circumstances over which they have some control be held accountable for harmful sex-related conduct. Our lives are dominated by our work, and we take our sexuality with us wherever we go—whether we are office workers, priests, or politicians. For government to be trustworthy, it must show respect for the privacy of ordinary citizens and public officials.[56] Likewise, ordinary citizens and public officials, because we all run this nation together, must strive to make honesty in their public roles and private lives a priority. Lying can undermine trust and render information unreliable. Until the links among sex talk, sexually hostile workplaces, sexual harassment, and sexual favoritism are broken, there is no alternative to public accountability for workplace-related sex.

Public officials are accountable to the press and the public; officials who unwisely mix business with intimate pleasure must accept scrutiny of their sex lives. They are not justified in lying to protect their sexual privacy in such circumstances, though they might be justified in lying to avoid disclosures concerning their sexuality that are unrelated to office. The public has no right to know about the remote infidelities and romances of political candidates or office holders. Probing into those attics and closets does harm to privacy without good justification. Probing into current sex lives is limited by the principle of commingling. For high-ranking national officials, there will very often be a credible nexus between responsibility and personal life, even in the absence of impropriety or misconduct. For typical public officials, however, there rarely is.

NOTES

1. Catharine A. MacKinnon, "The Logic of Experience: Reflections on the Development of Sexual Harassment Law," *Georgetown Law Journal* 90 (March 2002): 832.

2. An earlier version of my critique of Rosen appeared as "The Wanted Gaze: Accountability for Privacy Invasions at Work," *Georgetown Law Review* 89 (2001): 2013–28.

3. Jeffrey Rosen, "Fall of Private Man," *New Republic* 12 June 2000, 22–29. Federal antidiscrimination statutes 42 U.S.C. § 2000e-2(a) (2000) govern all workplaces employing more than a few workers. Accordingly, "It shall be an unlawful employment practice for an employer . . . to fail or refuse to hire or to discharge any individual, or otherwise to discriminate against any individual with respect to his compensation, terms, conditions, or privileges of employment, because of such individual's race, color, religion, sex, or national origin; . . . ." *Civil Rights Act of 1964*, Title VII, 42 U.S.C. 2000e, P.L. 88–382.

4. Federal regulations define sexual harassment as "unwelcome sexual advances, requests for sexual favors, and other verbal or physical conduct of a sexual nature . . . when (1) submission to such conduct is made either explicitly or implicitly a term or condition of an individual's employment, (2) submission to or rejection of such conduct by an individual is used as the basis for employment decisions affecting such individual, or (3) such conduct has the purpose or effect of unreasonably interfering with an individual's work performance or creating an intimidating, hostile, or offensive working environment" [29 C.F.R. § 1604.11(a) (2000)]. See also "EEOC Policy Guidance on Current Issues of Sexual Harassment," *EEOC Compl. Man.* (BNA) 3 No. N-915-050, at 4031, 4033 (19 March 1990). A leading case, *Meritor Savings Bank v.*

Vinson, 477 U.S. 57, 65 (1986), recognized sexual harassment as a form of employment discrimination and hostile environment as a form of sexual harassment actionable under Title VII.

5. See Symposium, "Strengthening Title VII: 1997–1998 Sexual Harassment Jurisprudence," *William & Mary Bill of Rights Journal* 7 (1999): 671–76.

6. For an insightful discussion of feminist critiques of privacy, see Debra Morris, "Privacy, Privation, Perversity": Toward New Representation of the Personal, *Signs* 25 (2000): 323–52.

7. Jeffrey Rosen, *The Unwanted Gaze: The Destruction of Privacy in America* (New York: Random House, 2000), 8–9. See also Erving Goffman, *The Presentation of Self in Everyday Life* (New York: Doubleday, 1959).

8. Rosen, *Unwanted Gazes*, 8–9.

9. A number of legal scholars have attempted to explain how sexual harassment is harmful. Professor Katherine Franke, "What's Wrong with Sexual Harassment," *Stanford Law Review* 49 (1997): 691, 693, explains that sexual harassment is wrong because it embodies gender stereotypes. It is not wrong because it would not have taken place but for the plaintiff's sex, because it is sexual in nature, or because it sexually subordinates women to men. Professor Kathy Abrams, "The New Jurisprudence of Sexual Harassment," *Cornell Law Review* 83 (1998): 1169, 1218, argues: "sexual harassment disadvantages its victims as workers," and "may compel choices that trade professional advantage for a more secure or peaceful environment."

10. See Catharine Mackinnon, *Only Words* (Cambridge, U.K.: Harvard University Press, 1993), 64–68. Contrast Anita Hill's book, *Speaking Truth to Power* (New York: Anchor, 1997), describing her testimony in Congressional hearings on the nomination of Justice Clarence Thomas and its impact, with Michael Wines's article, "The Thomas Nomination: Compelling Evidence on Both Sides, but Only One Can Be Telling the Truth," *New York Times*, 15 October 1991, A20.

11. President William Jefferson Clinton settled for $850,000 a lawsuit brought by Paula Jones. Jones claimed that while he was governor of Arkansas, Clinton summoned her from her work to a private room in a Little Rock hotel, asked for sex, and exposed his penis. Following his acquittal in impeachment proceedings in the Senate, Judge Susan Webber Wright of the federal district court in Little Rock issued an order on 12 April 1999 holding Clinton in contempt of court for "false, misleading and evasive" testimony about his relationship with former White House intern Monica Lewinsky in his deposition in the Jones lawsuit. See "Excerpts from the Judge's Ruling," *New York Times*, 13 April 1999, A20.

12. But for the opposite opinion see Anita Bernstein, "Treating Sexual Harassment with Respect," *Harvard Law Review* 111 (1997): 445–527. Bernstein argues that hostile environment sexual harassment is a type of incivility or disrespect that merits a Title VII remedy.

13. Commentators question whether Title VII has provided an effective remedy in hostile environment cases. See, for example, Susan Estrich, "Sex at Work," *Stanford Law Review* 43 (1991): 856–61. Estrich maintains that courts were "slower to recognize hostile environments in the first instance, and are now more reluctant to impose liability for them."

14. Rosen, *Unwanted Gaze*, 21.

15. MacKinnon, *Only Words*, 66.

16. Anita L. Allen, *Uneasy Access: Privacy for Women in a Free Society* (Totowa, N.J.: Rowman & Littlefield, 1988). The invasion of privacy torts are: (1) Intrusion upon Seclusion ("One who intentionally intrudes, physically or otherwise, upon the solitude or seclusion of another or his private affairs or concerns, is subject to liability to the other for invasion of his privacy, if the intrusion would be highly offensive to a reasonable person"); (2) Appropriation of Name or Likeness ("One who appropriates to his own use or benefit the name or likeness of another is subject to liability to the other for invasion of his privacy"); (3) Publicity Given to Private Life ("One who gives publicity to a matter concerning the private life of another is subject to liability to the other for invasion of his privacy, if the matter publicized is of a kind that (a) would be highly offensive to a reasonable person, and (b) is not of legitimate concern to the public"); (4) Publicity Placing Person in False Light ("One who gives publicity to a matter concerning another that places the other before the public in a false light is subject to liability to the other for invasion of his privacy, if (a) the false light in which the other was placed would be highly offensive to a reasonable person, and (b) the actor had knowledge or acted in reckless disregard as to the falsity of the publicized matter and the false light in which the other would be placed"). American Law Institute, *Restatement (Second) of Torts*, § 652b–e (St. Paul, Mn.: American Law Institute Publishers, 1965).

17. Cf. Gillian K. Hadfield, "Rational Women: A Test for Sex-Based Harassment," *California Law Review* 83 (1995): 1151–89, Hadfield rejects "tort-like treatment of sex-based harassment claims" and defines sexual harassment as "sex-based non-job-related workplace conduct that would lead a rational woman to alter her workplace behavior—such as refusing overtime, projects, or travel that would put her in contact with a harasser, requesting a transfer, or quitting—if she could do so at little or no cost to her" (p. 1156).

18. Wendy Shalit, *A Return to Modesty: Discovering the Lost Virtue* (New York: Free Press, 2000).

19. Shalit, *Return to Modesty*, 102, 147–48.

20. A proprivacy critic of the implications of certain forms of employer monitoring and conduct codes, such as forcing employees to sign dating waivers, need not advocate abandoning hostile environment law. See, for example, Niloofar Nejat-Bina, "Employers as Vigilant Chaperones Armed with Dating Waivers: The Intersection of Unwelcomeness and Employer Liability in Hostile Work Environment Sexual Harassment Law," *Berkeley Journal of Employment & Labor Law* 20 (1999): 325–59, "Current requirements for hostile work environment claims under Title VII are leading employers to take . . . undesirable and unrealistic . . . role[s] in consensual office relationships," but "recently elucidated employer liability standards for hostile work environment claims are proper. . . ." Nejat-Bina argued that alternatives to dating waivers include developing and distributing clear policies, educating workers about improprieties and policies, implementing effective grievance procedures and educating employees about their use, and finally, instituting employer measures to end immediately any ongoing harassment (Nejat-Bina, "Employers as Vigilant Chaperones," 358–59). See also Jennifer L. Dean, "Employer Regulation of Employee Personal Relationships," *Buffalo University Law Review* 76 (1996): 1051–74, defending employer

restriction of employee personal relationships but urging that dating outside of work and by persons not in supervisor-subordinate relationships not be a basis for discharge; Kathleen M. Hallinan, "Invasion of Privacy or Protection against Sexual Harassment: Co-Employee Dating and Employer Liability," *Columbia Journal of Law and Social Problems*, 26 (1999): 435–64, "If properly constructed, co-employee dating policies will . . . protect the privacy interests of employees."

A critic of the First Amendment implications of employer monitoring and conduct codes need not advocate abandoning hostile environment law either. See, for example, Deborah Epstein, "Can a 'Dumb Ass Woman' Achieve Equality in the Workplace? Running the Gauntlet of Hostile Environment Harassing Speech," *Georgetown Law Journal* 84 (1999): 399–451, "The current formulation of hostile environment harassment (which restricts the laws that regularly reach to the most extreme, persistent, and unwelcome forms of workplace harassment) strikes the best possible balance between the fundamental interests of equal opportunity and free speech thus far articulated."

21. See Vicki Schultz, "Reconceptualizing Sexual Harassment," *Yale Law Journal* 107 (1998): 1683–1805. Schultz argues that hostile environment law has been overly sexualized; some of the conduct that makes workplaces hostile to women "has little or nothing to do with sexuality but everything to do with gender" (p. 1687). See also David E. Bernstein, "Sex Discrimination Laws versus Civil Liberties," *University of Chicago Legal Forum 1999* (1999): 133–97, arguing that constitutional civil liberties should triumph over sex discrimination laws.

22. Many defend, for example, state laws that protect workers' off-the-job privacy rights to socialize with co-workers and to engage in high-risk and unhealthy activities. See generally Terry Morehead Dworkin, "It's My Life—Leave Me Alone: Off-the-Job Employee Associational Privacy Rights," *American Business Law Journal* 35 (1997): 47–104.

23. See *Chandler v. Georgia*, 520 U.S. 305 (1997).

24. Earlier versions of portions of this section appeared as Anita L. Allen, "Privacy and the Public Official: Talking about Sex as a Dilemma for Democracy," *George Washington Law Review* 67, no. 5/6 (1999): 1165–82; and Anita L. Allen, "Lying to Protect Privacy," *Villanova Law Review* 44 (1999): 161–88.

25. Gingrich's first wife was his math teacher at Baker High School in Columbus, Georgia. They began having an affair while he was a student.

26. See Alasdair MacIntyre, "Truthfulness, Lies, and Moral Philosophers: What Can We Learn from Mill and Kant?" in *The Tanner Lectures of Human Values*, ed. Grethe B. Peterson, 16 (1995): 342, quoting Kant's rejection of Benjamin Constant's view that "to tell the truth is a duty only towards a person who has the right to the truth."

27. Intent and deceitfulness are characteristics of lying. See Sissela Bok, *Lying: Moral Choice in Public and Private Life*, rev. ed. (New York: Vintage, 1999). See also Paul Ekman, *Telling Lies: Clues to Deceit in the Marketplace, Politics, and Marriage* (New York: W.W. Norton, 2001), 25–42.

28. Lying is ubiquitous and frequent. See F. G. Bailey, *The Prevalence of Deceit* (Ithaca, N.Y.: Cornell University Press, 1991), 27, 68: "The habit of protective

concealment . . . is ubiquitous, and there is nothing uncommon about it or about the accompanying itch to penetrate the privacy of others." See also Charles V. Ford, *Lies! Lies!! Lies!!! The Psychology of Deceit* (Washington, D.C.: American Psychiatric Press, 1996); David Nyberg, *The Varnished Truth: Truth Telling and Deceiving in Ordinary Life* (Chicago: University of Chicago Press, 1993), 11; and Bella M. DePaulo et al., "Lying in Everyday Life," *Journal of Personality & Social Psychology* 70, no. 5 (May 1996): 993.

29. Lying has a role in the learned professions and public affairs. See Alan Ryan, "Professional Liars," *Social Research* 63 (1996): 619–41, showing that physicians, lawyers, and politicians lie in professional contexts; H. Richard Uviller, "The Lawyer as Liar," *Criminal Justice Ethics* 13, no. 2 (1994): 105, opining that "purely moral considerations do not invariably command strict honesty," but lawyers' roles of influence "in the affairs of government, commerce, and the private lives of the people" demand scrupulous attention to accuracy. See also Jennifer Jackson, "Telling the Truth," *Journal of Medical Ethics* 17 (1991): 5, discussing how medical professionals lie. See generally James H. Korn, *Illusions of Reality: A History of Deception in Social Psychology* (1997), 1, discussing various ways social scientists deceive their research subjects. See also Nyberg, *Varnished Truth*, 185–88, commenting on deception in police work; W. Peter Robinson, "Lying in the Public Domain," *American Behavioral Scientist* 36 (1993): 362–66, commenting on lying in public affairs; and John Orman, *Presidential Secrecy and Deception* (Westport, Conn.: Greenwood Publishing Group, 1980), 7, discussing lies and withholding of information to maintain a positive public persona.

30. Robinson, "Lying in the Public Domain," 366.

31. Nyberg, *Varnished Truth*, 1.

32. See Ford, *Lies! Lies!! Lies!!!*, 197–235.

33. Lies are detected by body language and facial expressions. See generally Ekman, *Telling Lies*, 80–161; and Peter Robinson, *Deceit, Delusion, and Detection* (Thousand Oaks, Calif.: Sage Publications, 1996), 74–150.

34. The ethics of lying have been aired by many scholars, in addition to those cited in earlier notes. See Alison Leigh Brown, *Subjects of Deceit: A Phenomenology of Lying* (Albany N.Y.: State University of New York, 1998); Marcel Eck, *Lies and Truth* (New York: MacMillan, 1970); Timur Kuran, *Private Truths, Public Lies: The Social Consequences of Preference Falsification* (Cambridge, U.K.: Harvard University Press, 1995); Loyal Rue, *By the Grace of Guile: The Role of Deception in Natural History and Human Affairs* (Oxford, U.K.: Oxford University Press, 1994); Robert C. Solomon, "What a Tangled Web: Deception and Self-Deception in Philosophy," in *Lying and Deception in Everyday Life*, ed. Michael Lewis and Carolyn Saarni (New York: Guilford Press, 1993), 30–58; Mary Mothersill, "Some Questions about Truthfulness and Lying," *Social Research* 63 (1996): 913; Bernard Williams, "Truth, Politics, and Self-Deception," *Social Research* 63 (1996): 603; Perez Zagorin, "The Historical Significance of Lying and Dissimulation," *Social Research* 63 (1996): 896–904.

35. See Immanuel Kant, "On a Supposed Right to Lie from Philanthropy," in *Immanuel Kant: Practical Philosophy,* ed. Mary J. Gregor (Cambridge, U.K.: Cambridge University Press, 1996), 613, "To be truthful in all declarations is therefore a

sacred command of reason prescribing unconditionally, one not to be restricted by any conveniences." See also Christine M. Korsgaard, "The Right to Lie: Kant on Dealing with Evil," *Philosophy & Public Affairs* 15 (1986): 326, stating that Kant endorsed the claim that one must never tell lies under any circumstances or for any purpose. But see MacIntyre, "Truthfulness," 344–45, who cites scholarship suggesting that Kant's views may have been less extreme early in his career.

36. Works by these scholars are cited throughout the notes to this chapter; see note 28, for example.

37. Bailey, *Prevalence of Deceit*, 27.

38. Paul Ekman, *Telling Lies*, p. 83.

39. The purpose of this note is to convey the range of social science research lying has inspired. See Eck, *Lies and Truth*, 59–78, stating that all lying is done with deceptive purpose and that lying should be judged by the intention that motivates it; Ford, *Lies!*, 88–102, describing thirteen motivations for lying that may exist singly or in combination; Rue, *Grace of Guile*, 144, stating that people sometimes employ deception to achieve personal wholeness; DePaulo et al., "Lying in Everyday Life," 979–80, noting that many goals that motivate nondeceptive communication also motivate deceptive communication; Wendy Doniger, "Sex, Lies, and Tall Tales," *Social Research* 63 (1996): 663, discussing deception in the sexual behavior of humans; Paul Ekman, "Why Don't We Catch Liars?" *Social Research* 63 (1996): 801–17; Ekman, *Telling Lies*, 98, listing reasons people lie; John Hollander, "The Shadow of a Lie: Poetry, Lying, and the Truth of Fictions," *Social Research* 63 (1996): 643, stating that liars always perceive some advantage in telling lies; D. A. Kashy and Bella M. DePaulo, "Who Lies," *Journal of Personality and Social Psychology* 70, no. 5 (May 1996): 1037–38, stating that a person's motives for lying have a correlation with a person's personality; Robinson, "Lying in the Public Domain," 359–82, discussing motivations of public figures to lie to the public; Ryan, "Professional Liars," 620, analyzing lies told between spouses for purposes of saving a marriage; Leonard Saxe, "Thoughts of an Applied Social Psychologist," *American Psychologist* 46 (1991): 409, 412–13, reviewing studies of conditions that compel individuals to lie or tell the truth; David Shapiro, "On the Psychology of Self-Deception," *Social Research* 63, no. 2 (fall 1996): 785–800, discussing causes and effects of self-deception; A. F. Strichartz and R. V. Burton, "Lies and Truth: A Study of the Development of the Concept," *Child Development* 61 (1990): 211–20, studying children's conceptions of lies and truth; and H. Richard Uviller, "The Lawyer as Liar," *Criminal Justice Ethics* 13, no. 2 (1994): 102–5, discussing forces motivating lawyers to lie in violation of disciplinary rules.

40. Nyberg (*Varnished Truth*, 129) wrote:

A life without privacy is unthinkable. How could we make love? Reflect or meditate? Write a poem, keep a diary, daydream? How could we attend to those sometimes highly self-conscious requirements of skin and bowels? How could we expect to keep our intimate doings out of the newspaper? How could we pay adequate attention to our personal inner worlds, or find peace from the demands of daily living? We need a certain amount of privacy to maintain a sense of dignity and decency, to stay sane and happy. Civility itself requires privacy. . . . Privacy conveys advantage in achieving and maintaining a reputation, the difficulty of which for public figures is symbolized both by the highly prosperous gossip industry and by an increasing number of scandalous demeaning congressional hearings. The advantage of privacy extends beyond private life, to the world of employment, where competition for jobs, promotions, and other business associations is keen and mean.

41. Robert B. Reich, *Locked in the Cabinet* (New York: Vintage, 1997).

42. See generally Richard Ellman, *Oscar Wilde* (New York: Vintage, 1988), 307, 355, 389–91. Ellman documents Wilde's homoerotic lifestyle and relationships with John Gray, Andre Gide, Lord Alfred Douglas, and others. Wilde had a relationship with artist John Gray when he was young. Wilde's series of lovers also included Andre Gide, who was enthralled with Wilde. The lover who ultimately led to Wilde's ruin, though, was the Lord Alfred (Bosie) Douglas. See page 389, describing the relationship between Wilde and Douglas as "intense and romantic" although not monogamous. Ellman suggests that Wilde's "life with Douglas, including the publicity of their romantic passion, reflected his intention to oblige a hypocritical age to take him as he was." Ellman, on pages 390–91, speculates: "The excitement of doing something considered wrong, and the [vices of] faithless boys. . . may have been as important for Wilde as sexual gratification. . . . English society tolerated homosexuality only so long as one was not caught at it. His chances of being caught were enormously increased as he combined casual associations with his more idealized ones. . . . Wilde believed in his star. . . . But he was always bringing himself to the brink."

See pages 438–39, describing the initiation of a libel suit against the Marquess of Queensberry and quoting Wilde as saying, "What is loathsome to me is the memory of interminable visits paid by me to the solicitor . . . [where] I would sit with [a] serious face . . . telling serious lies." See also page 461, stating that Wilde did not practice "buggery" as such. On pages 439, 441–42, 460, detectives working for Queensberry uncovered evidence against Wilde through female prostitutes who complained about competition for male clientele "from boys under the influence of Oscar Wilde." See Bailey, *Prevalence of Deceit*, 37, stating: "[t]he prospect of losing face is, of course, apt to arouse nonrealistic sentiments, and a man can be moved to cut off his nose to save his face."

43. Ellman, *Oscar Wilde*, 438.

44. See Michael J. Chandler and Jamie Afifi, "On Making a Virtue out of Telling Lies," *Social Research* 63 (1996): 731, asserting that the good lie deserves a certain amount of respect.

45. Ellman, *Oscar Wilde*, 438–39.

46. Hill took and passed a polygraph test. See Anita Hill, *Speaking Truth*, 222–24.

47. See *Brogan v. United States*, 522 U.S. 398 (1998). The case held that the "exculpatory no" exception does not apply with respect to criminal liability under 18 U.S.C. § 1001 (1994) for making false statements.

48. "Public opinion is not easily avoided. If you. . . try to opt out of the game and be neither a talker nor a listener, the penalty is to be considered. . . not part of the community." Bailey, *Prevalence of Deceit*, 71.

49. Timur Kuran (*Private Truths*, 11) explains the dynamics of lying to protect oneself and to fit in:

> Talk being cheap, anyone can claim to be against this lifestyle or that political platform. An effective way of making such a claim credible is to participate in efforts to punish those from whom one is seeking dissociation. A closeted homosexual may become a gay basher to allay suspicions about his own private life. . . . [H]ypocrisy is a universal, and often successful, tactic of self-protection and self-promotion.

50. In September 1998, 49 percent of respondents to a *Newsweek* opinion poll conducted by Princeton Survey Research Associates (17–18 September 1998) said that they thought the president would be justified in lying to protect the privacy of his family, 46 percent said he would not be justified in lying, and 5 percent said they "don't know." See Poll, Roper Center at the University of Connecticut, Question No. 005 (1998).

51. DNA tests conducted at Oxford University indicated that Jefferson may have fathered a child in an intimate relationship with one of his black slaves. See Patrick Rogers et al., "All Tom's Children: A President's Presumed Affair with a Slave Gives New Meaning to the Term Jeffersonian," *People*, 23 November 1998, 77. Presidents who stray get away. Republicans hoped in vain that disclosure of Cleveland's out-of-wedlock son would cost him the presidency in 1884. See Harold Evans, *The American Century* (New York: Knopf, 1998), 31. President Harding maintained a secret relationship with Nan Britton and his daughter Elizabeth, whom he never saw, but the story got out. See Evans, *American Century*, 243. It is now well known that President Franklin D. Roosevelt concealed the extent of his disability from the general public.

Presidential deception can get out of hand and potentially imperil the nation. See Ford Burkhart, "Edwin A. Weinstein, 89, Neuropsychiatrist Who Studied President Wilson," *New York Times*, 21 September 1998, B12. Dr. Weinstein believed that President Wilson's denial of illnesses contributed to difficulties in office. President John F. Kennedy's sex-filled private life had an adverse impact on some of the people around him, according to Seymour M. Hersh, *The Dark Side of Camelot* (New York: Little, Brown, 1997) 229–30. A physician who studied Ronald Reagan's presidency concluded that he suffered from Alzheimer's symptoms, like loss of memory, that left him frequently unaware of world affairs. See Burkhart, "Edwin A. Weinstein," B12. Reagan privately worried about his failing memory and once failed to recognize a member of his own cabinet according to Melinda Beck, "Alzheimer's Terrible Toll," *Newsweek*, 2 October 1995, 36.

52. Sissela Bok, "Lies Come with Consequences," *Washington Post*, 23 August 1998, C1.

53. Jackson, "Telling the Truth," 5–9.

54. See Harriet Lerner, *The Dance of Deception* (New York: Harper Collins, 1993), 36–37 .

55. See Adrienne Rich, *On Lies, Secrets, and Silence* (New York: W. W. Norton, 1979), 185–92, who examined some of the psychological underpinnings of lying.

56. Bare truth can demean, humiliate, and prompt lies. See Kenneth Starr, *Referral to the U.S. House of Representatives Pursuant to Title 28, U.S. Code*, 595, Submitted to the Office of Independent Counsel, 9 September 1998. Bald-faced lying can hinder how organizations function and threaten the trust underlying relationships in organizations. See Steven L. Grover, "Lying in Organizations: Theory, Research, and Future Directions," in *Antisocial Behavior in Organizations*, ed. Robert A. Giacalone and Jerald Greenberg (Thousand Oaks, Calif.: Sage Publications, 1997), 68.

Conclusion

Accountability for and in private life is ubiquitous. As I have illustrated throughout this book, we constantly (1) inform, (2) explain, (3) justify, (4) sanction, and (5) remain transparent to others. Accountability in these five senses chills, deters, punishes, prompts, pressures, and exposes. These are evils when they amount to unjust domination or frank violation. They are not, however, always evils. Indeed, this book has emphasized that there are positive dimensions to accountability's qualification of privacy and private choice. Accountability protects, dignifies, and advantages. In closing, I bring those positive dimensions into bold relief, with the help of a final illustration. I end with some general observations about accountability in free societies.

The House of Prayer is a Christian congregation of African Americans who take seriously the biblical maxim that to spare the rod disdains the child. In March 2001, Atlanta police seized forty-one children whose parents belonged to the church, after one boy showed up at school with welts on his body. He said he had been beaten with a switch at church. They also arrested sixty-eight-year-old Reverend Arthur Allen and five House of Prayer members alleged to have encouraged or participated in child-beatings. In chapter 4, I briefly mentioned that Reverend Allen had been sentenced to prison in 1992 for beating a sixteen-year-old girl accused of premarital sex. However, sexual misconduct was not the only sin for which House of Prayer children faced church sanctions orchestrated by Allen. In trouble with the law again, Allen complained to a reporter, "We're getting persecuted. They want to dominate us with their way of life."[1]

To hold House of Prayer adults accountable to the state for their religious practices is indeed to dominate them with "our" way of life. But this is an apt example of the benevolent domination by the state that feminists have urged for years. Rip down the doors of "private" citizens in "private" homes and "private" institutions as needed to protect the vital interests of vulnerable people. It is also the kind of domination that should not much worry a political theorist for whom freedom in pluralist societies entails or consists in nondomination. The restriction placed on the House of Prayer is not an arbitrary, whimsical power play, but an attempt at humane law by fair-minded authorities.[2]

Accountability protects. That a society looks after health and safety by holding others accountable reflects the esteem in which its members are held. The forty-one Atlanta children were taken from their homes for a time because Fulton County values their well being. At first, parents whose children were removed from their homes refused to agree to stop church-supported corporal punishment. They eventually relented. Accountability (the threat of criminal punishment, the loss of parenting privileges, and the loss of reputation in the wider community) was protective of the children. It was also ennobling of the children's angry and befuddled parents. In the final pages of chapter 1, I asserted that accountability, if mutual and reciprocal, implies equality and inclusion. Accountability indeed dignifies. The society that holds individuals to account dignifies them by presupposing intelligence, rationality, and competence for dialogic social performances of reckoning. No one expects hamsters and centipedes to give account; that is one of the reasons they get squished and locked into little cages. The fact that we expect accountability of fellow humans is a measure of the seriousness with which we regard them. A parallel point is made by moral philosophers about moral agency in general all the time: ascribe moral rights, obligations, duties, or responsibilities as a measure of respect. Abstract moral respect is of little consolation to people who feel subjectively mistreated. The House of Prayer parents' anger may have stemmed from the nature of the procedures to which they were subjected in the name of state accountability. One could very well applaud the intervention but condemn the way in which it was undertaken.

Of course, accountability can be a feature of outright ignoble compulsion rather than protectionism or moral dignity. Serfs and slaves are expected to answer to masters, expectations that are enforced with whip and chain. The threat of brutality has led subordinated peoples to signal intent to cooperate, at a considerable loss to self-esteem. The accountability norms that deeply ennoble are egalitarian and reciprocal. Some African Americans interpreted the House of Prayer intervention as secular society's unequal, nonreciprocal subordination of blacks' minority culture. Reverend Allen suggested that his arrests for beating children were emblematic of the majority society's disrespect for African American religious and cultural traditions. Yet the laws that prohibit excessive child discipline apply equally to all racial and religious groups. White, secular child abusers get arrested, too, in Atlanta, a Christian-dominated city with a black mayor, black judges, and black police officers.

Even accountability demands that are not strictly reciprocal and egalitarian are potentially ennobling. They can dignify if they flow from the requirements of care and caretaking rather than from political domination. Accountability is a demand of love and nurture. The intense accountability for intimacies demanded by long-term lovers is missed when Alzheimer's, Huntington's, or senile dementia sets in. Intense accountability is part of the parent-child relationship, too. Parents need and want the accountability of their children. One of the saddest things about having a child who is mentally disabled is missing out on the experience of teaching the arts of description, explanation, justification, censure, etc. and seeing those lessons consistently put to work. A remote, autistic son speaks not at all; when manic, a bipolar daughter does not provide coherent reasons and explanations for conduct.

Physical discipline is a common expectation of good parenting in most African American families, communities, and churches, notwithstanding the opposition to corporal punishment in the wider society. It is not just the tiny House of Prayer that tells black parents to beat black children. The House of Prayer parents who subscribed to church beatings believed that physical discipline is and teaches accountability. They believed corporal punishment molds children into respectful youths and law-abiding citizens. But some forms of accountability proffered in the name of love and care are ill conceived. African Americans must understand that harsh physical punishment, though customary and biblical, is not a cause of good citizenship in a modern society. Moreover, children who are spanked, whipped, or beaten by even well-intentioned parents may be more likely to turn into abusive adults. There is absolutely no evidence that the factors that lead black youths to crime include parents' withholding the switch. Black church practices do evolve and change. In the meantime, black children remain accountable to black parents, who remain accountable to grandparents, neighbors, and churches for the choices they make concerning discipline.[3]

I have attempted in this book to display some of the old and new kinds of accountability that typify contemporary American lives. I have illustrated accountability *to* family, race, community, medical professionals, insurers, employers, and the general public; and I have illustrated accountability *for* drug use, child rearing, choice of intimate partners, health, and sex. Accountability norms profiled in this book are ties that bind. If you imagine lines drawn between each one of us and the people to whom we are accountable for personal matters, the resulting picture is a dense network of such lines—a web of accountability. The web of accountability relationships is both flexible and sticky. First mentioned in this book's Introduction, the intent behind this metaphor is now hopefully clear. The web is sticky in the sense that socially determined and reinforced expectations impel us. Expectations impel us, for example, to tell our mothers certain things, to explain certain things to our friends, and to justify much to our employers. The web is flexible in the sense that we have a good deal of freedom to stretch and mold these connections to suit individual taste. Not all accountability imperatives result from contract or choice. Still, it is oftentimes possible to avoid reporting, explaining, justifying, and so on, because we live in a society that permits a degree of "exit," economists' compact term for voluntary separation and self-isolation. It is not costless to escape societal accountability imperatives—the cost is sometimes loneliness—but we can often do it. We can work ourselves loose. We do not have to tell our mothers everything. We can compartmentalize our friends and get new jobs. We stick, but, the good news about life in the United States is that we are not generally stuck.

To be sure, some people feel more stuck than others. Just how stuck we are and feel is an empirical question. Faced with evidence of a great many people unable to express a core identity and associated preferences because of punitive accountability norms, I would abandon my belief that "we are not generally stuck." In liberal societies, political freedom limits accountability to the state. The extensiveness of political freedom in the U.S. underlies my observation that "we are not generally stuck." But in any society, including the most liberal, the combined force of accountability to state, community, kin, and friend will qualify both freedom and privacy.

Some cautionary points follow from the web of accountability relationships one observes in the United States. First, in the name of public health, safety, security, and morals, punitive legal accountability for certain forms of ordinary personal conduct have flourished in modern liberal societies. It was not so long ago that birth control bans, interracial marriage prohibitions, and sodomy strictures were pervasive in American law. We still live with criminal sodomy and adultery bans. Liberalism has never meant the end of accountability to the state for what a great many people consider their personal lives. A perpetual danger is that the ambition to protect will result in simple intolerance and oppression. A perpetual regret is that, in addition to affronts to privacy and freedom, affronts to culture and identity will be the costs of accountability to the state for personal matters. Ethno-racial, religious, and sexual orientation minorities pay such costs every day: sometimes for the better, as in the case of the House of Prayer's disciplinary violence, sometimes for the worse, as in the case of legal intolerance of gays and lesbians.

Second, although in liberal societies the government steps back from extremes of intervention, extremes of accountability are not limited to legal norms or totalitarian regimes. Unofficial, normative accountability in liberal democratic societies can be constraining in many of the same ways that official accountability to the state is constraining. A liberal society—or segments of a liberal society—may be a moralistic or clannish one, for example, in which people are bound to admit, confess, forbear, etc. because of their creeds and affiliations. Accountability is a device of group identity and solidarity employed by many familial, religious, and racial groups to positive effect. But suffocating, harsh, nongovernmental accountability can make a person wretched.

Finally, I have used the term "the New Accountability" to stand for the observed intensification of accountability experienced in the United States in the past decades. The New Accountability is a product of Americans' extensive social, economic, and political freedoms and our ambivalence about forms of privacy that hide truths useful to others. The fact that people in liberal societies are not generally subjected to state punishment for their beliefs or "self-regarding" conduct may perniciously heighten accountability expectations. Indeed, contemporary Americans are expected to exteriorize internal and intimate worlds in ways they would not if there were a price to pay. In Islamic societies in which sexually active unmarried women are stoned to death, no one would think to design a television program in which women are asked to talk about their sex lives. The New Accountability means a demand for bare private facts and then, inevitably, more. For with the revelation of bare private facts comes the call for detail. State that you have AIDS, and expect people to want to know how and why you contracted it. They will want to know what medications you are taking and your prognosis. They will want to know if you have a partner, and your partner's AIDS status. It feels good sometimes to speak intimate truths to strangers. It feels good to know that others take a compassionate interest in the details of your life. So you talk. But you are not always socially free to stop talking. The New Accountability means strangers may have no compunction about demanding more than you wish to tell and putting facts about you to uses that offend and hurt you. The freedom and openness of conduct means that numerous people witness and know about it. Many curious, interested, nosey, inquiring people liberally construe and exploit accountability-entitling ties. The ties they recognize may be as attenuated as membership in a public with a right to know whatever is interesting, educational, informative, newsworthy, or governmental. As America's New Accountability demonstrates, substantial accountability for personal life is a product of excessively tolerant and intolerant societies.

NOTES

1. Amanda Ripley, "Whippings in the Pulpit: A Congregation Loses 41 of Its Children to the State after a Boy Tells the Police What Happened at Church," *Time Magazine*, 2 April 2001, 47.

2. See Philip Pettit, *Republicanism: A Theory of Freedom and Government* (Oxford, U.K.: Oxford University Press, 1997), 4–12, arguing for freedom as non-domination and non-domination as the absence of arbitrary constraint.

3. In October 2002, I told an African American audience at Brown University that I had been whipped by my great-grandmother and mother. My great-grandmother beat me for pinching a bit of leftover ham from the refrigerator; my mother for throwing a pillow down a flight of stairs rather than carrying it. After my talk at Brown, a graduate student came up and suggested that I owed my unusual academic and professional success to strict physical discipline. I responded with an abbreviated version of my sister Gwen's story, narrated in chapter 2 of this book. If whipping explains my Harvard law degree, it must also explain Gwen's crack addiction. It is unlikely that corporal punishment is the single most important factor in determining a child's future success or failure.

Index

abortion: early laws, 36; Nuremberg Files, 48; procedure not fully private, 128; *Roe v. Wade*, 2, 11

accountability: benefits and burdens of, 41; children to parents, 24, 197; consent, as grounds for, 22; criminal sanctions as a type of, 152; cultural contours of, 28–30; defined, 14, 20–21; dependency, a grounds for, 22; as dignifying, 196; as domination and violation, 195; for drugs, alcohol, and AIDS, 30; effects of, 195; of employees, 10; equality, 41–42; excessive, 199; in explanation-emphatic sense, 16–19, 22, 25, 28, 37, 46, 54–55, 75, 98, 134, 197–198; family, 9; financial, 24; five forms of, 16–17; in friendship, 24; functions of, 26–28; to general public, 150; gender as variable in access to, 41; ground for, 21–22; groups, requiring, 27, 28; for health, 23, 115–140; in information-emphatic sense, 16–19, 26, 27, 28, 29, 35, 37, 46, 54–55, 82, 91, 98, 115–116, 126, 131, 142–143, 151, 198; interest balancing, 11, 14; internal versus external perspective, 21, 23–24; in justification-emphatic sense, 16–19, 28, 29, 45, 46, 54–55, 75, 98, 134; liberal spirit, 3–4; as normal, 3; old vs. new, 10–11, 199; to oneself, 25; parents to children, 22, 24; as performative and communicative, 25; positive dimensions of, 195; power 25–26, 78, 80, 129, 197; as a *prima facie* imperative, 24; as protective, 195; public need, as ground for, 22; in punishment/sanction-emphatic sense, 19, 21, 27, 28, 36, 39 54–55, 75, 98, 116, 134, 141, 174, 197–198; in relationships, 22; in reliability-emphatic sense, 20, 21, 30; reliance, as a grounds for, 22; required by law, morality, and etiquette, 116; responsibility, 27; as self-reinforcing, 28; for sex, 141–194; solidarity, furthered by, 27; as subordinating, 26; as tool of power, 26; trust, furthered by, 27; USA PATRIOT Act, 6; at work, 142–150. *See also* employment; family; race; responsibility; sex; trust

accountants, 43

adoption: confidentiality expectations, 128, 129; Indian children, 34–35; open adoption, 8–9, 34, 79–96

About the Author

Anita L. Allen is professor of law and philosophy at the University of Pennsylvania Law School. She is a graduate of Harvard Law School and the University of Michigan, where she earned a Ph.D. in philosophy. She has published more than seventy articles. She has also published three previous books: *Privacy Law: Cases and Materials* (with Richard Turkington, 2002); *Debating Democracy's Discontent* (with Milton Regan, 1998); and *Uneasy Access: Privacy for Women in a Free Society* (1988).